REMEMBERING GOD

THE STORY OF A VOLUNTEER AND HURRICANE KATRINA

BY: KENDALL A. KETTERLIN

Andrew;

Thanks for sharing in my story. I hope you enjoy me experiences

[signature]

REMEMBERING GOD:
THE STORY OF A VOLUNTEER AND HURRICANE KATRINA

by: Kendall A. Ketterlin

Copyright © 2009 by Kendall A Ketterlin
All rights reserved

Published by K2 Publishing; kketterlin@me.com
Printed by BookMobile; 5120 Cedar Lake Road, Minneapolis, MN 55416
763-398-0030; www.bookmobile.com

All Photos by Kendall A Ketterlin except where otherwise indicated
Katrina Support Report by Arthur Miller, printed with permission

Front and back cover designs by Kendall Ketterlin

ISBN: 978-0-615-33290-1

First Edition; November, 2009

For ordering information or to arrange for a discussion with the author, please contact:

Kendall A Ketterlin
141 County Rd 263
Armstrong, MO 65230
email: KKETTERLIN@ME.COM

CONTENTS

PART III: CATHOLIC CHARITIES
BILOXI, MISSISSIPPI

PART IV: AFTER MISSISSIPPI

PHOTOS

We should never forget that God is the source of all things, everything we do finds goodness so long as it is directed toward Him.

Within His goodness, I was able to experience the gifts of friends and strangers who made this time in my life unforgettable and truly life changing, turning my life rightside-up. For all of those who are named in these pages, you were each an invaluable part of God's plan for my life—THANK YOU!

But above everyone else, this book has long been dedicated to my father who said very simply, "Go for it."

In Grateful Memory

William Stephen Ketterlin
1949-2008

My one regret in life is that I failed to have this printed before he passed away on December 1, 2008. Though I am confident that he now knows more than I ever could have told him, I missed getting to see the smile of pride, love, and maybe a little surprise as well, as he opened these first pages. His encouragement and never failing support has been deeply missed.

INTRODUCTION

Like millions of people across this country, I stood in my living room, looking at the pictures of water rushing through levies and flooded homes in New Orleans with an awe filled despair. Although I was living in Colorado at the time, I had grown up in central Missouri and lived through the Mississippi and Missouri river floods of 1993, and then again in 1995. My stomach twisted at the memories of just how poorly pictures on a television screen convey the reality of what was really happening; how seemingly quiet waters were permanently chaneakging the landscape.

I remembered that once the waters receded, the cornfields we always drove by on the way to my grandma's house became popular fishing ponds. I remembered small towns that were forced to move, when Franklin, Missouri, became New Franklin. And I remembered how as children, my brother and I would hold our breathe as we crossed over the Missouri River bridge, and how small I felt as an adult when the river stretched for two, nearly three miles wide.

I also remembered the morning I was working at a local restaurant, when I heard the news about a major explosion at a Federal building in Oklahoma City, and how the following year, my stomach plummeted as a friend of mine drove those streets. She drove for block after block, first a half-mile then a mile, pointing to the buildings that had been damaged and windows that had been shattered. The pictures we see on television don't come anywhere near capturing the magnitude of life and the smallness you feel while paddling a canoe up to your front porch.

I was looking at a picture of a middle aged woman sitting on a bucket in a small john-boat, holding a cat or small dog in her arms and pointing to an invisible house off camera. A guy in a bright yellow life jacket, I think he had a short beard was looking toward that same direction, the top of his shoulder twisting as though he were turning the handle of an off board motor. I saw the weathered look of pitted ash on her face, the muscle worn exhaustion on his and the thought simply popped into my head; *I could go down there, find a job, maybe with an insurance company, and help in the recovery effort.*

It was early Monday afternoon, three days after the storm had passed, and I was supposed to be at work, nowhere near a TV or anything that would have brought hurricane Katrina into my life. As it had happened though, it had been 10:00 on Sunday night when my car inexplicable quite working. I had just left my local coffee shop, the Perk, when I turned the key in the ignition and nothing happened. I tried turning the key again, absolutely nothing happened. Then I checked to make sure I had put the car into park, made sure I had not left the lights on, and looked at the side of the steering column to make sure I was turning the key right, but still nothing happened.

"God Damnit!" I cursed as I hit the center of the steering wheel with my fist. I jumped out to run back to the now closed coffee shop, hoping that someone I knew had been slow in leaving. Fortunately, my roommate's brother had hung around past closing time and was able to give my car a jump, then follow me back home in case whatever had gone wrong, happened again.

The worst of my problem though, had very little to do with my car. The worst wasn't that I had not left the lights on, done anything else that should have left the battery drained, or that everything I knew told me that the jump from Robert shouldn't have been enough to get my car home. I had no clue as to why the car had suddenly just died (although maybe I should have paid more attention to the dim alternator light that had been on for the past few weeks.) The worst part wasn't the malfunctioning car, but had to do with my bosses come Monday morning. That night the bulk of our discussion at the Perk had been about how I wasn't going to be able to make a planned trip out to D.C. in a couple of weeks because my hypocritical bosses at the bank didn't think it qualified as personal business.

As far as I was concerned, and any reasonable person would be, *personal business* should have included anything that you needed to take care of that was not work related, like taking a couple of days to set up a few meetings and fly out to DC to raise funds for a nonprofit I was preparing to kick off. As I was told, however, *personal days* were for doctor's appointments and when "unexpected things came up"…like your car breaking down at 10:00 on a Sunday night.

When I was beating on the steering wheel, I knew that this wasn't going to look good. I could just imagine the look on my branch manager's face when I called her in the morning, *claiming* that my car wouldn't start, that I was going to have to use at least part of one of my personal days off, and "no, I don't know exactly how long it's going to take, but I'll call and let you know when I figure out what's wrong with it." It was exactly what I imagined someone would do if they were mad and simply wanted to throw the bank's own policies right back in their face, making sure that I had the last word and got my day off.

Even though I knew exactly how things would look from their perspective, at the same time, it made me even angrier with my bosses to think that they would just assume I was lying about my car, that I would be so immature as to concoct this story just to prove a point. But this wasn't an adolescent tantrum, just very bad timing.

Lying in bed that night, my mind flashing between images of what I would say when the branch manager accused me of lying and what could possibly be wrong with my car, it finally dawned on me that maybe I should have simply paid more attention to the alternator light that had flicked on a few weeks ago, rather than chalking it up to another glitch in a 15-year old car with 174,000 miles on it. The only thing that could possibly be wrong and makes any sense whatsoever would be if the alternator were out. Otherwise, nothing we had done would have done any good. So I came up with a simple plan.

I would get up at first light, take out the alternator, catch a ride to the parts store with my roommate Adriaan before he had to leave for work at 7:30, put the new one in and I could easily be at work by 10:00 am. For someone who was dreading another confrontation with his boss, it was a brilliant plan, that was, until some idiot was dumb enough to confuse the starter for an alternator.

Of course, I'm the idiot who had at least a few minutes of complete, inexcusable and unexplainable stupidity. By the time my eyes were opened enough to realize how stupid I was being, like confusing a coke can attached to the transmission for a small bunt cake near the engine, I had spent an hour trying to piece my starter back together. Then, after the ten minutes it took for me to pull out the right part, I had missed my chance at catching a ride with Adriaan. My choice was to either wait fifteen more minutes for my neighbor to come home, or jump on my bike and haul a 20-pound alternator to the store just over a mile down the road.

That fifteen minutes turned into just over an hour before he got home, and then he ran out of gas barely 20 feet from his drive. After a walk to the gas station and back and a couple more trips on my bike to pick up the right sizes of sockets that I never seem to have, yet always seem to be buying, the 30-minute job had quickly taken up the entire morning. The day had gone about as badly as it could have without someone actually dying. I had no other choice but to make the call to my boss Lil, "I'm not going to be able to make it in at all today." That's also when I finally gave up trying to argue in my head that it had been the worst possible time for this to have happened; just a day or two either way and I wouldn't have felt like my job was on the line.

I accepted that God had given me a much needed day off from work, time to clear my head a little from the previous day's frustrations and to go ahead and take care of a couple of other minor repairs that I'd been putting off. It was just a few minutes later, while I was waiting for some sealant to dry, when I saw the picture of a lady sitting in a boat in New Orleans with a small cat or dog cradled in her arm...

Although I was in no financial position to volunteer, I could certainly find a paid position cleaning up, and then working construction when the time came. As quickly as I realized what I could do, my decision was made. There was no debate or mulling it over. This was one of those very rare moments that I recognized at the time as a major turning point in my life. The decision itself, whether I chose to follow God and go, or to simply stay home and keep going on with my day to day life, was going to change the basic course of my life.

That night I called my parents, asking my mom what her gut reaction was to me dropping everything in Colorado and heading down for the Mississippi coast for a few months. It wasn't that I was questioning the idea myself, but my mom has a pretty reliable gut when it comes to making wild and crazy decisions, and I've learned the hard way that there's never anything wrong with asking someone's opinion who is smarter than you. She said it felt like a pretty good thing to do and since I was in a position that I could pretty well drop everything, it made sense. Ten minutes after we hung up she called again, "Your dad says 'Go For It!' That's all. I just thought I should tell you that."

There is a reason why I dedicated this book to him above anyone else. Whenever I think about making the decision to go down and help, I think about him saying, "Go for it!" and I want to tear up. It's as if no matter how certain I had already been that I was going to be leaving to help with the relief effort, that he was telling me it was the right thing to do, like every time he has told me that he loves me and is proud of the person I've become was poured into that one moment.

(Six months ago, my father died very unexpectedly. It was long after I had written these words and I thought hard about rewriting this part of the book, but in the end, the most important thing to remember is that these words were not written in the memory of his death, but in the experience of his life. My first regret in my entire life is that he did not have the chance to read this before he died.)

After that second call from my mom, I felt ready to rock and for the next couple of days I walked around with a rolling sense of confidence that I knew exactly what I was going to do, even though I still wasn't completely certain. The biggest piece I had left to find was a call from my friend Roy, a retired police officer and Vietnam vet who I had met at the Perk just a couple of months before Katrina hit. He was staying with his son, Roy Jr., in a place called Lafayette that I knew was somewhere near the Louisiana coast.

At the time, I didn't even know if their house was still standing or if their phone lines were even working, but part of what I knew was that my entire trip, or at least the first part of it, hinged on Roy. The last thing that I wanted to do, with all of the mess that I was sure they were having to deal with down there, was to add another person to the homeless population. My goal was to help, not to add to the burden. After leaving him a message on his voicemail Monday night, I waited. Tuesday and Wednesday came, passing without a word. I figured that if nothing else, he had a lot more important things to worry about than giving me a call. With ten minutes left on my lunch break on Thursday afternoon, he called.

At first, Roy tried to dissuade me from coming, telling me that everything down there was a complete disaster, "It's bad. It's real bad down here Kendall." He was saying that I didn't have a clue about what I would be getting myself into.

"I know Roy," I told him, "That's the one thing I know right now, that I have no idea what's going on and what I'm getting myself into. But I'm coming down."

The final decision came on Thursday night when he called back to let me know that his son Roy Jr. had said that it would be okay for me to stay there for a few days while I found something more permanent. On Friday morning I was regrettably forced to quit my

7

job, being told, "We're sending money, not people." Shortly after dawn on Saturday, I said goodbye to John at the Perk as I was heading out of town with everything I might need to live on for the next six months.

In fewer than 36 hours, I had found a place to stay, quit my job, had a farewell dinner with my friends, packed up the car that had died on Sunday night and left town. In less than three days, I had first thought about, and then left behind almost my entire life. The articles of incorporation for the Adams-Kennedy Society lay on the corner of my desk, still waiting for that next paycheck so that I would be able to afford the filing fees; my job was gone, not that I was upset over leaving the banking business, but I had hoped for a neater departure; and I was leaving behind an apartment I had moved into less than a month ago and one of the best group of friends I'd had in several years.

It had been barely seven months since I had pulled into the parking lot at the Howard Johnson hotel in Colorado Springs, having never visited the town and not knowing a single person there. I had simply overheard one of my friends say something about Colorado, and thought, "that sounds like a good place to go." Then I moved because I simply needed to get away from home, to get away from the voices of all of the people who had known me my entire life, or at least known me enough that I felt too much pressure to express my own opinions and draw myself out of a shell I had let them paint me into.

I was in Colorado because I needed to discover myself, to figure out what I wanted out of life and be free from the pressures of those who thought they knew me. As I was leaving, the one thing that I knew was that I had no idea what to expect, no clue as to just what I was getting myself into, but completely confident that I was heading to where God wanted me to go.

A little more than two months passed from the time when I decided to help with the Hurricane Katrina relief efforts until I returned home in the first week of November. With the time it took to drive between Colorado, Missouri, Louisiana and Mississippi, more car repairs, and a few days taken to visit with my family in Missouri, I spent seven weeks helping with relief efforts for both Katrina and Rita; three weeks at a Red Cross shelter in Lafayette, Louisiana and four weeks with a Catholic Charities distribution center in Biloxi, Mississippi.

As I had anticipated, it was a life changing experience that went far beyond having to quit a job I didn't want, or anything else I had imagined. I grew in courage, faith, my understanding of God, and personal awareness. There are deep-seeded friendships that I maintain to this day. I found a new level of confidence as experiences in the past, like my work with the Central Missouri Food Bank, offered surprising benefits.

The most significant change, though, wasn't a change at all, but a reminder to myself of a deeper faith I once had, and many of my personal beliefs that I had either forgotten, or had slid into hiding under the pressures of college and daily life. I understand that this sounds vague and what many might consider as trite and cliché, but like most every other volunteer I met in Louisiana and Mississippi, life changing experiences happened every day that I was open to them, and I learned more life lessons than I knew were even out there to be learned. That is why I started writing the journal that eventually became this book. Everyday I met so many people and experienced so many things that I never wanted to forget, that it was worth loosing an hour of sleep each night to frantically type as much as I could remember, and what I never wanted to forget.

This book began as a 30-page journal that I was posting on a website for family and friends back in Colorado and Missouri so they could keep up with what I was doing. But when I returned to Colorado in November, the questions kept pouring in. For one thing, most of my friends didn't have computers at home and they weren't able to keep up with the website. For another, when I went back to read what I had written, I even had to admit that it wasn't very good; just a spattering of notes I had scribbled down as fast as I could before going to bed. And then it seemed like everywhere I went everyone wanted me to tell them about all of my experiences, the variety of people I met, the incredible stories I had heard, the work I did and how it had changed me.

I wasn't ready to talk about it. I didn't want to talk about it. Not because it was a horribly tragic experience that I wanted buried in my deep subconscious for some shrink to uncover thirty years from now, nor out of a golden sense of humility that didn't want the attention and credit for giving up two months of my life. When I finally returned home, I simply didn't even know what had happened, much less, what to think about it.

I didn't have any problems remembering the people I met, the conversations we'd had or the events that transpired, I just didn't know how I felt about it or how they had affected me. I needed some time to figure out where I was and how to fit back inside my everyday life. The thought that started rolling through my mind was that I was having a hard time fitting the post-Katrina Kendall into my pre-Katrina life.

One of the most valuable lessons I learned was that if we believe that God gives us what we need, then it should follow that what we have is what we need. Unemployed, with very little work coming in through the three temp agencies I had signed on with, I looked at what I had; I had time. Time to sit in front of the TV, playing video games I had played through a hundred times, letting my thoughts wander into a void. And time to write. So I decided to take that time, go back through my scribbled notes, fill in the gaps and build in more detail.

Writing about what had happened, the stories I had heard and how I had felt at the time was more than just a way for me to deflect the questions, it also became a way to sort through and process it all. Thirty pages became forty, then sixty. Along the way I started talking with more and more people about what I was doing. People I didn't know would come up to me at the coffee shop, intrigued by what I had been spending so much time there working on. Somewhere in the mix of these 30-minute conversations I slowly got the idea that it would be worth putting into a full-length book.

What I've written is still about my friends, the ones back home and dozens that I made in Mississippi, but now it's also about opening a door for everyone else. More than simply sharing my own personal experiences, rather, this book is about bringing to light an aspect of Katrina's (and Rita's) aftermath that's been left in the dark. It's about the impact that Katrina made on the life of a volunteer and sharing the *life lessons* that I learned almost everyday; To inspire people to look beyond the tragedy and destruction, and think about the incredible impact Katrina had on the lives of the thousands of volunteers who came from all across the country to help.

Just the fact that so many people volunteered is phenomenal. The thousands more who stayed home and opened their doors to complete strangers is even more amazing. I know that most people didn't have an experience as profound as mine, but every person there was touched by an experience that will comfort them for the rest of their life. They tell the true character of the people of this nation and are an important part of Katrina's story. The part of the story that is more important, I would argue, than the floodwaters and the destruction brought by the hurricane itself.

In looking back on things, I'm tempted to say that Katrina changed me in ways that went far beyond having to quit a job that I didn't like and in ways that I could never have imagined, but every time I told someone how much Katrina had *changed* my life, a particular numbness twisted in my gut. It was the same feeling I remembered from several years back when I told people that I was planning on becoming a priest, something about that word just didn't sound right.

I came to realize that my experiences didn't change me, so much as they gave me the perspective to change my life. Last August, I was working at a bank; now, six months later, I'm teaching sixth grade special education. All of my free time last August was going toward forging a non-partisan political action group; now, it's going toward writing a book and possibly starting a publishing company. Last August, I was two days away from buying a house, only some last minute hitches in the financing stopped me from settling down permanently in Colorado Springs; now, I'll be spending the summer with my parents before moving to Minnesota. During those first days in Louisiana, I was adamant about not even thinking about the prospect of going to graduate school; this August, I will begin working on a Master's Degree in Pastoral Ministry. The very short of it is that six months ago, there wasn't even a vague impression of anything that's important in my life today.

The changes are not as simple as changing jobs and picking up a new hobby. Through all of the life lessons I learned, extraordinary people I met, things I discovered about myself, and some old ones that I was reminded of, Katrina made significant, deep-rooted impacts on my character and what I believe.

Part of that change came from the stories I heard; the lady who was holding on to the door frame and grabbed a bottle of holy water as it floated at eye level through her front door, or touring the different houses Mama Sau had recently lived in, and the apartment complex she was waiting to move into where dozens of people had been killed. Some things hit me on a personal level; the confidence the mental health workers showed in me and my resolve to confront the Red Cross and Sherri.

There were signs I witnessed; the crucifix and stained glass windows in St. Paul's that were left untouched, and seeing our prayers actively answered everyday, like needing ice and more volunteers at the Warehouse in Biloxi.

You could say that the changes came from an incredible experience in faith from the moment I quit my job and trusted in God, that He would provide enough money for me to stay down there for as long as He needed me to. But whatever you decide to believe, the bottom line is that when I left my home in Colorado Springs the only thing that I knew was that my life was about to change and I had no idea what I was getting myself into.

I was reminded of God.

PART I

The Road to Louisiana

Kansas

Sunday, September 4

Three hours after I left the Springs, and a few miles across the Kansas border, another thought popped into my head: *If I could get 300 people to donate just $10 each, that would give me enough money to pay all of my bills through the end of the year. Then I could spend all of my time volunteering and would be able to go where the help is needed most.*

It was a simple idea which, for the next several hours, ballooned into images of working with a car dealership to donate the use of a truck and then running a radio spot to have people fill the bed of the truck with donations that I would be able to deliver to Mississippi. And just maybe, if all went well, I could even convince the dealer to pay for a four-month lease on the truck since it would be used as a part of the clean up effort. Any pick-up, especially one with under 175,000 miles on it would have a lot more use down there than my tiny, two-door Sentra.

I could see the back of the black F-150 piling up with cans of food, tents, blankets, clothes and all sorts of things people would be bringing in for me to take. I pictured a 10-foot KPLA banner flying high above and could hear the radio hosts broadcasting live from the local Ford dealer. I imagined talking with Skip, the owner of a coffee shop back home, about putting up a donation display. Each week I would send a letter home with an update on what I had been doing and share some stories about the people I had met. It would be like Lakota Coffee had sent a local son down to the hurricane affected regions. The vision was incredible, and a far cry from where I had been just a few hours earlier; still talking to Jonathan at the Perk about how I would likely have to end up taking a job with an insurance company, but at least I'd be down there and able to do something.

Asking people to give me $10 so I could spend the next four months doing hurricane relief work may not sound like a big deal, especially when you consider that it had been less than 24-hours since I had made the final commitment to leave and had then quit my job without a second thought. But asking people for money would be a big step for me.

We've all heard stories about church groups making a decision to expand a building or start a new outreach program, trusting that God would provide the money that they were going to need. Then, a few days later, a check will appear in the mail for nearly that exact amount because someone had said a prayer and was compelled to make the donation. It seems impossible that we don't have to even ask people for what we need, and yet, God provides it anyway. Admittedly, I didn't really believe that things like that actually happen, so I challenged myself to accept something that I didn't really believe, to take another step and trust that God knew what I would need and that He would make sure that I got it. The thoughts about who I could talk to, what I would say in my radio interviews carried me through the next several hours and most of the way through Kansas. Then my brain got something new to puzzle over.

I was slowing down at the toll station near Topeka, Kansas, about 20 or 30 minutes after sunset. It was only three more hours to my parents' house which meant that I could be in by 10:00, maybe 11:00 at the latest. Then the radio sputtered into static, I hit the *scan* button, but it only moved up one number instead of jumping all of the way to the next station. I hit the button again and it toggled back down, then up one and back and forth each time I hit scan button. *Well crap!* I thought, *It's going to be a long drive without any music.* Then the whole car started lurching. *Did the lights just dim?* "I'm having some problems with my car," I asked the toll-booth attendant, "Do you know anywhere nearby where I can take it?"

He asked me, "What kind of a place are you looking for?"

"I'm not from around here so I don't know what's around here."

"Well, where do you want to go?"

There was no more sense of calm and politeness left my voice, and I knew it. "I don't have any idea what's around here." This idiot continued to act confused and threw in another question about which direction I wanted to go *Well duh! I'm headed east on a toll road and there isn't exactly anyway to turn around.* I didn't have time for such stupidity. My car was going to die on me at any time and I wanted to get as close to a mechanic as I could. "Just tell me where..." and then it died. I turned the key, nothing. It was just like Sunday night had been, there wasn't even a click.

I didn't feel an ounce of sympathy for the guy when he had to come out of his booth to help me push my car off to the side of the interstate. *If he had only not been such a buffoon I would have been...* It

17

didn't matter at the time that I wouldn't have been more than a quarter of a mile up the road and closer to nowhere. That was no excuse for this guy being such an idiot, and I was pissed because this was not the way to start a 1,700 mile drive to Louisiana. As soon as my car was far enough to be out of the way of traffic, the attendant rushed back to his post and another guy in a uniform popped out of an attached building to check on what was going on. An hour later I handed over 50 bucks to a tow truck driver who showed up just in time to do nothing. As mysteriously as the car had sputtered out, it started up again without any problem. *Had I imagined it? Did I not turn the key right?*

Nothing made sense. It was almost as if the car had gotten more power by just sitting there, but cars don't do that. If something had been wrong with the alternator, then the battery would simply be dead and there's no way that I would have been able to start it up again. The only other thing I could think of was that the problem had been with the battery, but then the car runs off the alternator when it's driving, so it shouldn't have spluttered and died like that. Plus, a dead battery usually means that a car won't start. What troubled me the most though, was that no matter what the problem had been, there was no way for me to find it while the car was running just fine. I was torn between a car that was now running perfect, and one that seemed to be destined to die out again at some point down the road. Just in case it reared it's ugly head again, I had the tow guy stick around for a good ten minutes, after all, he had just got paid $50 for showing up half an hour after he had said he would be there. Then he drove away and I pulled out.

Seven minutes and eight miles later, I exited at the next toll station. I had learned my lesson. The flickering radio meant that I was about out of juice. If it felt like my headlights had just gone a little dimmer, it wasn't paranoia, and there wasn't time to stop to ask for directions. "My car's about to die on me, I'll be right back." I had just enough umph left in the car to coast onto the shoulder and then walk back to pay my toll fee. I was definitely stuck in the middle of nothing Kansas and this was definitely not how my trip was supposed to be starting out. Fortunately though, something was beginning to make a little sense; when the car got too hot something, somewhere, was shorting out the electrical system.

I called my dad for a third time that night. He was at the local racetrack which didn't make an in depth conversation very easy, but by this time, there wasn't much to talk about. His brain was tapped out. With all of his experience, he has absolutely clueless as to what could be wrong, nothing was making sense to either of us. A few minutes later, I was fortunate that a local police officer stopped by who was kind enough to give me a jump so I could sweat out two more white-knuckled miles to the nearest Wal-Mart where I could spend the night in their parking lot. *If I had been able to make it this far into Kansas on my first run, then maybe I could be able to make it the rest of the way home in the morning.*

Shortly after I had made it to Wal-Mart, the security officer stopped by as I was half-way under the car, using my flashlight to stare into a big mass of "I don't know what I'm looking for." He was good enough to point me toward the nearest gas station and offer me a ride to get any parts I needed. I took his phone number, then walked to the nearby Village Inn for dinner.

The next morning, I finished out the last two hours with a tight grip on the wheel and a close ear on the radio. Although I made it the rest of the way without any more hiccups, I knew that I was going to be trapped in Missouri for more than just the long Holiday weekend. Rather than spending Labor Day with my family, then heading out first thing Tuesday morning, it was going to be late Tuesday before our mechanic could begin to look at it. *This was not how my trip was supposed to start out.*

10 Days in Missouri

Tuesday, September 13

I was in Missouri for far too long, wasted too many days sitting on my parents' porch swing waiting for Daniel, our local mechanic, to call and tell me that my car was finally ready to go. Normally, I would have been pulling my hair out by when he hadn't called by Tuesday afternoon to let me know what was wrong with it, and it was Wednesday before he even had a new starter ordered. Then the part didn't come on the truck like it was supposed to on Thursday and when it did arrive on Friday, someone had pulled the wrong part number. So it was wait around for another weekend plus Monday because the starter I needed had to be shipped from a different warehouse. It was the next Tuesday, a full week after I had planned on leaving, before anything came in. I had pressed so hard to leave Colorado as quickly as I could because they needed me down in Biloxi, not sitting around, wasting my time in the middle of nowhere Missouri.

I wanted to be angry, impatient and frustrated, thinking everyday that if I really cared about these people, then I should be pressing hard now and be more impatient. My mom has always told me that, "Patience is a virtue," but sometimes, it's better not to be. Like I said though, I *wanted* to be upset and tried to make myself feel it, but the frustration wasn't there. Everything inside me was quiet, and I felt calm and comfortable sleeping late and sitting on that porch swing.

A little before I had left, but mostly along the road in Kansas, I had made the conscious decision to live this trip as much by faith as I possibly could, to not make definitive plans of my own, see where things led me and accept everything that happened as a part of God's plan. We laughed at the Blues Brothers when they claimed to be on a *Mission from God*, but this really was my mission and the only thing I knew was that I needed to go and help, beyond that, I had no idea what I would be doing or what was going to happen. As I found out, I needed a little more than 24-hours to prepare and get myself ready to spend four months away from home.

On Thursday, two days after I had wanted to be gone, I borrowed my mom's car to meet my aunt Ann in Columbia. Her and my grandma had both seemed relatively unimpressed and unresponsive when my mom announced that I had decided to quit my job to go help with the relief effort. A few hours later, I had told my younger cousin how it hurt that neither of them had even hinted at helping me out. "Its not like I was expecting them to pay a month's worth of rent or anything, but they just sat there like my mom had told them I had got a job at a different bank. They didn't even offer to help me out with ten bucks and that hurts." Well, I was wrong and realized that I have to keep reminding myself not to take

21

things like that personally. It's just the way that part of my family is, expressionless and matter of fact about the most scintillating events. By Tuesday evening, I felt about 3 inches tall, and ashamed that I had felt so poorly of both of them.

First, my grandma had asked me to send her a list of all of the food and whatever else I was going to need. She was going to buy enough food for me to live off of for the next few weeks and that was the main reason for the trip to Columbia on Thursday. I needed to meet my aunt to pick up the supplies, along with some packets of clothes and a box of Bibles their Church wanted to send with me. (It was a far cry from my visions of a pick-up overflowing with donations, but it still felt good.) And then there was the check for $500 that had brought me to tears.

Tuesday night, a day after I would have left had it not been for the breakdown in Kansas, my aunt called me to let me know that their church council had met and she had asked them to give me some money so that it would be like they were sending a person down to Louisiana and Mississippi, instead of just another check, because what they needed most were people. New Hope is a small church, I think that there are usually around 30-40 people there on any given week, so I imagined marking off four or five more people off the list of 300. Then she told me that they had given her a lot more than what she had been expecting. "A lot more! I mean, Kendall, I was prepared to go in and have to make a presentation and tell them how wonderful of a person you are, but as soon as I told them what you were doing…"

So I thought, *Okay, maybe it's closer to $100*, which would be incredible. Then her words struck me, "They're giving you a check for $500 Kendall." I cried and was stunned into complete silence. I had heard of stories like that, like this, happening for other people, but I didn't remotely believe that it was something that really happened. New Hope had just given me enough money to pay my bills for a month and for the first time since leaving Colorado I thought: *Wow, this is really going to happen.*

Those extra days at home also gave me time to work with my mom on sending out a letter to everyone she knew, asking them to help her son do this extraordinary thing. I talked to Adriaan, my roommate back in Colorado, about asking people to help out as well, figuring that maybe there would be another dozen people at the least. I thought about calling Doreen and some of the other ladies I worked with at the bank. A couple of my bosses may be heartless and greedy, but most of the people I worked with wouldn't have thought twice about putting ten bucks into my account, but for some reason, it never felt right calling. I also bowed out of directly asking Skip for a donation and putting up some sort of donation stand at the coffee shop. I had told him about my idea of getting 300 people to donate $10 when I stopped in for a bit on Thursday, Lakota Coffee is one of those places you stop in whenever you're in town just to see who might be there.

Skip is a wonderful man, so I figured that if he had wanted to, he would have stopped and given me ten bucks. Plus, by that time I had made the conscious decision not to push anyone too hard. The idea had been given to me. My job was to pass it along to people and to accept that God would take care of the rest. That's also the reason why I didn't worry about following up with my cousin Eli. The last time we had talked, I had felt let down by my grandma and aunt, so I had desperately asked him to talk to his church to see if they would be able to do anything to help me out, but I hadn't heard anything back from him. I even thought for awhile about what I might be able to do as far as giving people a tee-shirt, or something to show my appreciation for what they were allowing me to do, but then I realized that spending money would defeat the whole purpose and no matter how uncomfortable it felt, I was going to have to learn to accept what people were giving me…but even at that, with so many wonderful things already happening and accepting that I was on God's timetable, the wait seemed interminable.

First, there had been the wait through the long Holiday weekend. Even arriving home on Sunday meant that I had to wait through Monday until Daniel would even have a chance to look at my car on Tuesday; and then it was a week filled with missed shipments and wrong parts. I spent one more weekend sitting on the porch swing in the middle of the corn and soybean fields of Missouri and it was Tuesday morning before Daniel called to let me know that my car was finally ready to go, with time for one more surprise. All of this time that he had put into my car, dealing with idiots not shipping, then shipping the wrong part, and getting to the shop at 6:30 Tuesday morning wasn't going to cost me a penny. My parents, even though they are far from wealthy, took care of the cost of the parts, and Daniel took care of the labor. "It's the least I can do to help you out," he told me.

Maybe what I'm about to do really is something special.

PART II

THE CAJUN DOME
LAFAYETTE, LA

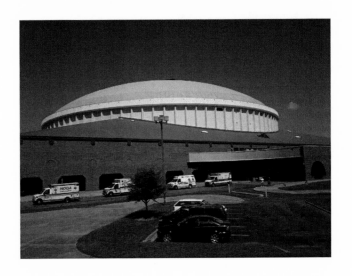

Arrival in Louisiana

Wednesday, September 14

At some point in our lives, most of us have driven on snow-covered roads or at least been caught on the road during a heavy thunderstorm. We are familiar with that gut rolling fear brought on by rain so heavy that you can barely make out the front of your own car, or that snow covered bend in the road that looks just like the cornfields off to your right. You turn the wheel, nervously hoping that you guessed right and the road doesn't disappear from under you as the car noses down into the ditch. Having spent much of my youth living in the flood prone country, it's the same feeling I got as I attempted to drive across the flooded road, the corner of the car door scraping across the water's surface as I opened it to check the water level.

Some would describe the feeling as highly caffeinated butterflies dancing in their stomach. I liken it to my insides being turned into a mass of ground beef; a gut that feels as sturdy as jello with the sensation of tasting raw meat. From the moment I crossed the Mississippi-Louisiana border, to when I pulled into the parking lot at Roy's townhouse, this is how I felt. Never knowing, and always expecting to see roofs blown off, trees scattered and the occasional building collapsed. But like the vast majority of those nervous filled drives, this drive also ended uneventfully. Despite knowing that I had no idea what I was getting myself into, I was stunned that up to this point, everything seemed very normal. That changed in just a few hours.

After a brief pit stop at Roy's house to drop off a few things and have a quick bite to eat, he took me to the Cajun Dome, the University of Lafayette's athletic center, where the Red Cross had set up a shelter. The stomach churning picked up its pace. I was minutes away from coming face to face with thousands of hurricane victims. I thought of the Super Dome in New Orleans. Visions of the Superdome in New Orleans came to mind; of loud, dirty conditions; of people and beds crammed into every corner; and of bathrooms wreaking of overflow. Once again, I was surprised.

I was in awe at the cleanliness and apparent organization. Even the air seemed quiet, which was extremely surprising given that three thousand people were making the Dome their home. In order to go inside, you have to have a Cajun Dome security i.d. card. Getting my badge was the main purpose for the trip tonight, that and allow me the chance to get a general feel for just what I had gotten myself into.

At the first checkpoint, Roy introduced me to one of the National Guardsmen as a new volunteer. The fully armed guardsman directed me to a registration table off to the side were I waited for a Red Cross nurse to run through his litany of questions: Did I have any open wounds? No. Any coughing, sore throat...? No...

After passing his tests, we were directed to a second checkpoint. Short of the x-ray machines, this one was just like going to the airport. The contraband list was even much the same: no guns, knives, alcohol or lighters. I was pleasantly surprised that despite having to empty their pockets and walk through a metal detector to go inside what was now their house, nobody seemed bothered by the extra ordeal. I guess that's one good thing the coverage on CNN did, everybody understands that the tight security really is for the best.

After passing the second checkpoint, it was time to get my i.d. card. The area looked like a miniaturized local DMV. A dozen or so chairs were lined up off to the side of a rope line that led to a row of cameras an attendants constantly calling out, "Next!" I was immediately impressed by how well organized the place was. Across from the i.d. area was the health center were people could meet with a doctor or talk with a counselor if needed. Roy led me around to see where they had the distribution area set up for new arrivals. Here they could pick up their cot, bedding, hygiene products and clothes.

There was a snack stand that was open between meal times and a stand designated for handing out supplies for babies. We walked by the daycare center, a phone bank, a post office and areas designated for employment, housing and financial assistance. FEMA had a table set up to assist with people's claims. I noticed signs scattered all around for daily and Sunday masses, and even haircuts. I am impressed with how much seems to be going on under this one roof. *We're just a Starbucks short of having an entire city in here.*

During the walk-around tour we stopped to pray with a lady in her early twenties. Still overwhelmed by the mass of beds crowded onto the gymnasium floor, I stood back and let Roy do the talking and comforting. She was a single mother with a 3-month old baby girl. The father had disappeared long before the hurricane, and she was simply lost, not really knowing where to go or what to do next. She asked for a prayer for guidance and we obliged, before heading home to relax and prepare for a very long, full day tomorrow.

The Ardoines

Thursday, September 15

My first job when I arrived at the Dome was to assist the families who were just arriving to check in and get settled into their new home. I was surprised to see that three weeks after Katrina, people are still coming into the shelters for the first time. Some have been staying with family for a couple of weeks, patience and tempers now beginning to run out. Others have been sleeping in cars, on porches or had found a spot of ground to pitch a tent. Whatever the case may be, it's been a little more than two weeks since they lost their home and the reality of their situation is beginning to settle in; it will be quite some time before anybody will be able to move back home. And whatever their reasons may be, living side-by-side, cot-to-cot with 3,000 other people was never their first choice. It shouldn't be difficult to imagine the drooping faces and blankness in the eyes of most people I see. The Ardoines, however, were a pleasant exception to that.

Mr. And Mrs. Ardoine and their three children were the first family I welcomed, they turned out to be the last as well. Their house was in East New Orleans and they were in the biggest group of those still arriving. Mrs. Ardoine's sister had been letting them stay at her house, but the two-bedroom apartment was just too small for a second family with three kids to stay for very long. Mrs. Ardoine was also concerned about the added burden placed on her sister and her own family, "Better to make use of the Red Cross than abuse her family," she thought. That was the smallest part of their reason, but it provided cover for Mr. Ardoine's real reason for wanting to move out.

As I have said, it's been two weeks since he lost their home and he felt like it was time for him to start taking back the responsibility of taking care of his family. Coming to the Dome was a step in that direction. So here they came, mismatched suitcases and garbage bags. Everything they now owned was dropped at the curb by their brother in-law, then carried in with assistance from the red-vested volunteers (these are the 'official' Red Cross volunteers.)

Just like I did yesterday, their first stop was to face Gary's short barrage of health questions. Next was the brief registration process and then they were handed into my personal care.

The hour I spent with the Ardoines is already a blur, flashing in my memory from moment to moment, out of order and filled with lots of holes. To put it in a little perspective, here they were having arrived ten minutes ago, and there I was, fewer than fifteen minutes into my first day and I was the expert they were looking to for all of the answers to their questions. To say that I was nervous, insecure and dazed by my surroundings is quite an understatement. *Thank God Roy brought me down last night in order to get my bearings!*

Our first challenge was to go through the security station manned by National Guardsman and metal detectors. Every bag had to be searched for lighters, alcohol, weapons (including pocket knives), scissors, etc. After everything that happened at the Super Dome, no one is taking any chances, and that's a good thing. After the security check, the first stop for everyone arriving is to get their security badges, again, just like I had done fourteen hours earlier. During, this time Mrs. Ardoine kept asking me about something, I think it was how to find a job or a babysitter. I don't really remember because it was something that I wasn't real sure about and we had other things that needed to get done first.

Instead of all of us standing and waiting for the badges to get printed, we left the bags with the three kids, the oldest son being 14, and went to get their cots and bedding. As we were walking, I went over the few things I knew that I knew; when and where meals were served, the main information table, where jobs were posted (so I guess that wasn't the question she was asking and I have no idea what it was) and where church services were held. We talked more about their experience, I told them about meals and where the snack stand was. All of the time, trying to keep the focus in mind that what they needed most from me was a sense of warm welcome, sincerity and a source of confidence in this new and very strange environment.

I did the best I could to give them my complete attention and hope that it was enough. The cots, I found out, would be delivered to them once they had found an open spot in the gymnasium, so we gathered a handful of bedding materials, made the five-minute walk back to the Dome from the attached Convention Center and found a corner area big enough for the five of them. I didn't know how to leave the Ardoines, but their i.d. badges were ready and it was time for me to head back outside and be ready for the next family. Mrs. Ardoine was still asking me her question and I had to give up, tell her she would have to check in with the information table later and say good-bye. Hopefully I will see them again so I can follow up on how they are doing.

Within a few minutes of returning to the registration area, I was assigned to work the front information table. Different from the information table inside, this one was set up outside the Dome in order to help those who are not actually living at the Cajun Dome. Some of them are continuing o stay with friends or family, others found an open campground to set up a rented RV and many more are staying at an area hotel. There are even people who don't really have a place to stay, but cannot mentally take the idea or stress of living in a shelter with so many strangers and no privacy anywhere.

Sent by television and radio reports, friends or the hopeful reputation of the Red Cross, there was a steady stream of people coming looking for assistance. But the unfortunate truth was, there was no help for them at the shelter. It was very quickly and sternly communicated to me that the Red Cross was not set up here, only that they where here to help provide shelter to the Katrina refugees. The impressive luster I felt last night wore off very quickly.

The biggest part of my job really was to tell people that the Dome was not actually a Red Cross Center, meaning that if you weren't staying here, they had nothing at this location to give you. There were index cards printed up with a 1-800 number for me to give to people who needed to sign up for financial assistance (it took me two hours and talking with a dozen workers to figure out that this is the only assistance that the Red Cross is providing for people right now) and a helpful packet with several phone numbers for them to call for help with finding clothes, food and anything else they might need. We had several maps, including one to the local FEMA office where they could go to check on the status of their FEMA application, along with a dozen other fliers with information on everything from childcare to finding a job and even transportation around the country to reunite with separated family members. Like the impressiveness I felt last night, the awe at how much information I had to give out quickly waned under massive confusion and disorganization. Within 20 minutes of joining the two ladies running the table, I've long since forgotten their names, I was left on my own with a vague mention that someone else might come out to help me.

Fortunately, although I had been left to myself, I had Officer Steve at hand to help with directions, after all, I hadn't been in Lafayette for 24 hours yet and didn't even know the name of the cross street 200 yards in front of me. Other people did show up throughout the day to help out. After about half an hour of being on my own, a man named Paul came out to give me a hand. He turned out to be the first of a new group of Mental Health workers that were taking 2-hour shifts helping me work the information table.

I'm already finding it difficult to keep track of where they are from, much less what people's names are. Paul is from Montana. There was someone from New Jersey, Connecticut, Wisconsin, Kansas, Illinois, Nevada and of course Colorado, if I'm including myself. Each one has said pretty much the same thing and expressed what I had felt; the situation down here is bad and the people here need all of the help they can get. It's amazing how many people have come from all across the country and I think that I would have enjoyed this job today if it weren't for two things.

First, I was the expert that all of these people, everyone of them older than me and a trained counselor, looked to for answers to their questions as to what was going on and how to answer peoples' questions. Second, it feels like I spent the vast majority of my time dolling out bad news. Telling people that nothing was being distributed at the Dome and fighting off an endless number of rumors to the contrary. There was one woman, in particular, whose face I will surely never forget, even though I never got her name.

Her tears started flowing as soon as I mentioned that there was nowhere here for her to sign up for the financial assistance. Like so many people that I talked to throughout the day, she had already spent three days calling that 1-800 number we were handing out, getting nothing but a busy signal for three days. I had no idea how to comfort and console her beyond saying "I'm Sorry" as sincerely as I felt it and asking if there was anything else that I might be able to help her find. She had food, clothes, a place to stay and had already talked with FEMA. But she didn't have any money for gas or the many other things that a family with three kids, who were cowering in the arms of their grandmother 15 feet away, needs. After I had said a final, futile "I'm Sorry," Bob took her aside.

I was so thankful that he was on hand and tried to pay attention to what he was saying, learn from a professional so that I could do a better job the next time this situation came up, but for the life of me, all that I can remember at this point is that she left in a much better mood than when I had first seen her.

Thank God I had people like Bob, Paul and Officer Steve around me today. If it hadn't been for them I don't think that I would have made it through, and tomorrow is just a few hours away. At least by then I will have a day behind me and I did a good job today of figuring out as much as I could about what's going on at the Dome, so tomorrow I might at least feel like I know what I'm doing.

The Mental Health Workers

Friday, September 16

When I arrived at the Dome this morning, I asked one of the Red Cross ladies at the registration booth if she wanted me to go back and work the information table until they needed me for something else. She gave me a blank nod that seemed to say, "Uh, yeah, whatever. Sounds good to me." It was with that roaring injection of confidence that I grabbed the box of papers from behind the table and nervously began arranging them on the two tables pushed up against the portable guardrails.

I had absolutely no idea what I was doing and was still fumbling through the stacks half an hour later when a guy in a red vest (indicating he was an official Red Cross volunteer) walked up to me, "I hear you're the expert around here." There was absolutely no question in his voice and no matter how humbly I tried to push that aside, it didn't take long to realize that I really was the expert. Somehow it doesn't seem right that having not even been in town for two days and having never experienced anything to do with disaster relief, that I am the expert. But as the day wore on, my hopes for a Red Cross person who did know something to join me continued hoping. I realized that having worked the information table yesterday for only a few hours, I did have more experience than anyone else who was going to show up.

Aside from trying to *feel* like I knew what I was doing, the other big challenge for the day was to actually get a better handle on what is going on and just what services are being offered here at the Dome. I found out that there's a free city shuttle bus just a hundred yards down the drive that anyone can use. I still haven't found anybody who knows what its schedule is or where it goes.

People seem to have different ideas about where people can go to get healthcare assistance. Yesterday afternoon, I was told that people can go to the University Medical Center, a tall brown building 3/4 of a mile directly in front of us and receive whatever assistance they need. The only thing they have to do is show proof that they were living in any one of the affected counties. Several Red Cross people have told me that they can also have existing prescriptions filled there, and some others are saying that they have to go to the county health department if it's a prescription that has already been written. That small distinction has caused a lot of headaches today, whether people are simply needing a prescription filled, or if they need to have one written. Since we can see the medical center and the county building is a few miles away, I'm just sending everyone to the University Medical Center. I'm hoping that tomorrow I'll be able to get the real scoop figured out.

I can't remember if I have already mentioned this or not, but this job is extremely stressful and exhausting. Most of my time is spent trying to console and explain to people that they need to be persistent and keep calling the 1-800 number to register for the financial assistance. More than once, we were told that the number simply doesn't work and that there must be some other number to call. What can I say other than, "keep calling and you'll eventually get through?" I have been told that there are people on the phones 24-hours a day, "so maybe take a nap early and try calling at 2:00 or 3:00 in the morning and you'll have a better chance of getting through."

I spent a lot of time also making sure that people have checked in with FEMA and asking if they needed any other assistance: food, clothes, baby supplies...The most frustrating part is that although I was passing out a small packet that had phone numbers and addresses of agencies in the area, I had absolutely no idea how to give directions to people on how to get there. Someone had drawn up a map that could get people from the Dome to the local FEMA office, which was really helpful. What was most helpful though, was a local police officer, Steve who grew up here in Lafayette.

People were constantly coming up to ask us where the local Wal-Mart was, or how to get to the Salvation Army location that I was sending them to. Steve was standing by and always alert to helping out. Little by little, I listened in and by mid-afternoon was able to at least point people a mile down the road to the Wal-Mart store, or hand them a map to the FEMA office and point to a spot across the street, where the Food Stamp building is located. I don't know what I would do if it weren't for Officer Steve—some expert I was?!

After talking with dozens more people who are still unable to get through on the phone to sign-up for Red Cross assistance and consoling many more who are getting absolutely nothing from the Red Cross, the impressiveness of their operation when I first walked in Wednesday evening is long gone. Adding to this feeling is that as I've gotten to talk with the Mental Health workers over the past two days, there is the universal feeling on their part that their time and services are being wasted. They're trained to be counselors and help people through the mental trauma of such a catastrophe, and yet, outside of their two hours spent helping me, they talk with maybe one or two people a day.

I'm not arguing their point, but at the same time, I am extremely grateful to have them around. While they tell me I've been doing a good job of listening and being very helpful to people, I still don't know what to say to someone who breaks down in tears when I tell them that the Red Cross is not registering anyone for financial assistance here. The mental health workers are professionals and maybe they don't know what to say either, but it's a lot better than what I can come up with.

All is not bad though. It largely seems like it because by the end of the day I need my own comfort of letting out some of this stress on paper, and for the smaller part, each day has been so mentally draining that I need all of the time I can get to shut down and sleep for nine or ten hours everyday. I will offer a few moments here though, devoted to some good things, one being the mental health volunteers I work along side with every day.

I have long had difficulty remembering people's names, and I'm already having trouble keeping track of where people from. It is simply amazing to find out how many people have taken time off from work, mostly a week or two weeks, to come down here and help. There's Paul, a counselor from Wyoming who decided this would be a good way to spend his vacation. More than anyone else he has helped show me the importance of exuding confidence in instilling a sense of confidence in people. Bill from Iowa has an extraordinary ability to empathize with people and turn tears into laughter. Michelle from New Jersey, who my mom would be happy to hear has proposed marriage and a little less happy that I turned down the offer, never gives up on trying to find help for someone.

Then there's Anna from Wisconsin, who I really wish would propose marriage. No more than 26-years old, she's the boss of the entire shelter. I have seen the tears welling up in her eyes whenever she hears that the Red Cross is failing to help someone, and witnessed her willingness to fix a problem that is brought to her attention. In many ways, even though she is nearly my age, I feel that she is a child trying to be President of the United States. That's not to say anything against her, or her character, she just doesn't have the experience or knowledge to be running such a large, chaotic operation, and should have never been put in this position.

Roy pressed me hard again today to talk with the people at PRC, the Pastoral Resource Council. It's a group of churches that have gotten together to send people out, *closer to the action*, amidst the cleaning crews where Katrina actually hit. I am extremely grateful to have him in my life right now. Not only has he given me a place to stay for as long as I am down here, but I'm relying on him as a source of God's guidance. Even with that though, I have this gut feeling that it's not time yet to talk with the PRC yet. So I tried to gently express to Roy that while working the Information Table isn't what I had in mind when I left Colorado and is extremely stressful, I'm confident it's what I need to be doing for at least a few more days. Then I'll talk with the PRC and hopefully put these youthful muscles to work. I do hope he doesn't think I'm upset with him, or that I don't trust his high opinion of that group.

Frustration

Saturday, September 17

We usually think of Saturday as a slow day. After all, it's the weekend and under normal circumstances, most government offices and nonprofit agencies are closed. The weekend is our normal time to relax, catch our breaths and do all of the things we didn't have time to do during the workweek. But life is anything but normal right now, and so coming into the Dome this morning, I really didn't know what to expect; whether or not we would have much to do.

I arrived around 10:00 am, which seems to have become my regular starting time, nervous and unsure. It didn't take long to dawn on me that even though the rest of the world slows down on the weekends, this is home for hundred's of people. The Dome is where they live and life doesn't stop simply because a few offices are closed. Things were quieter with fewer volunteers having come to help, but the Dome itself was just as active as it was through the week. Nothing was all that different today.

Late in the morning, a lady from New Orleans asked me about getting a pair of glasses for her ten-year old son. Complicating the situation, she was staying with her sister-in-law and was not an actual Dome resident, and since this was the first time I anyone had asked us about eyeglasses, it took me a bit of running around to figure out what we could for her. After 20 minutes of asking questions, I was able to track down a lady with the Red Cross who knew where to get glasses inside and since it was the weekend, it was slow enough that she had time to take care of the lady herself. But that left one more major hurdle to overcome. Since she was not a Dome resident, she couldn't come inside in order to talk to the *right* person.

Once again, Officer Steve proved his worth and character. Even though she wasn't technically allowed in, he allowed me to escort her and her son inside, "so long as someone from the Red Cross is with her at all times." I took her inside, passed her off to Linda, and returned to my table outside to help the half-dozen people who had been waiting for the twenty minutes while I had been helping her. Sadly, half an hour later I saw the lady and her son walk out without any glasses. I asked if she had been able to get anything and she said quite plainly that she had not.

A man had stopped in a couple of weeks ago who was handing out donated eyeglasses. He was long gone and the Red Cross itself was not doing anything to help out. I quickly spotted Anna, the young lady from Wisconsin who is in charge of running the shelter, and asked her if she knew of anywhere for this lady to go. She had no ideas and no suggestions to offer us. The lady was very kind and grateful for my attempts to help, but I could feel the frustration and despair in her voice as she walked away with her son empty handed.

It wasn't very long after the eyeglass lady had left that an older lady came up to ask us about getting her family registered with the

Red Cross. She had just a touch of grey in her otherwise very black hair and as soon as I moved my hand toward the stack of 1-800 placards, before I even had the chance to say anything myself, she spoke up, "Don't you be thinkin' about giving me one of those things and tellin' me to call that number. I been calling for three weeks..."

Unfortunately, neither her words nor the harshness in her voice are unusual now. I've had a dozen people stick their phone in my ear yelling "See what you get! That number ain't no good!" (It wasn't until this morning that I made the connection between their busy signal and the problems I've been having when I try to call my own family back in Missouri. This part of the problem, at least, is a cell tower issue, not the Red Cross'.)

Their attitudes are understandable and expected given their situation. They're homeless, nearly penniless and three weeks is no exaggeration. The harsh attitude and near yelling voices only bother me to the extent that it makes it more difficult for me to calm them down and help them find what we can for them. This time however, went well beyond a distressed outburst. This lady was pissed, now shaking one of those 3"x4" cards we've been handing out and demanding to speak with someone from the Red Cross. She wanted them to give her some answers for the way they've been treating people.

I don't have the writing skills to describe her anger, frustration, or the frantic way that she yelled at us about not telling her to call a phone number she'd been calling for so long. "I know it's not your fault, your just volunteers and they don't tell you anything, just what they want you to know." She also mixed in a reference to us just being pawns as she paced back and forth in a small arc about fifteen feet from the table. This lady wasn't without a point and I could empathize with her, yet she is also wrong.

I have come to describe a significant part of my job as playing interference for the Red Cross, but my primary goal is to do whatever I can to help people out. Had this been the first hurricane relief effort for the Red Cross, their own behavior and apparent confusion might be understandable, but as they say, "this isn't their first rodeo." When I go home to Roy's each night, I see commercials touting how the Red Cross is the expert in helping Americans through difficult times. They ask, "When America faces disaster, who do they turn toward for help?" and then a big Red Cross fills the screen. It is ridiculous, but as I explained to her, I could take the time to track down an *official* Red Cross person, but she would be getting the same answers.

Her voice had settled somewhat to more of an angry discussion than pure yell, allowing the 50 or so nearby residents and other volunteers to sneak in a relaxing breathe. Then Bob from Oklahoma jumped in with his own tirade before I had a chance to start thinking about how to respond. I do need to make a point here that this is not the Bob who I met on my first day, the one from Nebraska who I have wonderful conversations with. This Bob took everything this lady said personally, telling her how he had come down here, "all the way from Oklahoma," to help her and was good enough to volunteer his time and doing the best that he could and deserved more respect... The two of them were going full force at one another and I was trapped in the middle, feeling like a kid trying to push two giants back to their corners. Bob, not me, is the trained professional and should know better than to mix it up. After all, isn't he supposed to be helping her, or at least trying to.

For a moment, I was in shock and stood silently until Bob had effectively pulled her back toward the table and I could try interrupting the argument without yelling across the drive; which would have only tossed me into the heat of the moment. With an unargumentative tone, I agreed, nodded and consoled with the lady, but forced my way over Bob's retorts to insist that the only people around here who did not have to register through the phone line were the residents who were living in the Dome (I was hoping that she would pick up on the hint, a suggestion at how we could help her. I didn't feel like I could come right out and say, "Come over here, pretend that you are going to stay here, register for financial assistance and then leave." She was in no mood to listen, so it went right over her head.

It seemed like minute after minute went by, me trying to verbally pry her away, and Bob vehemently pulling her back in against me. After a few more minutes, she had finally backed away from the table again, turning around every other step to throw a non-insultive complaint in the air. But she was leaving and that was my unfortunate goal. Nothing against her personally, she is just one of the many who have reached their breaking point and happened to do it in our presence. Fifteen feet, twenty feet, then thirty. She was a good forty feet away, no longer saying a word and Bob tossed out yet another, "I'm down here trying and you're telling me!!! I didn't come here to be treated!!!" That was it, child or not, untrained versus trained, I yelled at Bob to shut up. Out of the corner of my eye I saw the lady start to turn back around, but my focus was entirely on Bob, yelling and gesturing for him to leave it alone.

I can only guess that seeing me helped to hold her tongue and she finally left. I wish Bob would do the same and never come back. If it were up to me, the idiot would be locked up inside the Dome and allowed one trip out, to get on the bus and catch his plane back home. Our job here is to do whatever we can to help these people. Sometimes that's as simple as giving a phone number or address, at others it involves a consoling moment and embrace, and there are a few when we need to be a verbal punching bag to let them blow of some steam. I'm sure that Bob knows that, on a normal day. He's a trained professional who didn't come down here to yell at people and pick fights, rather, he came out of the goodness of his heart. I am confident that he knows better, but the stress and our growing frustrations have turned him into a counseling buffoon.

You may be asking why I didn't just get someone from the Red Cross to begin with. There are two reasons why I was reluctant to do that. First, we have been told as bluntly as possible that they won't tell people anything that they haven't told us, so there is no real point to making that effort. Second, and this is the main reason, while trying to calm and council people who have lost their homes is difficult enough, many of them have told me that they don't even know whether or not they've lost their house, the most stressful part of my job is actually having to deal with the Red Cross. Over the several days that I have been running this information center, I have gained a firm grasp on what people need to do when it comes to working with FEMA, finding some food, clothes, housing and jobs locally, but the Red Cross remains a grating mystery.

Finding the right person is nearly impossible. Deanna from the Louisiana Council on Child Development came up to the table today and asked to speak with Eric. She had scheduled an appointment with him to talk about putting on a presentation for parents with younger children to share with them what childcare resources are available in Lafayette. Common sense would expect that an organization experienced in disaster relief would have a system in place for the workers to get in touch with one another. Even if it was something as simple as having radios for the key volunteers working with the Red Cross, but apparently they haven't figured that out. From what I could gather, there are about four people equipped with a radio at the Cajun Dome, and who those people are changes almost hourly. That's four radios for a crew supporting over 3,000 residents. For the rest of us, we have to rely on the arena's built-in paging system. It takes about ten minutes to walk a handwritten message from our table outside to the other side of the Dome where they set up the paging table. Of course, there's no way of knowing whether or not the page was even heard by the person, so we usually wait for fifteen minutes for them to show up and then it's another ten minute walk to have the page reread. After an hour of waiting, re-paging, more waiting and asking around if anyone had seen or knew who Eric was, I happened to bump into the right person, "Yeah, he's not here, but should be back at some point." Another hour later, another *right person* happened to overhear why Deanna was waiting for Eric. Fortunately, this guy really was the right person and he was able to schedule a time for her to come back and meet with parents.

That was well over a half-hour of my time wasted, while more people were waiting in line for me to help them out, because the Red Cross isn't organized enough, or smart enough to have radios for their key management people. Even without radios, there should be a roster of the people in charge of each area so that when I went to the Administrative Center two hours earlier they could have told me, "If Eric's not here then she can talk with Aaron." The worst part of it is that their ineptitude goes beyond simply making my job more difficult. Deanna was the one who had already taken the time to schedule an appointment and still had to wait for over two hours in order to do something that took less than a minute to get done. It's a good thing that she is as patient as she is because most people would have left after the first half hour, leaving parents and kids out in the cold.

On the first day I was here, I was told that if anyone not living inside needs healthcare of any sort that they could go to the University Health Center. Late in the day on Friday I heard an older man tell Nancy that when he got there they wouldn't do anything for him because he didn't have his insurance card. Needless to say, that didn't sound right, so I told him and Nancy to hold on for a second while I dug around to find out exactly what we needed to do. For two days, it turned out, we had sent a countless number of people to the wrong place; the county health department was now taking care of all of the hurricane victims. We had been sending people to the wrong place for two days because no one bothered to tell us, the information table, that things had changed. It's been the same story with finding eyeglasses for people, trying to figure out what the scoop is on getting prescriptions filled, distributing the debit cards that have been sent here for people to pick up, and just about every other service that the Red Cross has provided at some point. Things change and the only way we find out about it is if I hunt someone down after we start hearing conflicting stories. I physically cringe now whenever someone asks me a question and I realize that I have to talk with someone from the Red Cross.

With so many problems and such a low opinion of them, one could easily argue that at this point I should step away and have nothing more to do with Red Cross. After all, had I been an employee who thought this poorly of his employer, I would have been gone long ago. However, I find some level of contentment in knowing that I am working alongside the Red Cross, and not for them. Mostly though, I thought about what would happen if I were to leave, to go and volunteer my time somewhere else, and I see Oklahoma Bob with no one to stand between him and the next upset person who walks up to the table. The people coming to the Dome need someone like me here to do whatever I can to help. That being said, they are going to have to get by without me tomorrow.

When I left Colorado I had in mind that I would be working daylight hours, seven days a week and it's one more thing that hasn't turned out like I had imagined. Seven to eight hours of working at the Dome has been as much as I can handle each day and even at that, I've gone from needing only five to six hours of sleep a night, to easily sleeping ten hours strait and in desperate need of a day off after working just three full days. Maybe driving from Missouri on Tuesday has added to the weariness so I can count it as closer to working a full week. However, the bottom line remains the same. Even though life at the Dome keeps going on Sundays, they're going to have to fend for themselves. I'm going to have to take the day off tomorrow and fight any temptation to go in for a couple of hours. My brain needs the break.

A Day of Rest

Sunday, September 18

Being Sunday, Roy and I began the day by going to his church. It was a nondenominational service and I've already forgotten its name. The preacher, whose name I never caught so I'll call him Jordan, spoke for a little more than an hour about finding God's message amidst the disaster of Hurricane Katrina. At the core of Jordan's message was that events like Soddom & Gommorah, Noah's flood, the enslavement of the Jews in Egypt, etc. weren't merely about the expression of God's wrath and dolling out punishment, but were a way for Him to communicate with us. He asked us: "What is God trying to communicate to us through Katrina?"

Jordan's idea was that we need to pay closer attention to the depravity of events like New Orleans's Mardi Gras celebration, which feels uncomfortably close to blaming the hurricane as God's judgment against New Orleans. I don't think that God looked at the earth, saw New Orleans, and decided to stick His thumb in the ocean to stir up a hurricane. I do think, however, that there are greater questions Katrina should inspire: How do we treat the poor? How quickly are we to throw blame at others, rather than address the problem at hand? Are we more concerned about our own personal gain or the *Common Good*? Jordan did have one good point though: As members of Christ's church and body, we should be asking ourselves how we are responding to the growing immorality around our daily life.

For once, the announcements were the best part of the service. Jordan is one of the founding committee members of the PRC, the orange shirt crew at the Dome that Roy has been nagging me to team up with. As soon as the words came out of Jordan's mouth, Roy winked and gave me a nudge. *I wish he would just leave me alone.* I really do know what I'm doing and listening to God on my own. I don't need him to be telling me what to do, especially after I've already told him a dozen times that I am going to do it!!! That sounds harsh, but each day it's more and more how I'm feeling. There's quite a bit of difference between feeling that Roy is fitting into the plan God has for me here and following everything that he suggests. I'm digressing and should return to announcement.

Jordan claims that the PRC is the only significant organization that is sending individuals and work crews out into the field. This just confirmed what I have been thinking the last few days...to keep working with the Red Cross at the Dome for a few more days and then, later in the week, I'll talk with someone from the PRC about joining one of their crews. I really feel like everything down here is coming together in its own time. So it was with a mixture of a high note and feeling of empty wanting that church ended. It just doesn't feel like I did much of worshipping God without partaking in the Eucharist/communion.

After church, Roy drove me to Iberia Parish for my first taste of real Southern Cooking. Naturally, I told him it was great, but in all honesty, it was nothing to write home about, or in a journal. We did however, run into a good friend and mentor of Roy's, Brother Dave, as Roy enthusiastically calls him. Brother Dave is what I would consider your prototypical southern minister, hefty in appearance and voice. If the meal at the restaurant was a let down, the hospitality from Brother Dave wasn't. He invited us strait over to his table to join him and his wife where we continued to eat for a second hour. Even growing up in the Midwest, I'm used to an attitude of non-intrusion and letting the couple enjoy a Sunday afternoon with themselves. There, we would have stopped by their table for a few minutes, caught up briefly and then motored on out the door.

As it was, I sat relatively bored while Roy and Brother Dave talked about local business; so maybe Southern hospitality isn't all that great. After all, I was the 'guest' and sat quietly for the better part of the hour, wondering if it would be alright to get another plate and hit up the buffet some more. I probably would have, but the food hadn't been worth it. After they had finished their meals, it was back to Roy Jr.'s place to relax for the rest of the evening.

A few hours later, Roy tried to get me to join him for an evening church session with Steve, a Pastor he had met at the Dome. But I'd had enough fill of being Roy's lackey for the day, and needed some extra rest for tomorrow.

The Rumor Mill

Monday, September 19

I feel like a big part of my job here is to play rumor control, the biggest rumor being that people can come to the Cajun Dome and sign up for, or get assistance with the Red Cross. This is not just another rant against them because this time, it's not the Red Cross' fault. At least one out of every five people I talk to have come to the Cajun Dome in order to get help because someone else has told them to. It almost seems like everyone who comes here has gotten their information from a different source and has a different story about what we are doing here.

Just the other day, I asked Anna to get on the phone with the local FEMA office and 'clarify' to them that we were not distributing any money or supplies at the Dome. I've had people come directly from the Salvation Army, their local church, Goodwill, the Social Security Office and even Wal-Mart. The most frustrating thing is that it's not just individual people we are fighting. More than one person has come to me because they had read it in the paper or heard on either the local news or radio that the Red Cross was giving out assistance. Nobody seems to know what's going on down here and for some reason, it's always harder to stop a rumor than it is to get a dozen started. Today, however, it was my turn to turn the tables and try using the local media to start my own rumor. Of course, this rumor would be true.

The number of people coming to the information table every day and asking us about registering with the Red Cross has not changed. It's been nearly four weeks since Katrina hit and I still talk with dozens of people everyday who have spent hours trying to get through to the 1-800 number, which is the only way that they can register. That is, unless they are living in the Dome. For a few hours each day there are a few representatives signing up Dome residents to receive their financial assistance.

It's understandable that people can't get a call to go through; cell towers are crippled and millions of people are trying to register. There are legitimate reasons why the phone system isn't working, but each day we've tried finding a new, creative way of getting people the help they need. For the first day or two, we talked with Anna and others to let them know how much difficulty people were having. We suggested that they try calling late at night and tried to comfort them by explaining that 4,000 more operators had been hired. But we spent most of our time during those first days really trying to convince the Red Cross that they needed to come up with a new system. Then, when we realized that wasn't going to work, we started *letting it slip* that residents were able to meet with someone and register for assistance inside.

By Thursday, I was making sure that the *slip* became a part of our standard spiel and on Friday, people were walking up to the table and flat out telling us that they knew other people were able to register inside. Nancy, Paul, Bill and I were absolutely thrilled that the word was getting out and gladly pointed them in toward registration. Aside from helping these people, we were hopeful that if enough of them were coming here to stay just so they could register for the financial assistance, that the Red Cross would be forced to do something. Today, they did. Only it was something none of us imagined would happen, and brought their actions here down to a whole new low.

As of this morning, and due to the increasing number of people who have been signing up to stay in the shelter but not actually taking residence, the Red Cross will no longer be conducting any on-site registration whatsoever. Just like everyone else now, the people living in the Dome will have to start calling that blasted 1-800 number. Outrage seems too kind of a word. Evil feels appropriate. The official word that filtered down to us, we weren't actually directly informed of the change in policy, was that they no longer had enough volunteers to continue the financial registration...HORSE SNOT!!! I know at least a dozen people who would have been more than glad to set up a tent outside the Dome a week ago and register people. There are more than enough volunteers to take care of it. Furthermore, we also heard the whispers that they were concerned about people coming here just to register for the financial assistance. You're bloody right that's what they're doing, because they have no other real option. On TV, The Red Cross begs the question, "Who do Americans turn to when they need help." On the street, they tell people to be patient and keep calling. *How many more weeks should a person who's lost everything they owned be patient?* It's already been four.

About an hour after we had heard about the decision to close down the financial registration, I saw a camera crew walking around the front of the dome and asked Paul and Nancy if either of them could see a network logo on the camera. I'd already met with more than one journalism student who had been working on a class project out here and didn't want to go through very much effort just to end up on some professor's desk.

The next thing I knew, I was running to catch up with Paul. No word between us was needed. Within 30 seconds, the two of us had the cameraman and reporter cornered against the side of the building and didn't let him go for at least ten minutes. "If you just stand out here for five minutes you'll meet a dozen people who have worn their fingers raw from trying to get through to register with the Red Cross...We've done everything we can think of to try and pressure them from the inside, but nothing's worked. We need you guys to run the story and put some outside pressure on them. Maybe then they'll change things."

Sadly, it was a failed attempt. John, the reporter, informed us that he had run a story on the difficulty of people getting assistance from the Red Cross just a couple of days earlier, so "there is no point to running it again." When our appeal to his greater humanity failed, I tried to use my Mizzou Journalism School swagger, the University of Missouri is the topped ranked broadcast journalism program in the nation, into convincing him that this was the moment for the media to shine, we needed him to put the pressure on the Red Cross and he would be a lead on what would surely, needed to, become a national story. As I said though, our efforts failed and the best we got was a, "Maybe we'll run it again toward the end of the week." *Maybe he could tell the hundred people I talk to today why their story isn't important, why they're not worth 30 seconds of time on the local news.*

Going to, and challenging the reporter was another big step for me. I was proud that for once, I really had said to heck with the system. My pulse picked up an extra few dozen beats a minute. I felt the urge to whisper and kept looking over my shoulder just in case we caught the attention of one of the higher ups. If trouble did come, I was ready to point out that I was not affiliated with the Red Cross and under no obligation to blindly support their policies. Typically, I defer to the stronger powers and toss my hands up helplessly in the air, assuming there's nothing that I could do. Aside from a large measure of confidence that I've gained over the last week, this experience really is making an impact on my life.

Hopefully by tomorrow morning I'll think of something else to try.

First Signs of Rita

Tuesday, September 20

Last night, the news broke that Hurricane Rita is coming and today, you could feel it on every face. It was like one morning years ago when a nineteen-year old cook for the restaurant I was working at didn't show up to open the store. Within an hour after opening the store, it took one look at Melissa and the group of other servers and cooks huddled by the manager's office door and I knew we were never going to see James again. He had lost control of his pick-up on the way in to work, crashed into an embankment and was killed instantly.

That was how things started off this morning, even without a word of news from TV or radio, you could sense that something had changed and gone terribly wrong. Blood has drained from peoples' faces, the eyes have drooped and shoulders are hunched in futile surrender. It's as if their whole body is asking, "Where can we go now? How many more times am I going to loose everything I own this year?

More than depression, the look is fear. Forecasters are already describing her as bigger and stronger than Katrina, but I don't think that her size and power matter very much. She could me a lowly Category 1 storm and I think that she would inspire the same cowed reaction by the people here. It brought me to wondering what things were like in Florida last year when the third, fourth and then the fifth hurricane hit. At this point, a hurricane is a hurricane, and that simply terrifies people. But that is still a few days away and we still have work to do from Katrina.

Since our attempts to garner support from the news crew failed yesterday, Bill, Nancy, Nebraska Bob, not the one who caused so much trouble on Saturday, and I spent the morning trying to come up with some other way to help people register for financial assistance. I don't know if it's true or not, I heard Bob tell someone this morning that one of the reasons why people are having so much difficulty getting through is that all phone calls to a 1-800 number originating in Louisiana are routed through one central juncture, which just happens to be in New Orleans and under ten feet of water.

I know well enough to be weary of rumors, especially if I'm going to start spreading one, but this one makes sense with the hundreds of stories we've heard about people in other states having a much easier time. It also seems reasonable, given the little I know about how the telephone system works. More than anything else though, since our efforts to get the Red Cross to change things ran out yesterday with our news crew failure, this gives us something concrete that we can explain to people and at least give them some ease of mind. Sure the Red Cross is most definitely to blame and should have to answer for their actions, and this should encourage them to find a sensible way for people in Louisiana to register, but anger toward them isn't going to accomplish anything right now.

More importantly though, understanding this new obstacle sparked a few ideas that we began suggesting to people today.

The challenge is to make the phone call from somewhere outside of Louisiana. There are two ways this could be done, well, three really. The most obvious solution is that if someone wants to, they can take the time and expense in gas to drive out of the state. They can go to Texas or Arkansas (Mississippi might not be any better than here,) place the call from there and should be able to register within a few hours at the most, instead of at least a few more days. Second, is the third party option. If you call someone outside of the state, in Texas, Oregon, or just about anywhere other than here, you're bypassing the New Orleans router. Then have them dial the 800 number and conference you in once they get through. The only drawback to doing it this way is that not everyone has someone who would be able to conference them in and they would have to check about extra fees and expenses from the phone company.

The third option, I have to credit to both my pride in not being an actual Red Cross volunteer and my growing assertiveness. "If a person were to call with their vital information, social security number, license number, number of people living in the household, their ages and the addresses where their home used to be and where the debit card should be mailed to, then that person would be able to call and get registered."

Like the early days when we began to *let it slip* that residents in the Dome could register, I was very careful not to suggest that people try this, only to insinuate that if a person had a close family member living in another state who they could absolutely trust, that they wouldn't have to worry about trying to circuit around New Orleans. For their part, the rest of my crew, who are Red Cross volunteers, stood quietly by and had no part in this. Even when someone asked them a question while looking directly at them, they gave their shoulders a slight shrug and looked my way.

It's something that I know could be considered as bordering on fraud and is a risk that I certainly wouldn't have considered taking just a few days ago. But then, this is something that the Red Cross has promised to provide and is taking the credit for giving to people. We've already tried everything else we can think of and they simply haven't left us much choice. Then there's also the question as to whether or not it would be fraud for one person to call in and register someone else. It's not as if they are trying to take their money, just trying to help a member of their family because they've been trying unsuccessfully for over three weeks with no end in sight and another hurricane squarely between here and there. Unfortunately though, not everyone fits into any of those three options.

What do you say to a woman standing six feet in front of you, who has spent three weeks trying to register for financial assistance, and is tearfully asking: "What is the Red Cross doing to help people?" Despite our best efforts, Gloria was still standing in front of me, no money to drive to Texas, no family and no one else she could roll a conference call through.

Years ago my dad taught me never to tell a customer no, or that there was something that you couldn't do for them. No matter what the situation is, there is always something that you can do and should offer them that alternative. If we're not signing people up for financial assistant, "Have you registered with FEMA?" or "Do you have a place to stay, need food, clothing...?"

Gloria and all of the other people I see everyday are my customers. Not that they are purchasing something from me, but they look to me for help and are my responsibility to take care of.

My heart more than goes out for all of the people who are still unable to register for financial assistance. Time and time again, they ask me where all of their money is going and I've learned to respond time and time again with a shrug of my shoulders. I wish that I had confidence in the Red Cross, that I could share that confidence with others so that if nothing else, they could walk away with some confidence and hope of their own, rather than an added sense of hopelessness. It's not that I have any desire to spin a bright face for the Red Cross, everyone reading this by now knows how I feel about them and that I'm not holding back any punches, but these are the people I am taking care of. If I have no answer to give them on where they can turn to help or what exactly it is that the Red Cross, the organization they have always believed they can turn to for help, is doing for them, then I have no answer to help ease their burden.

With a heavy heart, I've started taking the approach that the dollar amount that the Red Cross will be providing isn't all that much (in truth it really is only about $300 per person) and they might be better served spending their time now getting help from other places and coming back to the Red Cross in a couple of weeks. My hope is to bring their expectations back in-line with proven reality. To help them feel less dependent on the Red Cross specifically. That way, it doesn't hurt as much when they fail them. For Gloria it was a soft hug, a very small comfort for finding out that Santa Clause isn't real. Unfortunately, I found out later that the saddest part of the debit card ordeal isn't just that people haven't been able to get registered, but that actually getting the card once they've registered is turning into yet another fight.

Sharon came to us today looking to pick up her debit card. She explained to me that her family had stayed at the shelter a couple of weeks ago, but were now living at a hotel. She had received a message from the Red Cross that the card had arrived and that she needed to come down to the Dome to pick it up. Since no one had passed along any word to us that people would be coming and about how they are to pick up their debit cards, I had to work my magic and track down someone who knew what we needed to do. Once again, it would have been nice had I been able to go to a central person, perhaps someone at the administrative office, and directly ask who was in charge of distributing the cards, but that has been too much to ask for. After a long half-hour of asking around, I was able to find out that Security is responsible for taking care of the debit cards and it took me another twenty minutes to track down Mike, the head of Security. When I told him about Sharon's situation and asked where she needed to go, he looked puzzled for a brief moment before simply saying, "I don't know."

"So how can this lady get her card?"

"I don't know." He was casual, like I had asked him where I could get a can of soda. I pressed him to find out who would know and got the entire scoop on why Security is in charge of handling the cards and how everyone else could get them, but for Sharon, "We haven't figured that out yet."

"So what do I tell this lady?" I asked him.

Mike, the person who is in charge and responsible for taking care of this, wouldn't even tell me who she could call to figure out what to do. He just tossed out a final, careless and unemotional, "I don't know." I had tried, gone strait to the top and there was nothing else for me to do.

When I finally got back to Sharon I had one last trick in mind, "You don't happen to still have your I.D. badge do you?" She didn't. With it, she could have gotten inside and possibly picked up her card just like everyone else. But without it, no one would even give her a chance at getting inside. Needless to say, I did the best I could to commiserate with her and help her out with anything else she might need. But in the end, another person walked away from the Cajun Dome upset and angry with the Red Cross.

On a positive note: I did finally find out today what the real story is for people to get their prescriptions filled. As I mentioned on Saturday, I was just then able to get clarification from the Red Cross that anyone who needed medical attention or a prescription written could go to the County Health Department, however, there was still confusion as to where a person who already had their prescription could go to have it filled. Unfortunately, this good news comes with some bad. I had been informed and passed along that they could go to CVS, Walgreens, Wal-Mart or Revco. The whole story is that once the Red Cross starts distributing vouchers for medications, they can then get them filled at any one of these four places. However, and this is an enormous HOWEVER, the Red Cross hasn't started distributing vouchers yet. Until then, the only store that they have a contract with to go ahead and fill prescriptions without the vouchers is Wal-Mart.

Everyone who I sent to CVS, Revco or Walgreens, because an official from Red Cross had told me to do so, would have been told that they had to get a voucher, then come back to ask us about getting a voucher and be told that the Red Cross wasn't giving any out.

I want to feel guilty about giving them the wrong information, sending them in more circles to get nothing. But once again, I only had what information I had fought for and it all goes back to the Red Cross's ineptitude and complete disorganization that has put me in this same position time and time again. Forget frustration, I am furious with them. Fortunately though, Seattle Maggie has arrived. She's the person who clarified the drug situation for me and is the first person from the Red Cross who seems to really know what's going on and cares enough to put forth the effort. Even though she's not in charge, I actually haven't been able to figure out who that is since Anna left over the weekend, she's going to be my new Anna.

On a side note: I attempted, albeit to no avail, to make progress on the PRC front today. With so much going on throughout the day, I didn't have a chance until later in the afternoon to get over to their table and ask about getting on one of the work crews. The young lady there, she may be 19 years old, spent a couple of minutes trying to track down someone over the radio named Jeff. It didn't take long for a half-dozen, "Don't know where he ises" to come back to her over their radios. Jeff is the person who would know, so we figured that he was out for the day and I should check back early tomorrow. The entire process took less than three minutes. *Now that's how things are supposed to work!*

Rita Bears Down

Wednesday, September 21

Today was an odd and uneventful day. On the one hand, I feel like I'm finally getting a firm handle on what's going on and how to get things done, on the other, there's still a feeling inside me that I haven't been doing everything I can to help out, that I'm not as committed as I should be to finding out the real scoop on things: getting FEMA to pay for their hotel room, having prescriptions filled, where people can get their immunizations, where the transit bus leaves from and how often it's operated… The list of questions I didn't follow up on as thoroughly as I should have is endless, but the one thing that I am proud of is that I am stepping out of my childish shell of uncertainty.

When I was first assigned to assist with the information table I was as lost and confused as the people I was supposed to be helping. By the next day, I was the person training new people, and for the past several days they have constantly come to me when all else had failed. It's one thing to have people say kind and confident words to you, and something entirely more when they come to you for answers. One could simply be a matter of being polite, but the latter comes from genuine trust and respect.

With Rita bearing down, the crowds coming to find help at the Dome had almost disappeared by mid-afternoon. As it was, only a heavy trickle of people came by in the morning and almost all of them were asking about the financial assistance. Out of those who came, only a small handful are still trying to get settled into the area, needing everything from clothes to furniture and silverware. With so much hopelessness, it is heartening to see people who are really beginning to start their lives over, rather than the hundreds whose lives seem to still be falling apart.

For the people trying to register, all I could think about is how much worse things are about to get for them. Even if they don't get caught by Rita, she's going to hit somewhere hard, meaning that if it's difficult for people to get through to the Red Cross now, it's going to be impossible with the thousands of additional people who will surely be trying to get through after she hits. So I took another step in trying to get around the Red Cross and the crippled phone system here in Louisiana. Last night I wrote that I was only insinuating that another person could place the call for them. Today, I came strait out and the very first question I asked people was, "Do you have a close family member or friend who you could trust with your personal information. Someone who lives outside of the states hit by Katrina?" 90% of the people answered 'Yes.' I flat out told them that the best thing to do would be to pass their information along to them. With each person, I stressed many times that it needed to be someone they could absolutely trust because it is sensitive information. For those who didn't seem to catch on, I also reiterated the point that the Red Cross wasn't allowing someone else to call and sign up for them. "If they call and say, 'My name's John Smith and I'm calling to get Charlie Jones registered,' then the operator will tell them to have Charlie call and then hang up."

For the people who didn't have anyone that could help them out, and there were a heart wrenching few, I could do nothing more than shrug, and provide as much consoling as possible, often falling back on Monday's strategy of telling them it really wasn't that much money and the best thing they could do would be to look for help from somewhere else, then try back with the Red Cross in a couple of weeks (The last thing they needed to hear was that no matter what happens with Rita, even if turns and hits Texas, it will be a hundred times harder to get through next week.)

Fortunately, I heard and confirmed with the local Salvation Army that they are assisting with $50 debit cards. Once again, this is information I should have had when I started last week and I could immediately think of a few people who could have used this money for gas. But I guess it's better late than never, and $50 is still enough to make or break a lot of people. Another thing that I was able to get nailed down yesterday, is that there is no special paperwork or voucher needed in order to have FEMA to pay for a hotel room. All a person needs to do is find an available room and provide evidence that they were residents of one of the affected counties. Most hotels will take care of the billing from there and at worse, a person might have to get some information from the local FEMA office to pass along to the hotel management. Dozens of faces flashed across my eyes when Margaret from FEMA clarified this for me; all of those people I've talked to who are living in tents, rented RVs, on their porch, in a crowded room with ten others and even some who have been living in their own vehicle. *If I had only known and been doing my job right, they could have moved into a hotel room weeks ago.*

With such a small scattering of people coming in, Paul and I had a chance to sit back and talk. He asked me point blank; "Have you ever thought about being a counselor or minister?" (During my senior year in High School I had a close experience with God and spent a few years working toward the goal of becoming a priest. But something about that prospect didn't quite sit right, and after a failing my first semester of college with a 0.69 GPA, I gave up the idea and hadn't given it a second thought for the last ten years.) Of course, that all changed on the drive down here. Shortly after I left my parents' house, the thought popped right back into my head and as soon as the words came out of Paul's mouth, I quietly thought: *Yeah, I started talking with my priest three weeks ago about becoming a priest.*

There's still a lot of turmoil going on inside about that prospect. I don't even know for sure yet what I think about it and I want to be able to ponder it quietly to myself without any interference or outside pressure. I'm not talking to anyone about it except for Fr. Mike back in Missouri and only mentioned it to my mother after she told me about a *relevant* conversation her and my dad had recently had. Needless to say, I didn't mention any of this to Paul, even though he broached the subject.

We mostly discussed my abhorrent feelings toward college. It had taken me nine years to get through eight semesters of undergrad work and I'm nowhere near ready to even entertain the slightest thought about graduate school. Along with Nancy and New Jersey Bob, Paul is among the volunteers here who I respect the most. So it feels very good that he has such a high opinion of me, and my ability to listen and comfort the people here.

Everything is mixed, including my emotions. I'm excited to finally get to experience my first hurricane. Not in any demented way that I wish for another hurricane to come through here, this is the last place that should have to deal with even the threat of one coming, but if there's going to be one, then I want to be in it. I am also worried about my car. I may have a place to stay at Roy's, but beyond that, that car is my lifeline down here and one tree branch could wipe it out. And then, there's also the internal devastation I feel at seeing the affects Rita has already wrought on the people around here.

The slower day did give me more time to work on finding a way to Mississippi. I managed to track down a phone number for Rob with the PRC, he is in charge of organizing the work crews. I also don't know if I should be frustrated at my laziness or comforted by faith. My original plan had been to be in Lafayette for a week at the most, but finding a place to go to in Mississippi has proven to be harder than expected. And I can't forget about that week stuck in Missouri with a broken car. All in all, I feel like I should be long gone from this place. But then, maybe I'm not supposed to be.

Over the last day or so, I've gotten the sense that I'm here, right when I need to be. Although I came down to do the physical work of helping people recover from Katrina, they may end up needing my help more in recovering from Rita. Then again, maybe I just haven't been as persistent as I should have been in getting a Mississippi contact. I don't know, but with Rita looming, it's best to wait and see where she hits and how bad the damage is before making any plans. *Everything is simply mixed-up.*

Life has essentially stopped, waiting to see what Rita's going to do. Here at the Dome I've heard rumors that the Red Cross has developed an evacuation plan and to their credit, at least one lesson has been learned from the Super Dome debacle in New Orleans. The word is that the Cajun Dome is only rated to stand up to a category 3 storm, Rita is already well beyond that and we're sitting well within her projection cone. The decision as to whether or not we will evacuate everyone from here up to Shreveport will be made sometime tomorrow. It seems as though she's put everything on hold. *There really is a calm before the storm.*

Evacuation

Thursday, September 22

Today was one of those days that feels like you're walking in soup. When I first arrived at the Cajun Dome everything felt nervous, tight and a little darker than normal. The chatter seemed louder, people moved more quickly, some with a purpose, many tottered back and forth between taking a step, standing still or trying to figure out which way they wanted to go. I suspected that the evacuation had already started, but no one at our information table had heard any official word. Half an hour later, after I had given up trying to figure out what was going on, Nancy walked up and asked me, "Have you heard what's going on?"

I was disappointed at first. *No. I hadn't heard so I had nothing that I could tell her.* It turned out though, she had made a special point to find me because she had realized that I wasn't at the staff meeting this morning, probably because I had no idea there was such a thing. Nancy wanted to make sure I knew that the evacuation had been ordered. The Red Cross, however, was going to wait another hour or so to make the announcement so they would have time to get everything ready (which I agree with completely.) The problem, however, is that as the person who is in charge of the information table, I should have known and had it not been for Nancy's thoughtfulness…well, you get the idea.

If I had felt like a third rate volunteer before, I don't know how to describe what it felt like today. While I was talking with a few of the volunteers in the staff room, a guy came by passing out procedures so everyone would know what to do. He started to hand me one, but when he noticed that my I.D. badge was green, indicating I was a local volunteer and not with the Red Cross, he took it back, telling me that it was for Red Cross personnel only. I couldn't believe it! And I don't think Maggie could either. When he handed her a copy, she passed it strait to me and immediately asked him for another copy. I'm glad she was there. As I told her, "Words were going to fly. I don't know what they were going to be, but they were about to start flying."

Not long afterward, the announcement was made. With all of the services inside shutting down and most of the town in the process of closing as well, there wasn't much more for me to do than stand around by myself, waiting for something to do. The mental health workers were off taking care of shutting down and packing up the Health Center. There was almost a steady stream of residents coming through the doors, arms full of mismatched luggage and trash bags. Most of them hobbling under the weight as they carried them the 30 feet from the Dome entrance to where a car had stopped right in front of me. A lot of people were moving out and I wonder how many of them will be back here after Rita, or if they all just needed a heavy hand of motivation to find another place to stay. Then, in the middle of that very thought, I was pulled inside to help someone check in. On the day people were packing up to get away from one hurricane, someone had finally hit their breaking point from the first one.

His name was Guy and he was one of those people who I have
heard ridiculed for continuing to stay in New Orleans after the
storm hit. A graying man in his mid-50s, he had been able to take
care of himself and chose to stay home. A week after the storm,
however, he decided to leave because he found out that it would be
several weeks before any water or power would be restored and he
has been living in his pickup ever since. He would still be there
except for the fact that two days ago, he had surgery on both his
knees, finally surrendering to the reality of moving into a shelter the
very day it was being evacuated.

Needless to say, there wasn't much to the orientation. No cot to
pick up or need to find a spot to make his home in the gymnasium.
It was all a matter of getting his I.D. and helping him transfer the
things he needed most into one bag that would sit on his lap for the
eight-hour bus ride to Shreveport. The rest of his things went into a
garbage bag, then tagged and strait into storage. I wheeled him over
to the TV area where a handful of guys were watching CNN track
Rita. Even after everything I've seen this week, I can't imagine the
thoughts that would be running through my head if I were checking
into a shelter and had to immediately turn around, pack what I
could fit on my lap and put the rest into storage for whenever I got
back, especially since no one knows when that might be. This is
what Guy, and to an extent, everyone else staying at the Dome, was
going through.

Although most of them had been settled for some time and
started accumulating their life again, they were only allowed to take
whatever they could carry on their lap and had to leave the rest
behind. I don't know which emotion was more powerful today, the
sadness I felt in seeing the mechanical looks in their eyes, or my own
fear in experiencing a monster like Rita as my first hurricane. (Even
though she's still projected to hit Galveston, she is so big and her

winds are so strong that we are expecting 120 mph winds here. Of course, she could still turn and hit closer.)

As if watching people pack up the rest of their newly begun lives in garbage bags wasn't difficult enough, today turned out to be a day of goodbye's to a lot of people. The Red Cross volunteers work in two-week stints before heading back and, while they're in Shreveport, the end of that two weeks will hit almost everyone I've worked alongside. Today is the last day that I will get to see them.

I forgot my camera, once again, making it even more of a final *goodbye*. Paul, Bill, Richard, Nancy and Paul from Ohio will be greatly missed. Aside from their friendship and support in managing what is widely considered the most difficult and stressful job at the Dome, they have spurred in me a tremendous growth of confidence. And even though today I found who I could, Paul had mentioned he was working the late shift last night so I didn't get to see him at all today. Then it was time to say goodbye to the Dome itself.

All of my papers had been boxed up and packed in the van going to Shreveport. Even the registration table was packed and shutdown when one more lady came needing a place to stay. For a moment I actually thought she would be turned away, after all, that's what happened to Jimmy when he didn't have an I.D. and Kenneth, the new registration head, told me they weren't registering anyone else. Fortunately though, he meant that they weren't going to do any of the paperwork. She was still able to go with them on the bus and would just have to fill everything out when they got back.

After that, there really wasn't anything else for me to do and I couldn't handle any more random milling about. I gave Kenneth my phone number, asked him to give me a call to let me know when they returned and finally headed back to Roy Jr.'s. It was a slow walk. It wasn't even 2:00 pm and I didn't want to leave, but had to face up that I had done everything I could do there and it was time for me to get myself ready for Rita. I am still nervous about staying around town, afraid that something might happen to my car and to be honest, I am only staying because I don't want to be the fool who ran away from a little thunderstorm.

Later in the evening, Roy Sr. and I made the supply run to Wal-Mart. Unlike most people, we didn't actually need very much. Thanks to my grandma, I already had all of the food and supplies I'd need to live on for a couple of weeks, so it was mostly a matter of getting a couple bags of ice and some food for the next couple of days. Then there was nothing to do but go home, watch the weather and wait for tomorrow to come.

Landfall

Friday, September, 23

For the last few days, I've been trying to balance the emotions of fear and excitement. Excitement, because this was going to be my first hurricane. Fear, because a monstrous hurricane was heading my way and I could already envision a tree or stray branch crushing the roof of my car! For all intents and purposes, that car is my home now and I haven't the slightest clue as to what I would do if something happened to it. This morning, most of the fear was gone though, along with Rita's big punch. Instead of facing winds of at least 100 mph, we began expecting something closer to the 60 mph range, helping turn what I had been anticipating as the big day of my first hurricane into little more than rainy, windy and progressively boring.

Except for Senior cooking up a roast, the day was as far from extraordinary as sitting around in front of the TV could be. Roy Jr. owns a townhouse that sits on the backside of a building he shares with one other person. It's a relatively small place. From the door, it takes two steps to pass through the dining area into a kitchen that's more like a short hallway with a sink and dishwasher on one side and stove and refrigerator on the other. Behind that wall is the couch Sr. sleeps on. Roy's futon is up against the adjacent wall, the bachelor's version of a sectional, and Sr.'s favorite recliner sits in the middle, the perfect video game distance from his 30+ inch TV. With a coffee table sitting between the three, there really isn't much room to do anything except sit.

Every hour or so, we'd go outside and sit on the porch, a short five-foot plot of concrete under the cover of his second-floor deck. His back yard is slightly bigger than the living room; a small 20' x 20' corner, enclosed by a six-foot high picket fence. The back fence row looks like there's supposed to be a couple feet of flower beds with shrubs and manicured plants. The yard itself is so rough that even though there's grass between here and there, Roy doesn't even own a lawn mower. Every month or so he borrows a weed whacker from a neighbor to chop it down, but with so many trees overhead, the patchy grass doesn't look like it needs cutting that often, more than sufficient for an off-shore bachelor mechanic. We'd talk and watch the trees sway, a row of palms off to the left, a willowy looking tree almost directly overhead, and a pine tree or two scattered about. Every once and awhile my legs would get bored so I'd walk over to the gate, fold my arms across the top ledge and strain to see anything resembling a storm in the distance, but that would last only a few seconds before the rain became too much of an annoyance and I'd go back inside to catch up on Rita's progress.

By 7:00 pm, Roy Jr. and I had had enough of the boredom that we both simply needed to get out of the house. For one, I wanted to see what was going on in the rest of the town and Jr. figured that driving around, looking for anything that was open would be better than doing more nothing. I think we saw two, maybe three, other cars on the road. Along with the radio reading off a list of curfews for nearby towns, we didn't hear anything for Lafayette, the few twigs scattering themselves in the road, finally started to give me the feeling like we were in the middle of something big and my nerves started to come back. Something was building.

Before we left the house, Jr. had mentioned something about stopping to check out Jack's, but there really wasn't anything open. Then he pulled into an empty lot next to a squat, mustard colored building made out of cinder blocks. I didn't know what he was doing. There may have been a metal painted sign or two on the outside of the building, but I remember not being able to see a sign and there weren't any lights coming from inside. Nothing about the place looked like it was a place of business, much less a bar or that it was open. Then I realized there were a dozen full-size pickups parked in a gravelly mudded lot. Jack's was clearly a place that I normally wouldn't even think about going into, but it was the only place in town that was open, and the full lot meant it had to be the place to be for all of your hurricane fun.

Once we were inside, I saw that Jack's may be a place I would go to after all, not every week and I do prefer places with at least one window in them, but it does have a good, local character. It was an insubstantial small bar with a pool table off to the side and a backroom dart game in progress, just a couple dozen working class people loudly enjoying themselves. The good times, however, came to an abrupt end only moments after we arrived. With my beer in hand, and the man behind the bar turning to make Roy Jr.'s Beam and Coke, the lights went out. Cheers roared through the crowd as lighters flicked on. In a matter of a few seconds, we could hear the rumble of a small generator and the faint glow of emergency lights pop on.

With the loss of power, Rita had been ordained a real hurricane, but Roy was in no mood to join the celebration. As one of only two sober people on our side of the bar, he knew that there was going to be no Beam and Coke for him tonight. I saw a couple of people head toward the front door and could make out the silhouette of their cell phone. For the most part though, the cheering continued. Most of the crowd had been there long enough to be clueless as to what no power actually meant, which was a good thing for the two guys behind the bar. The one remaining bar still open in Lafayette would be open just long enough to get all of the generators started and close up shop.

After Jack's, there wasn't much choice but for us to head back home. Not only was there nowhere else to go, but the bar was less than a mile from his house and, with the power out, Jr. was concerned for his dad. As we drove down the completely darkened street, we slowly started seeing a faint glow coming from around the corner and the first light we saw just happened to be coming from the house next to Jr.'s. We still had power for a few minutes before they went out.

I was a half-step from my gas lantern, which was ready to light with a turn of the dial, when they came back on. It seemed like that happened every ten minutes. The lights would go out, we'd stop talking, listening for them to come back on, catch an extra breathe and then they'd come back. After a half-dozen times, the conversation wouldn't even skip a beat.

We spent a couple more hours watching Rita's progress on TV. The experts/idiots where still predicting that it would take a sharp turn toward Texas, but we had already figured it would hit within 30 miles of us, somewhere around the Louisiana-Texas border. Then, sometime around midnight, we realized that the lights had been off for almost a full minute. *They weren't coming back.*

Rita's landfall was weird. Her eye was just hitting the coast, but the rain had already stopped where we were and there hadn't been any thunder or lightening all day. (That's when Roy Jr. told me that hurricanes don't have lightening.) So instead of either going to bed or sitting on the back porch, we did what any other twenty something guys would do; take a walk around the neighborhood.

It was invigorating. Everything was dark, but there was enough light glowing against the clouds that we could see there wasn't any debris flying around. The only sounds we could hear were the rustling of trees and a rhythmic banging of metal on metal, which after several minutes I eventually figured out was a lid beating against the back of a garbage dumpster.

On the way out from the house the wind was just strong enough that I had to push against it to walk. The hardest part though, was after we had turned around to head back toward the house. With our backs to the wind, I had to lean back a little to keep from being blown forward. Then every once and awhile, it would die down without warning and nearly pull me over backward without that extra force to hold me up; it felt when you're walking down stairs and that next step isn't there.

A couple hundred feet from the house, I noticed a large, black something flapping in the wind. It took me a few seconds to realize that it was the roof to Sr.'s jeep. We had noticed on the way out that he hadn't done anything to tie it down. Whatever his reason had been, whether it was because he had been too tired, lazy or just irresponsible, it didn't matter. Jr. was tired of taking care of someone who didn't care enough to take care of his own stuff. When we had first walked by, it had been breathing wildly, but it was still attached at all the corners so we left it as Sr.'s responsibility and continued walking.

I haven't written much this week about the strain between Roy Jr. and Sr., largely because I've had other things on my mind, and mostly because it's a personal issue of confidence, but it's something that definitely added to the color of the day. To put it in short terms, there is a huge strain on the father son relationship. Roy feels like Sr. still treats him like a five-year old, and Sr. doesn't think Roy treats him with the respect due a father. Like any familial trouble, it's not that simple, but that's enough to give an idea of the underlying tension in spending a day trapped with each other. Sr.'s neglect of the jeep had sparked a lot of the conversation Roy and I had while walking around, but no matter how fed up he was, he still wasn't going to let it fly away. Fumbling in my trunk for a flashlight, some rope and fighting 50 mph winds to secure the soft canopy was our big excitement for the night. *He probably doesn't realize it, but Sr. is fortunate to have Roy as a kid.*

Sometime after 1:00 am, we were able to call it a night. By our best guess, the eye of the storm had passed, meaning that the worst was over. I figure maybe the wind made it up somewhere between 50 and 60 mph, but nothing much beyond that. It was just a very long, drawn out thunderstorm, without any thunder.

The Farm

Saturday, September 24

Trudging through water that rippled against his chest, Roy Jr. made one final scan of the horizon. "I just can't believe it's this bad!" He was looking for signs of any of their animals: goats, horses, their bull, calf, or anything else with four legs that was still standing. We had already spent a couple of hours at the farm, been in and out of every building, so by this point it was more a look in futile hope than it was any kind of a sincere search.

I had come with Roy to the farm in order to survey the damage from last night's hurricane. The damage from Rita's wind had been minimal, but a small bayou backed against one side of their property. Her course and direction of the winds had been just right for the worst-case scenario and the combination of storm surge and heavy rains had simply been too much for the land to handle. No one in Roy's memory had ever witnessed floodwaters that had been so high. "Not even when Andrew went right over us." He told me.

At first, I made an attempt at sharing some feebly comforting words. But after the fifth or sixth time, I realized that there was nothing for me to say. The former marine was in shock and truly couldn't believe that the water had risen so much that their once above-ground swimming pool was now under four feet of water.

As Jr. was turning to make his final look around the property, Tiny, their goat-herding dog, and I were waiting impatiently on the back porch. The cloud-covered sky had started dimming, meaning that the sun was on its way down for the night. The water had been rising all day. Where I had once walked with my arms raised to keep them out of the water, I was hopping on tip-toes in order to keep from swallowing farm/bayou water. And just in the last half-hour, both Jr. and I had noticed a steady increase in current's strength as well.

We weren't in any immediate danger yet, but that was ready to change at any moment. For the first time in my life, I felt the nagging concern that I was putting my life on the line, and there was still a mile of water between us and the truck. It was time to leave, with or without Roy Sr., who had vanished 20 minutes earlier. *We had to leave, immediately.*

****

As usual, I had awoken frequently throughout the night and for the past several times, I halfway saw the morning light streaming in through the double glass doors. Even though we were well on the backside of Rita's punch, I heard the sounds of the wind still rustling. Outside, small twigs and leaves were swirling in the corner of the deck. The cloudy sky made me feel like yesterday was preparing to repeat itself, but any notions of complete boredom were almost immediately pushed aside by the anxiousness of Roy Jr.'s voice coming up the stairs.

He was talking on the phone with his mom, and I truly wasn't awake enough to understand what he was saying, Yet, it was one of those rare moments when no words were needed. I was leaning on the bed as he entered the room, hanging up the phone and I simply asked, "When are we leaving?"

"About ten minutes, if you can be ready." Roy fits the prototypical description of a 5'7" Marine, just add a twinge of red to his closely cropped, brown hair and you have as good of a picture of him as anyone could paint. His mom and step-dad own a farm about 30 minutes strait to the south with a bayou marking the eastern edge of their property. Someone needed to go down and see how the house had weathered through the night, along with their many livestock: goats, horses, bull and calf. This was the reason I had made the 1700-mile drive from Colorado, not to sit at a table giving people directions to the local FEMA office, which any idiot could do. It's not that I haven't done a lot of good with my time spent at the evacuation shelter, but this morning is the exact picture I had in mind when I left home; helping a family that may have lost their home to a hurricane.

Just as quickly as he had come in, Roy turned around and headed downstairs to finish getting ready. Five minutes later, I followed, joining Roy and Sr. in mid-discussion. Unfortunately, Sr. was going with us to the farm.

It may seem odd for me to use the word 'unfortunate,' however, in addition to the ever-growing strain in their relationship, Sr. is on poor health. The accumulated wounds of a soldier and life-long police officer have taken a hard toll on his legs. Every good day, which meant that he could spend three or four hours at the Dome ministering with Katrina victims, was followed by at least two bad days when he could only muster being up with his cane for an hour or two. After that, he was completely wiped and would sit in his recliner for the rest of the day. *How on earth was he going to be any good out at the farm?*

Of course, I had no real idea of what to expect when we got to the farm, but it was already clear that today was going to be physically taxing and would demand all of our attention to the work at hand. As harsh as it may sound to even have this thought, this was going to be a day of taking care of Roy, the farm and the animals. There would be no room for babysitting stragglers, no matter what their intentions may be. But what can you say to a father who is trying to make up for his past mistakes; who only wants to be there to help his son; and who had given me his bed to sleep on at night? "No, Roy. You can't go because you're too old and will only cause more problems for us," wasn't something I could say. It just didn't seem right, so Sr. grabbed a few REMs, Ready-to-Eat-Meals, and we headed out the door.

It was 10:00 am and we were still a mile from the farm when Roy pulled his truck off to the side of highway. Across the road, a pickup had backed up to the water's edge, where a couple men in their forties were leading a pontoon boat off its trailer. These were the loading docks. The steep embankment off the side of the highway made for a nearly perfect place for rescue crews to launch and load their boats.

"This is bad..." Roy was simply shaking his head, "I can't believe the water is up this high. It wasn't even like this when Andrew came through...This is really bad." Three men in one boat were just beginning to accelerate through a back yard, pointing and fumbling around at their gear, much like they were heading out to fish for the day. The entire scene was odd, but the fact that the front yard of an 80-year old man was being used as a launching point felt perfectly normal. Sr. mumbled a few words that I imagine to be of a comforting nature, but too much of my focus was on the water surrounding us, and nothing intelligible came through...*Perhaps I wasn't feeling as normal as I thought I was.*

For a couple of minutes, we sat in the truck, reluctantly debating our options. Most of the talk centered around how many road signs, mailboxes or other roadside markers might be sticking up out of the water, allowing Roy to get a good feel for where the road was. We decided that in the worst case scenario, I could jump out of the back of the truck and use my feet to feel for the edge of the road. Even with the road-side loading dock, everything Roy knew was telling him that the water couldn't possibly be too deep for his truck to make it through. Not even the gaggle of men and half-dozen trucks already surrendered to parking would tell him otherwise. And if nothing else, he knew he could drive at least another half-mile, which meant that much less we would have to walk.

The looks on the men's faces as we drove by, Roy gently waving a request for them to move out of the road, were the one thing out of the entire scene that felt strange. I couldn't imagine what they were saying or thinking, I didn't even know what I was thinking, just meandering through visions of what the next mile was going to look like.

Crouching over the steering wheel, our adventure was ready to continue. Roy eased the truck into the water, sticking his head out the window after we had gone just 50 yards. He took a quick check of the water's level, "Any water coming in on that side?" The water was already over the bottom edge of the door. The street sign ahead warned of a sharp curve, and judging from the water line, another hundred yards would be the best we could hope for. Even if that was far enough to make it worth the risk, the inside of the truck would be flooded as soon as anyone cracked open one of the doors, and I doubt Sr. would have been able to crawl out through his window. *We were done.*

Having finally accepted that the truck wasn't going any further, Roy had to figure out how to back up without driving off the side of the road. I climbed through the window, fond memories of the Dukes of Hazard flashing in my head, plunked down into waste high water, and scooted away from the truck, scuffling my feet to feel for the edge of the pavement. The crowding of strange faced men hadn't moved since Roy had ushered them aside two minutes earlier. Still engrossed in their conversation, they barely spared a glance at the truck as it backed out of the water.

Everything was normal today, even if, and especially because nothing was. There were no ornery grins; no one was shouting, "I told you so."; no one laughing at obvious futility; or shaking their head at the foolishness of youth. Everyone knew youth when they saw it, even if it was on a 30-year old face. They had known that our trip was going to be a short, and understood that everyone needed to make the attempt. Today was a day of trying what you can and doing what you have to do; of figuring out what the situation is and feeling your way through events; one of the few days when we see and realize that everyone is in the same, unimaginable situation.

Parking his truck along the shoulder, a good 30 yards from the water's edge, the three of us prepared for the mile-long hike through the water. For once, I actually thought strait and remembered to leave my phone, camera and everything else I didn't want to get wet, in the truck. As I was digging my wallet out of my jeans pocket, I held onto a last hope that Sr. would realize some ordinary sense and stay behind. There is no way he could make it a mile on dry land, much less wading through water that was at least waist deep. Not to mention that the only way back was going to be to walk a second mile and if his legs collapsed, there would likely be nothing that Roy and I could do. I hoped, but seeing as how he won't acknowledge any of his physical limitations, even at the best of times, I couldn't think of anything to say that he would listen to. Especially since he had one more huge reason not to admit his problems today. In Sr.'s eyes, his son needed him, and there's no father who wouldn't at least try to make this trip...and few friends with the heart to try stopping him.

The walk started and it didn't take long for Sr. to fall behind, so I found myself, once again trying to be a bridge between them. For the last two weeks I had been listening to the two of them complain about the other. During the day, I would hear stories about how one wasn't being a good son, and at night, about how the other was treating his adult son like a twelve-year old child. To my surprise I didn't mind that they were dumping these things on me. Even after spending a stress-filled day of counseling dozens of hurricane victims and trying to decipher the Red Cross, I have thought of listening to them as another job I was down here to do. I still haven't figured out yet how to redirect their relationship toward healing, but am confident that it will come with time. This morning, I had already been trying to keep the communication between them soft and the focus on the farm.

The absolutely last thing that I wanted to do was to slow Roy down, even the tinniest bit, but the idea of abandoning the old man still tugged at the corner of my conscience. I found myself bouncing from wading next to Roy, then falling back 10, 20, 50 yards, depending on how far Sr. was trailing at the moment. It was close enough that Roy kept trudging along at his pace, and Sr. should have been able to tell that he wasn't forgotten. Then we stopped at a pickup tilting off the side of the road, water covering half the dashboard, plastic paper wraps hanging from the mirror, and a three-foot tall stack of today's edition of the *New Iberia Gazette* that filed the passenger's seat.

The best that we could figure, there were one of two possibilities; either the driver had been too inebriated to keep his truck on the road, suffering the misfortune of getting stuck on the same the day that Rita moved through, or there was an idiot now walking around who had been out delivering newspapers in the middle of a hurricane and simply lost where the edge of the road was. Whichever the case, the truck gave Roy and I a small laugh, as well as something to lean against. To his credit, he suggested that we wait a bit for Sr. to catch up a little. Then, as Sr. popped around the bend 30 yards away, we started up again and the water level started going down.

The drop in the water level wasn't noticeable at first, actually, I didn't realize it until after I noticed the water was only coming up to Roy's knees; then he started lifting his feet out of the water; I started seeing the faint yellow of the lines on the highway and then he was waiting for me on dry land. It was a cozy island, a slow rise in the land that made me realize just how flat this part of the country is. Rising two or three feet made a huge difference, and even a couple of inches became noticeable. We were still waiting on Sr., who had just turned a corner a couple hundred yards away and I started wringing out my clothes, thankful that we were dry again, and completely ignoring what lay a short distance ahead. Another few hundred yards down the road, it reentered the water and the tree line veered off sharply to the right.

"I hope the house is okay. I still just can't believe it's this, bad." Roy said as we had some time to kill before Sr. came closer to catching up. He also sprinkled in a few more complaints about the old man, how slow he is and how he never thinks of anyone else, "What was he thinking coming out here? I can't be babysitting him." He was saying nothing that I disagreed with, so I just listened as we slowly headed toward the other side, enjoying the ease of walking on dry land. We stood at the edge of the water for a few moments, then as Sr. stepped onto what had become the little island, Roy's patience was done.

"Don't worry about him. I'll wait for him to catch up and then catch up with you." He turned and walked on ahead.

I took a moment to look around at the three houses that had been fortunate enough to be on this stretch of land. It felt like it was the only dry spot for miles, yet aside from a few dogs scattering around, it was just as quiet and abandoned as everywhere else. The driveways were empty and the grass was mushy.

"Where's Jr.?" Sr. asked as he had finally caught up with me.

"He's pretty anxious to get to the farm," I told him, "so he went on ahead."

"That boy, I tell you...Couldn't he at least...?" I didn't hear anything else that Sr. had to say. Roy was beginning to disappear around the bend, a good 400 yards down the street and we were both there to help him. Sr. asked about taking a break since he could finally sit on dry land and I simply told him that I needed to get going to catch up with Roy. He protested faintly, but in the end, we both stepped back into the water at the same time. Within a few steps, he was already falling behind. I was completely focused on catching up to Roy, ignoring how far Sr. was dropping back, but within a quarter mile, I had to do the last things that I wanted to do.

From the front porch, a woman in her early fifties yelled out for help. Having already walked by her house, a single story, suburban home with a three-foot step up into the front door, so I had to turn around and couldn't quite hide the flash of disgust at the situation. If I had been on the way to my own parents' farm, she wouldn't

91

have even had to ask, and I most certainly would not have walked by her and her husband, trying to pass off in quiet ignorance of their need. But this wasn't my family's farm, this wasn't my trip, and I wasn't on my timetable. Today was Roy's and I had long seen the anxiousness growing in him with every minute that passed. *How long had we been walking? How much further did we have to go? And were any of their animals still alive?*

I was trapped between Roy's family and this man and woman, two faces staring at me in undeniable need. While walking by without making eye contact was one thing, there was nothing I could do to make myself tell them no. I gave a yell out to Roy, who I had nearly caught up with and was now just 80 feet ahead, "Hey Roy! Do you mind if I stop and help these people out real quick. I'll catch up with you later." He turned around, and to my surprise, he didn't yell back, but started walking toward us.

The lady and her husband, I never asked them their names, were moving their dogs from his pickup, back into the house. While backing out of the driveway, he had been a foot too late in stopping the truck. It slid into the ditch and now sat much like the newspaper truck we had walked by a half-mile earlier. He was standing in the back of the truck, one foot braced against the side rail, the other was in the middle of the truck bed, standing nearly ankle deep in water. There were over a half-dozen pet carriers, which he had already moved to the driver's side that was nearest the road. They were stacked three, sometimes four on top of another in order to keep them out of the water that was rising on the other side of the truck. It was obvious that he hadn't been stuck for long as the truck itself was slowly slipping further down the steep embankment.

One by one, he handed the carriers down to myself, Roy, and his wife. Then we would walk them over to the house, letting them float on the water, and nervously keeping an eye on their driveway in order to avoid a surprising fall into the ditch. After the first trip, the lady stayed on the porch so Roy and I could pass the dogs up to her. It took us three more trips to get all of the animals. The last to come was their prized black lab. Bounding out of the truck with a splash, his tongue hanging from a grinning mouth, he looked like he was out for his weekly swim. It was good to see someone enjoying the extra water.

It was about that time when Sr. finally caught up with us. From what Roy was saying, the farm was just past the curve in the road ahead, not quite another half-mile, and given Sr.'s current pace, I no longer felt bad about not wanting him to come along. He was an adult and would have to live with the consequences of his own decisions. From that point on, I looked back to make sure he was still standing, but put no more effort in trying to hang back, or otherwise be the bridge between him and Roy.

Right before leaving, as Roy was starting to take off, I asked the lady, "What are you going to do?"

She said plainly, "I don't know." It had been one of those futile questions that you go ahead and ask even when you already know the answer, or when there's nothing you can do, no matter what the answer is. It's asking the question that matters most. For two weeks, I had been the information guru. It had been my job to have an answer for everyone, even if it wasn't what the person was looking for, or if I had to spend 30 minutes tracking down an answer. But there wasn't a local police office at hand for me to ask directions, or a phone in hand for me to make a call. The day, and this lady, was something entirely different and a part of me felt pure failure. So I only did the best that I could. I extended a hand, turned a warm handshake into a friendly, one-armed hug, wished her the best of luck, and hurried off to catch up with Roy, who was already a hundred yards down the road.

The last leg of the trip was marked by steadily deepening water that gradually reached waste height, then mid-torso; increasingly large islands of fire ants floating up the road toward us; and a darkening sky aided by a canopy of trees lining both sides of the road. If the brief respite of dry ground had felt adventurous, this part of the trip was a foretaste of the severity and a reminder of what we were doing out there, why we were hiking through over a mile of water.

A dog started barking just off to one side of the road. He was still locked in his kennel. Across the way, the line of trees had abruptly disappeared, adding a false sense of a brightening outlook. But it wasn't entirely false. We had arrived at the farm and since the kennel was on a shallow rise and the short, yellow mutt was standing on dry ground, he would have to wait until the trip back.

What is there for me to say to describe the farm? I could say that when we first arrived the water was flush with the threshold of the house, none had gone inside yet; the front half of the hood to the car Roy's mom had bought a month ago was underwater; the windshield wipers on his step-dad's truck were slowly scraping across the window, too weak to move a even a single raindrop; their workshop, that unlike the house had not been built four steps off the ground, was flooded nearly to the bottom of the knob on the side door; or share the image of the side of my ear skimming the surface of the water as I stretched my arm to its full length, fingers desperately feeling along the grassy bottom for the keys to Roy's truck that he had dropped. But the picture that I think best captures those first few minutes of discovery is Roy sitting on the roof of his step-dad's truck, hammer in hand, having to take three swings to break the window to the workshop.

94

Aside from being his parents' property, it was an ordinary window, possibly a little dustier than what most of us are used to. It was neither extra thick glass, nor made from any kind of high-density, break resistant material. It was his parents' window, and no matter how many times he had already muttered, "Everything's ruined," the thought of himself doing more damage, even if it was just a window for him to crawl through, was painful. Without any keys to either the house or the workshop, breaking the window was his only way in. After a few deep breathes, Roy swung the hammer and the glass broke. Sr. was standing a couple hundred yards away, likely in the middle of the road, waving his arms.

With everything covered in Bayou water, it was easy enough to assume that Sr. had no idea how to safely get from the street to the house. "Where's the driveway?" he yelled across the yard.

"By the trees!" I was yelling as loudly as I could and very deliberately pointing to my right. Just on our side of the road there were a few small trees, eight-foot sticks with a couple of sprouting branches and leaves. Most of them are spaced about ten feet apart, and then there was a noticeably larger gap between the last one and line of full grown trees running alongside the driveway.

"What? I don't know where…"

"You can come strait across." The steady wind in my face wasn't helping. I tried yelling louder as I took a few steps toward him. "There's no fence! Just come strait across!"

"What?" He responded. Roy was still sitting on the roof of the truck, picking the last shards of glass out of the window frame.

"Strait this way!" I had gone a third of the distance, and that was as far as I was going to go. I didn't have time to walk all of the way out there, take him by the hand and escort him safely over flat ground, even if he didn't know it was safe.

"How do I..."

"Come strait!" I tried using the hand signals my dad had taught me to use when we helped him back up trailers. Extending both hands in front of me, I motioned in a strait line back. But nothing was getting through and Sr. stood there looking like a perplexed child. It was my final straw. Roy was waiting on me to go in the workshop and Sr. was playing the part of the incompetent infant. I yelled as loudly as I could one last time, "It's flat! Come strait across!" I turned around, motioned Roy to go on in, and then followed, crawling through my second window of the day.

Inside the workshop, it was readily apparent that Roy's parents took great care of all of their belongings. Although normally crowded, the building was kept very neat. Equipment for his step-dad's band filled the corner next to the window we had gone in through; drums, amps and microphone stands were standing in place, all set and ready for their next party; Three 4-wheel bikes neatly parked out of the center, next to the music equipment; An under repair, black, antique horse buggy was parked in the center of the floor with several feet of space on each side for easy access; Another buggy, white with dirty gold trim was stationed at the far wall across from us. Both of them looked as slick as the day they were made nearly a century back. To the one side of the white buggy sat their chest freezer full of fresh beef from cattle they had raised, and the other corner had been designed into an open-air tool shed where a wooden stairway led to a second floor walkway. Clean and organized is how the shop had looked yesterday, but even taking away the fact that we were walking in water up to my waist, every step let us know that things were vastly different today.

Sodden dog food floated on the surface of the water, reminding me of handfuls of the fish pellets we would throw into the water at bass farms as a kid. Broom-less handles stuck out of the water at awkward angles, blocking our path. Amplifiers and half-full buckets bounced around like bumper boats and the chest freezer tilted with the bottom edge of one end at eye level with Roy. Nearly every step encountered some sort of random, unseen shape below the surface.

From the window, the path wound between the bikes and music equipment, curved around the black buggy, then split into two branches: one leading to the nearly upended freezer and the other to the tool corner. Frequently, the path was too narrow for either of us to walk through, forcing us to twist and scoot along sideways, using our feet to feel for any unmovable objects. At any time, taking a full, normal length step could send either of us hurling face first into the water.

For the first few minutes, Roy wandered mostly in silence, finding a dozen new ways to utter that everything was ruined. I trailed behind him, searching for anything that I could save, something to rescue that would give myself some meaning for being there. I wasn't there to gawk and observe a family's life washed away. I was there to save something, to save anything. Failing to be the hero, I helped Roy lift the front end of his bike and rest the front wheels on the seats of the two other bikes. The bike was Roy's baby.

The first conversation that I had with him last week was 30 minutes of him talking and me asking questions about the new methanol carburetor he had just put on. Since methanol burns much hotter than regular gasoline, the extra revs would come in handy while racing with his friends, but it had been running too hot and he was having a hard time adjusting the air intake. Tuning the new carburetor had been the final piece to a multi-thousand dollar puzzle and he had just proclaimed her finished and ready to go. That was four days. Today, he was pouring oil into the cylinders and draining the fuel tank; desperately doing whatever he could to salvage one thing from the utter ruin he had found.

"Could you hand me that screwdriver?" I made a few other trips to the standing tool chest for wrenches, but mostly though, I stood quietly for nearly half an hour, watching Roy, busying my hands by scooping aside an endless supply of wet dog food, and at some point, I realized that I did have a real purpose for standing there: I was present for Roy. If not for myself, he would be more than alone right now.

For all I knew, Sr. was still worthlessly standing outside in the middle of the road. More than worthless, he was making the situation worse. It's one thing for a friend to be able to put another person out of the mind, letting them *fend for themselves*, but it can be something entirely different for a son to leave a father to suffer through his own decisions. Amidst the mumblings of disbelief, Roy had started tossing in, "What the hell is he doing?" Roy finished doing all he could for the bike and it was time to move on.

Shutting the door to the workshop, both of us checking to make sure that it was unlocked, we had to put aside any more stalling and checked for whatever traces of the animals may remain. Against my greatest hope, the goats we could hear bleating from a small barn next door belonged to the neighbors. It seemed as though Roy had already resigned himself to a total loss of all animal life.

"Roy.....Kendall...." We could hear Sr. yelling at us, unseen from the front yard, his voice carrying in the strengthening wind. But that stronger wind carrying his voice, also meant that there was no chance that he could make out any reply we could offer. Of course, that would have mattered if Roy had even the slightest inclination to offer one. He was beginning to simmer down from his earlier anger at the old man, asking, "Am I being unreasonable or overreacting?" *No, he wasn't.* He still had more to focus on, and wasn't nearly ready to talk to the man.

For my part, I did actually consider yelling back to let Sr. know that we were on the other side of the workshop, we were okay and he didn't need to worry. But, I decided that there was really no reason to respond. Most likely, he wouldn't hear a single word, but in the event he could make out some sound, it would probably be enough to confuse an, "We're fine!" for a call for help. It didn't matter how inconsiderate or unthinking he had been up to that point, I had learned a lesson when I was five. I had accidentally tricked my father into believing I was drowning once in an effort to get my older brother to give me my turn on the air mattress. He had nearly broken his nose, diving in to save me.

That was over twenty years ago and I can still remember the terrified look on his face as he was threatening to paddle me if I ever did that again. There was no way I was going to try yelling anything that might make Sr. think his son was on danger. As for walking around to talk to him, going across the front yard hadn't been a possibility before we climbed into the workshop, and the only thing that had changed since then was that he had become worse than useless. Worse than having to make an effort to ignore him, his yelling only added tension to a situation that was about to get much worse.

We came out of the workshop directly across from the front steps leading into the house. From there, we could see their barn hiding behind a sparsely treed fence row, just a few hundred feet away. A small, square island deck was floating halfway between us and the barn. *Odd,* is the best word that came to mind. First of all, what was a deck doing four feet off the ground in the middle of their yard.

Secondly, the deck wasn't even level, half of it gingerly bobbed in and out of the water, giving it the impression of an anchored raft wobbling in the current.

When we took our first steps off the concrete patio between the house and workshop, the water was at thigh level, the further we walked, the deeper it became. I had to left my arms awkwardly to keep them out of the water; then it was up to my waist, then over my stomach. *What do I do with my arms?* It was an unusual question to ponder, but along with wondering what that deck was doing there, it was the biggest question on my mind. At first, it had been no effort to lift them a couple of inches, but as the water passed waist level, the angle became awkward and feelings of slight embarrassment at how I looked, holding my elbows parallel with the water, creeped in. But the thought of dragging them in the water also felt odd.

A few feet from the deck, Roy began shaking his head again. It had not been something that floated in from a neighboring farm, rather, it was nearly right where it was supposed to be. A couple of inches below the surface, I could just make out the muddy edge of an above ground swimming pool. If it had been nowhere else in this mess, there had to be some irony in walking up to a swimming pool that wasn't as deep as the water that we were standing in. We took advantage of the time to take a brief pit stop to catch our breaths. Although it was only mostly dry, the pool deck offered the first opportunity since leaving Roy's truck for us to sit down on a dry seat.

With no watches, clocks or visible sun, time had no real meaning this morning, only goals. The first had been to get to the farm. In the workshop, it was to do whatever could be done to salvage the bike. Now, our break finished, it was time to get inside that barn.

Not long after leaving the deck, that tinge of embarrassment crept in again as I realized that I was walking with my arms held strait in front of me, virtually parallel with the water. I don't know why I was still concerned about keeping my arms dry, yet it was with some reservation that I finally gave in and let them sink into the water as well. Roy's shoulders were completely underwater.

I have never had an easier time climbing over a four-foot high fence. We didn't have to give any attention to footholds, and there was no real climbing effort involved. It was simply a matter of feeling for the top of the cattle gate, placing one hand for support and swinging one leg over at time. On the way over, within an easy arm's reach, I caught the sight of coarse, brown hair, floating against the fence. I barely paused a moment. It was the first sign confirming what we had already tried to accept; Not all of the goats had survived.

On the other side of the gate, I found myself even more thankful for every inch of extra height that I had over Roy. Within a few steps, he had started swimming, while I was still able to walk on tip-toes. A few more feet, he continued swimming in front of me and I began a half-swim, bouncing on the furthest tips of my toes, using a modified breaststroke to pull myself forward with the current. After another 15 feet, I had lost all of my height advantage. With a fresh taste of hurricane/bayou water dribbling in the corner of my mouth, I gave up and swam the final ten yards, before seeing Roy put his own feet down and walk into the barn.

Even though we were still in high chest deep water, the combined relief of finally making it there and being able to walk normal again, made it feel like I had stepped onto dry ground. And then, there was one other reason to feel very good right then.

"Hey Tiny. Yuh ok, bud?" Trailing behind, I heard Roy before catching sight of the white head of a human sized dog sticking out of the water. Their sheepdog Tiny was pinned in the six-inch space separating the wall and a length of vertical pvc plumbing pipe. He was not shaking, was not excited to see Roy, had absolutely no appearance of energy in him. *How long had he been pinned like that? With the water up to his neck, how much longer would he have survived had we not come?*

Roy and I took a moment, since we were only standing up to our chests in water, to comfort Tiny. Then, seeing as how he wasn't hurt, wasn't panicking and not likely to go anywhere, we took some time to look for any of the other animals.

The stall where they kept the chickens had enough shelving and bare wooden beams that the chickens had just climbed to higher levels as the water rose. Even though they had less than two more feet between the water and the ceiling, there was a hole in the barn that could possibly serve as an escape route; and seeing as how there wasn't exactly any dry ground around, we had to hope that they would continue taking care of themselves and march on.

As we had begun to expect, especially after passing within arms reach of a drowned goat on the way to the barn, none of the goats were found. We looked for any sign of the horses, Roy wasn't sure how many his parents had right now, walked through the length of the barn, out the other end to check the fields that were on the opposite side from the house. A few hundred yards toward the horizon, we could make out two shapes standing up to their chests in water. They appeared to be safe for now.

There was nothing left for us to look for outside. All of the goats were gone, Roy's parents either had just the two horses or they had more, and their bull was either somewhere safe or it wasn't. Those are hard decisions to force yourself into accepting, but there was a massively terrified dog who had spent the night pinned against a wall, and absolutely nothing we could do for any of the other animals that may, or may not be out there. By the time we had completed our circuit around the barn, noting his step-dad's boat that was sitting on its trailer, firmly tied down and half-sunken, we noticed a considerable change in both the water's level and the strength of the current. It was time to get Tiny and head back to the house.

Even though we had earlier checked to make sure Tiny hadn't been significantly injured, I still thought that his ribs should have been bruised, if not broken, it wasn't until then that we took the time to make a closer inspection and figure out exactly what we had to do in order to free him. His weight, and likely the reason he had not been either crushed or drowned, was supported by a valve pipe running horizontally into the wall. In order to get Tiny out of there, one of us would have to bend the plastic pipe holding him against the wall, while the other would need to physically lift Tiny's front legs over the valve pipe and back him out. As for who did what, we had the former Marine, a scrawny runner, and a nearly 150-pound, soaking wet dog to lift.

I grabbed hold of the plastic pipe, unconcerned about bending it too far, Roy lifted Tiny and the three of us began an entertaining, albeit painful dance. Just when we needed Tiny to be lifeless and let us do the work, he showed his first signs of energy. Our original plan was that Roy would lift Tiny high enough, which was nearly over his head, to clear Tiny's front paws over the valve and then slowly back him out to safety. Unfortunately, as soon as Roy lifted Tiny's front legs, his rear tilted deeper into the water and the massive dog began to panic. Rather than allowing Roy to ease him backward, he began kicking his paws, propelling himself forward.

Not only was Roy not prepared to carry Tiny that direction, but forward was exactly where I had to stand in order to bend the pipe

Tiny was throwing Roy into me, but I couldn't move without letting go of the pipe and likely crushing his ribs. Roy wasn't able to both lift and force Tiny backwards. I struggled keep the pipe bent, bracing myself with one arm against the wall and balancing my weight to keep form falling into the water. Once again, I found myself taking advantage of my height and Roy's shortness. As he struggled to completely lift Tiny over the valve, I stretched my shoulder as high as it could go, Roy squeezed underneath my arm and between me and the pipe, as I switched hands and blindly found an underwater board to brace my foot against. Now free, Tiny returned to his perfect calm, resting in Roy's arms.

With myself on one side, Roy on the other, we began escorting Tiny to safety. It had only taken us ten minutes to rescue him, but once we stepped out of the barn, our surroundings took on a whole new level of concern for me. The combination of the rising level, a much stronger current, wind and misty rain had reached a critical point. For the first time, the thought seeped into me that we needed to hurry up and get out of there. As if this new fear wasn't enough to raise my pulse, Tiny had again stopped cooperating.

As soon as we took the first step outside the safe enclosure of the barn, he started kicking. I wrapped my arm tighter and pressed my body harder against his side, thinking it was a matter of soothing his panic at being outside and seeing nothing but water surrounding him. I wanted to give him some sense of a firm foundation. Roy observed otherwise. As far as Tiny was concerned, even with the two of us carrying him, he was floating in the middle of an endless lake. His instincts were telling him to swim. A fence post, tree or anything else that stuck out of the water was a point of refuge, something safe for him to swim toward. Short of blinding him, there was nothing for me to do but take a firm hold of his paws and endure the pain of inch long claws driving into my side whenever that grip would slip.

Like before, Roy's feet stopped hitting bottom after just a few steps. He had to let go of Tiny, swimming against the current toward the cattle gate. I was thinking that if I played my cards right, I would be able to hold onto Tiny and not have to break into a full swim. Perhaps the massive dog would add some buoyancy and I could use him as a semi-floater, skipping on my toes, and pulling myself forward with one arm through the deepest parts. Most likely though, I hadn't begun to think things through before telling Roy to go on ahead. "I'll take care of Tiny."

He hadn't finished his second stroke before I lost all contact with the ground and I was swimming with one arm, holding Tiny close with the other, while also trying to push him as far away as possible in order to keep from getting kicked by those claws. I felt like a real lifeguard, flashing back to images of the pool at Boy Scout camp where we learned life-saving techniques.

Unlike the trip out, when we had been heading for a large barn, strait into a barely noticeable current, now we were trying to go cross current, and there was a narrow, eight-foot window of safety that we needed to reach. On either side of the gate was the unseen, barbed wire fencing, with at least one goat already trapped and tangled in its mesh.

We were trying to swim across a river. Not only did my arm begin to tire out because of how much further we were having to swim, but with each stroke, we drifted nearly as far downstream as we did in the direction we were trying to go. Even when I was able to resume walking on my tiptoes, just halfway from the barn to the cattle gate, I was trying to figure out just where along the fence row the gate was, weighing how much I was being taken downstream with each step, and trying to calculate just when I needed to start trying to walk toward the gate.

Walking past Roy, I looked over at him and he was still swimming. While I was on my feet and able to somewhat brace myself against the current, he was still loosing more ground, heading downstream further than what he was gaining. *He's not going to make it.* Concern entered my head, he was going to float past the gate and dangerously close to the underwater fence. Using my experience from canoeing as a child, I looked for the characteristic rippled edge that would indicate precisely where the gate was. Then I somehow managed one of those three-armed maneuvers that we can never figure out how we did it. At least six inches under the surface, I grabbed the top of the gate, pulled myself toward it, reached a hand out to Roy and pulled him in, all while still managing to keep a tight grip on Tiny.

The most difficult part was over. Once we hauled Tiny over the cattle gate, it was a simple matter of trying to keep his legs from kicking as we crossed through chest deep, then waste deep water on our way to the back porch. Raised nearly three feet off the ground, the water was inching over the edge, yet there was still a small patch of dry floor at the back corner. Roy and I guided Tiny's front paws to the edge, halfway expecting him to use them to pull himself up, but while the worst had ended when we crossed over the gate, we still had to face the most difficult. Soaked to the core, it felt like the man-sized dog weighed 200 pounds and had gone back to acting like a limp sack of potatoes. We struggled, each pushing one of his front paws onto the porch, then it took the last of my strength to help Roy push Tiny on up from the rear.

I needed a moment to recover on dry land, tried joining Tiny on the porch, and was painfully reminded of both how physically tired

I had become, and also how careful we needed to be when attempting even the simplest of things...like walking up a few steps. Hidden underwater, I missed the steps to the porch by a few inches, unexpectedly catching my foot in a hole in the lattice work underpinning, ripping it loose from the house and scraping a loose nail down my leg. After three more attempts, and a four-inch slice down my shin, I finally joined Tiny on the porch. Fortunately, Roy had been distracted by something toward the neighbor's farm, sparing me the embarrassment, as well as the shame of damaging part of the house that had survived. It's likely though, that already underwater, all of the latticework will have to be replaced anyway. At least, that's convincing enough of an argument to give me a little comfort,

I stood on the porch for a brief minute, Tiny remained quiet and motionless, his eyes bewildered with a touch of fear still in them. The sky seemed darker, water colder and heavier. I had just come as near to having to swim for my life as I had ever been, and even though we were completely safe, I began to realize that the safety was temporary. We still had to walk back to the truck and for the first time in my life, I could feel real life threatening danger closing in. We had to leave immediately!

****

Before leaving, we made a final quick trip back into the workshop to find a cooler that we could pack up with some of the meat from the freezer. Not only was Roy out of food back at his place, but anything left there would simply have been abandoned to ruin and there was over a full head of cattle in there: T-bones, sirloin steaks, ground beef and roasts. Everything was still solidly frozen, but we had to be careful not to take anything that had touched the farm-bayou water that had flooded in when the freezer tipped over. Once the cooler was full we went back outside. The water was at

107

least a foot over the threshold of the house, confirming that it had not been my imagination; the water was definitely rising and it wasn't taking its time. With the cooler in hand, floating on the surface of the water, we walked around the back of the house, drug Tiny back into the water, and went to join Sr. by the road. He was nowhere to be seen.

"Where the hell is he?" Roy said, "What the hell is he doing?"

I was actually worried. Neither Roy nor I had given much thought to the fact that we had not heard any sign of Sr. since we first left the workshop for the trek out to the barn. He had been standing in what looked like to the middle of the front yard, yelling like a helpless child, but he was the parent who should have known well enough to take care of himself. "Roy!" I yelled. "Roy!"

"He probably got tired and went on back to the truck." Roy said as he continued walking. He didn't even slow down a step.

"Roy!" I called again, but faintly softer. I was torn between being worried, being angry and being helpless. I wondered if his legs had given out, or some debris floating by had knocked him over. Earlier, I had seen a snake or two, possibly one could have bitten him. *But what if it had? What's there for us to do?* We were standing in the middle of a huge lake, with a few houses, out buildings and cars periodically poking up out of the water. *If he had slipped and fallen, he could have washed a mile away.* "Roy!" I halfway spun around, as I continued walking, scanning for any sign of where he may have been. Roy Jr. was already turning down the street with Tiny slung over his back. I had nothing but to hope that Sr. had just decided to leave without telling us and began walking, still twisting my head around, reluctantly searching, equally prepared to either see him, or not.

The hike back to the truck was much like one of those dreams when you are looking down on yourself. Before turning down the road to follow Roy, I stopped to free the dog from the kennel across the street. While he had been standing on dry concrete when we arrived at the farm, he was now standing in water up to his knees. It was obvious that the people were gone, the house was standing in over four feet of water. I said a small prayer while crossing the yard, that his idiot owners had simply left the gate latched. But then I saw the padlock and begin trying to imagine how I could use my bare hands to tear open the chain link fencing. Fortunately, they hadn't clamped the lock closed. With a simple swing of the latch, I opened the door and let the mutt run loose. There was a small rise that gave this side of the road a stretch of about 100 yards of dry ground. *Running free, he knows how to take care of himself.*

A short distance down the road I had nearly caught up with Roy when I caught sight of a scraggled mess of fur trapped on the roof of a pickup. The water was less than an inch from going over the tiny, red metallic island. I walked up the drive, which fortunately had the tips of a couple red reflectors sticking out to mark the edge, and set the gray cat on top of the cooler. A helicopter passed overhead. I could imagine whoever was in there laughing at the pale-chested idiot pushing a cooler with a well-drenched cat sitting on top. (Somewhere among the mounded islands of fire ants floating in the water I had picked up a few in my shirt.) Roy was not far in front of me and I quickly had caught back up with him.

"How do I tell them that everything they own is gone?" I couldn't think of an answer, so I remained silent. Not everything was truly gone, only those things in the house that were on the floor, but Roy was in no condition for a pep talk. He was in shock and needed time to grieve in silence. *Perhaps later, after the water recedes and he returns to the house, he'll feel better when he sees that things weren't as bad as he thought.*

Near the halfway point, the once small stretch of dry road was nearly gone. On the way out, if had been nearly a quarter mile long. This trip, however, it barely took five steps to cross. It was still large enough though, for me to drop the cat off. A good sized part of my heart hurt to leave the tattered thing along the side of the road. It felt like I had driven ten miles into the country and dumped it. But I know that I had done what I could. He very likely wouldn't have survived the night on the roof of the truck and this was close enough to his home that his family would stand a chance at finding him when they came back.

As I was setting the cat down, a large flatbed truck pulled out of the water from the direction of the farm. They had hoped to be able to make it all of the way out, but after making it this far, decided making it all of the way wasn't looking very promising. That, and the transmission had locked up at some point. They were stuck in low gear and were debating whether or not four men could push it into one of the driveways.

"Do you need any help?" A man yelled from the other side of the rise as two guys pulled up in their fishing boat.

"I think we need all the muscle we can get to push this thing off the road."

"We'll tie up and be right over." They offered to give us a ride, once they were finished helping with the flatbed. Even though waiting to catch a ride in the boat would have been quicker, Roy was anxious to get back to his truck and talk to his parents. I could also sense that Roy felt much better walking, rather than standing around and waiting on someone else.

"Go ahead." I told him, "I'll stay and help these guys out, then catch up with shortly." He took hold of Tiny again and started walking toward his own truck. The guys were having a hard time tying the boat up to a speed limit sign. I trudged over to the ditch and held the boat steady as they stepped onto the side of the road.

To my embarrassment, I had to let the 'strong' men push while I stood idly by at the corner of the drive to mark the ditch. I felt pathetic, like I was simply standing there, watching six men struggle to push the truck. Yet it was one of those jobs that needed to be done...no one wanted to take any chances of slipping something that size onto the mud. With the truck safely parked, I loaded the cooler into the boat and we headed back to the truck.

Surprisingly, Roy was only 50 yards from the truck when we caught up to him and as I had reluctantly assumed, Sr. was sitting in the cab. The truck itself was sitting in six inches of water, at least 30 yards from dry ground. When we had left, it had been at least that far from the water's edge. It was another sign that we had gotten out just in time.

Much of the conversation that passed between the two of them is easy to imagine. Roy did a fine share of yelling and Sr. put on a look of innocent confusion. Just like when we were at the farm, my thoughts jumped back to the time when I had faked drowning in order to get the air mattress from my brother. But the tables had flipped. No longer was I concerned about how afraid Sr. would be for his kid. Sitting in Roy's truck, I remembered how scared I had made my dad, how Sr. was acting like the five-year old who had just faked his own drowning, and how I couldn't ground a man in his 50s.

"Why is Jr. mad at me?" He stared, clueless that he had done anything wrong, why either of us would be upset that he simply disappeared. I was thinking: *If he was twelve and pulled this, I would be spanking his butt right now.* But Sr. isn't a kid, no matter how much he had been acting like one all day. It was simply absurd that he could truly have no idea that he had done anything wrong, or what that may have been. To simply disappear when you're standing in floodwaters over your waist, to not tell anyone or leave any kind of a sign that you hadn't fallen over and drowned is simply wrong. There's no other way my mind could put it; no way that it could form a way to explain to Sr. how stupid, inconsiderate and self-centered he was being. I said nothing. *We are going to have a talk later.*

Since we were back inside the truck, the events for the day were done. I could hear Roy talking with his parents on the phone. He was telling them: "everything is gone…the water is over the pool in the backyard…the bikes are all underwater…the cattle gate going to the barn is completely under…" Even though things are bad, both of their vehicles are ruined, the workshop is destroyed and they had lost nearly all of their animals, except for possibly two horses. I really don't think that things are that bad. I know that Roy feels like everything has been lost, I would likely feel the same way, but I had hoped he would have been a little softer with the news for his parents. "Everything is gone," was just too blunt.

It was nice though that he followed the one suggestion that I was able to offer him when, for the seventh time, he had asked me what to tell his parents. Immediately after he told them how high the water was, and before he told them that the only goat we had seen had been floating against the fence, he told them, "We found Tiny." That is the kind of thing I left Colorado to do: *We saved Tiny today.*

A Horse Rescue

Sunday, September 25

The plan for today was to meet with Roy's parents, his mom and step dad, then go out to the farm so they could check on the two horses and begin salvaging whatever they could. Until this morning, all they had to go on were Roy's descriptions and the sound of near hopeless shock vibrating through his every word. Even if it meant coming to the harsh reality that none of their animals had survived through the night, they simply needed to see the destruction for themselves.

About the only thing that knew last night was that I was sure of was that there was no way possible the horses could have survived the two more feet of water that the forecasters had been predicting. When we had left them yesterday, they had been standing on the highest point of the field and the water was already halfway up their chests. I had no hope inside and was fully expecting to find two more bodies tangled up in the barbed-wire fence. Their only hope was that the news reports were wrong and the water did not rise as much as they were calling for. Making matters worse, in my mind, was that they were also predicting that it would take 3-4 days before the water levels would begin dropping by any significant amount.

I don't know if he asked, but even if he had, there was not a chance that Sr. was going to join us today. One day had enough to humor an ailing relationship between father and son, a second day would have been too much and I was prepared with a speech already in mind to forcefully tell him that there was absolutely no chance he was going. I'm glad that I didn't have to say anything. At 7:00 am, Rick, one of Roy's best friends, arrived at the house with the scuba gear so we would be able to dive under and cut the cattle gate open. Reality and hopelessness seeped in just a little deeper. Then the three of us left.

Even after everything that happened yesterday, I still felt that soupy air of surrealness, like I was a ghostly observer unable to interact with what was going on around me. I think this added to the lack of welcoming I felt from Roy's parents when we met up at a roadside restaurant. One of the first things that I noticed was that their faces looked a lot more hopeful than what I felt. After a few hours, and what I am sure were several phone calls, they had been able to find a boat, horse trailer and a long-term place for the horses to stay. It seemed to me that they had in mind that they were going to pick up the horses, check on the condition of the house and take out a few things if possible.

We met with little more than a "hello," punctuated by Roy's description and gestures of how high the water was. But as I told Roy, it doesn't bother me in the least, "they have much more important things on their minds." For all his parents knew, they had just lost everything they owned, except for their dog Tiny, and just like yesterday, I'm here to do whatever I can do to help out, not to be entertained.

114

The half-hour ride from the parking lot to the farm was quiet as Rick, Roy and I followed his parents. As soon as we arrived at the highway turn-off though, everyone's spirits raised and as shadowy as things had begun, it quickly turned into a very good day. Not only had the water not risen an additional two feet, but it had actually dropped a couple. The only downside was that the highway put-in was a little more difficult than expected. Whereas boats were plopping in with ease yesterday, it took all four of us to work the boat off the trailer, then we walked it several yards through two-foot deep water, before it was deep enough for Roy's dad to lower the motor. We floated off through backyards and over roads before catching the bayou that bordered the back of their farm. I was so impressed at the new hope that despite floating chairs, piles of clumped lumber and other household debris, the sun, wet breeze, and lush trees along the banks of the bayou almost felt like I was out on a Sunday fishing trip.

When we did arrive at the farm, we found both horses to be in better shape than any of us were, along with their lone bull that we all thought had been lost. One of the neighbors had left the gate to a neighboring field open. At some point during the night, all of the area livestock that had survived, which is probably less than a third, were able to make their way into a field that was now dry ground. After a very short discussion, it was decided that we would leave the animals there, where they had room to roam freely and plenty of hay to eat, rather than taking them to a strange stable. It was obvious that no one was home so Roy and I spent a few minutes looking around for food to leave out for a dozen area dogs that had taken up residence. Maybe two of them had lived there two days ago.

We only spent a half hour with the horses, but already found ourselves in the same precarious position we were in yesterday of having to leave quickly, or not being able to leave at all. Ironically though, it was because the water level was dropping so quickly that we were concerned about it being too shallow for the boat. Even as it was, we had to climb out and portage the boat 50 feet down the driveway where the water had fallen to just a few inches deep; *so much for the 3-4 days that the weatherman had warned it would take for the waters to recede.* Once the boat had cleared the shallowing driveway, Roy's dad took us for a winding tour of their own property.

Their own boat was still tied down to their trailer, now poking it's nose out of the water. Where yesterday we blindly sat on a pool deck that we couldn't see under the water, today we could see the top few inches of the pool. The deck looked more like a broken pile of pallets than the firm platform we thought we were sitting on yesterday, infinitely grateful for a secure place to sit and rest on our way to the barn. Circling the pool, Roy and I pointed to the muddy stain of the water line just a foot from the roof of the barn, "Wow!! It was that high?!" The water had dropped nearly three feet, but even with the clear, muddy evidence, the reality that we had worked and swam in water that deep just doesn't fit with the reality that I remember. I wish I had taken my camera with me today.

We made a very quick pit stop to check on things inside the house and take a few with us. The water was just lipping over the second of four steps, meaning there was still a good six inches standing in the garage/workshop, but the house was dry except for a damp film of bayou laying across the floor. It seems that Roy's exaggeration yesterday turned out to be for the best. The relief on their faces after expecting the worst was incredible, much better than if he had tried to soften the blow and they had found things to be worse. We took things that had been on the lower shelves throughout the house and found scattered surfaces to lay them on so they could at least try to air out. Roy's mom found a brand new horse bridle that had been on the floor of their closet, and I spent most of my time arranging several photo albums that had

116

unfortunately been stored on bottom shelves. I can't be for sure, but I don't think any of the pictures, or the horse collar, were ruined since they were only under water for a few hours.

I found out that one of the most important things we had come out there to do was gather up and remove all of their guns. Even though the water level was down and dropping rapidly, it could still be several days yet before they will be able to move back home. Not that it's a big concern, but some basic steps do need to be taken to protect against looting. Once we had the guns on board, I untied the boat from the front door rail and we hurried on out.

Roy's parents were in high spirits as they looked in awe at what surrounded them. In less than an hour they had gone from knowing for certain that everything they owned was lost to the gleaming thought that things really aren't that bad. They had started the morning with little hope of even finding their horses, much less that they would be standing next to the bull Roy and I was sure had been lost. Now, they know they have a few days of waiting and then a lot of work to do in the coming weeks. We immediately headed back to the highway where the trucks were parked. Roy's dad backed the trailer off the shoulder, dipping into the water and we heaved the boat on up. Even though we had rushed to get out, the water had fallen enough that it took six men, the four of us plus two neighborhood strangers, to pull the boat up the trailer.

****

It's amazing just how soothing the sensation of stepping onto underwater grass feels after walking a barefoot mile on pavement. With the boat loaded, Roy, Rick and I decided to drive the back ways and find a place to park that would be a little closer for a return trip to the house. Unfortunately for my feet though, I had discovered on the first trip with his parents that a good pair of boots left alone for a year in the back of a closet can suffer the same dry rotted fate that the tires on a car will if you leave it parked for months on end. The soles had lasted only long enough so that I didn't notice them dissolving away until after we had arrived at the highway put-in, but by the time I had jumped in the boat there had been very little left of the once three-inch thick rubber soles. For most of the first trip, I had been flopping what was left of the cardboard and rubber liners underfoot and trying to stay away from gravel. When we were finished loading the boat, there was nothing left to flop. I had thought very briefly about the need to go home and get some shoes that would actually stay on my feet, but once again, I had come along to do what I could to help, not to add any more burdens. I wasn't about to make Roy take over an hour to drive me home simply because I no longer had any shoes.

I have the sense that the second trip was a lot like the extra time Roy spent working on his bike yesterday, just as much therapy from the comfort of being around the farm and doing something as it was actual help in getting some needed work done. The bulk of our time was spent cleaning out the freezers in the garage and refrigerator in the house. It may seem trivial, but just imagine the stench and ooze of dumping over 100 gallons of bayou soaked and rotted peppers, homegrown vegetable soup mix, fresh cut beef, chicken and wild mushrooms; much better to take care of while everything was still mostly frozen. We also used the water to our advantage, floating their picnic table and benches the 100 yards back toward their porch, instead of waiting for the waters to recede and have to carry them possibly further. I was amazed, and a little grossed out by the dog food that still seemed to be floating everywhere. I'm sure that there are much worse things floating around in that same water, but for some reason, wet dog food throws my guts into a crinkle.

For the trip back to the truck, I grabbed a pair of house shoes out of the closet. Not exactly the best for trekking through water, but the dark red blisters growing on my feet weren't up to handling the rough hardness of regular shoes. Within the first quarter mile, one of the neighbors picked us up in his tractor. Why he had driven right by us without offering a ride on our way out to the house was a mystery to us all, but then, anyone of us had plenty of opportunity to ask for a ride and I didn't want to admit that I couldn't handle a little barefoot walking. I settled for walking along the center lines of the road, quietly celebrating every time the doted line become solid (I had never noticed just how smooth those lines really are.) So it was with extreme comfort and relief that I stepped up into the bucket attached to the front of the tractor and in short order, we were back at Roy's truck, laughing at the dilapidated remains of my boots. It was a very good day!!!

Breakdown (Again)

Monday, September 26

Roy Jr. woke up early this morning to go out for another day of work out at the farm. I had entertained thoughts of offering to go with him, but shied away at the prospect of waking up at 5:30 am. I was physically exhausted, not to mention still uncertain that my blistered feet could handle putting on a pair of shoes, much less walking in them. So I waited for Jr. to ask, and he never did.

I also haven't heard back from any of the Red Cross volunteers that are supposed to call me when they move back from the evacuation to Shreveport, so today was a day of rest and Roy treated me to what he claims is the best coffee in the world, Mello Joy, a Louisiana specialty. I will admit, it was better than any Starbucks I've ever had, but nothing can compare to Lakota Coffee back home in Missouri. Unfortunately though, the restful part of the day came to an abrupt end

On the way back to the house the radio in my car went quiet. *I can't believe it*!! The mystery with my car that cropped up three weeks ago just outside Topeka, Kansas has returned. I fiddled with the tuner for a bit, and quickly noticed that it was only toggling between two numbers. I yelled out, "*CRAP!!!!!*" The car was almost out of juice and we were a good two miles from Jr.'s house yet.

With any luck, I thought, I could nurture it as far as I could, and maybe, just maybe, get close enough to pull into a lot, park, walk and then wait for him to get back from his parents' place. Less than a quarter-mile further, the car died. We didn't make it anywhere near close enough to walking distance, but we had at least just passed the exit to a mall. So, with an extra wide shoulder, I pushed and Sr. steered the car backward into the parking lot next to a Buffalo Wild Wings. If history held to form, an hour or so of letting the car cool down would free up enough juice for us to make it all of the way back.

An hour and three glasses of water later, neither of us enjoying the awkward wait of sitting there without enough money to buy a soda, the car started right up. There was no question about it, whatever the problem had been, it was the same thing that had me waste a night in Kansas and over a week in Missouri. I thought, *What in blazes is going on? Why has the car worked great for the past three weeks? Why, now that I've finally made contact with someone to work out in the field, has it decided to flare up again?*

Unfortunately, things didn't continue to go according to form. The car had started without any problem, which meant that we should have been able to make it all of the way back to Jr.'s. However, less than another half-mile down the road, the radio bean sputtering again and the car lurched into a small parking lot by some doctor's offices. *Now what do we do?* Jr. was still out at the farm, we had no idea how much longer he was going to be there and we were still too far from his house for Sr. to walk. I called Roy; I simply had no other option.

121

"Roy, how are things going out there." After a very short greeting, "Sorry to bother you, but my car's broken down and I was wondering how much longer you were planning on being out there..." It was going to be at least a few more hours and once again, I knew that his parents needed his help a lot more than I did. I wouldn't have even bothered him, but I knew that there was no way Sr. could have made the walk in this heat. Fifteen minutes later, his friend Rick showed up in his pickup.

At home, I called Rob with the PRC, who I had finally made contact with on Sunday night and had to cancel out on meeting them tomorrow. My next call was to our mechanic Daniel back in Missouri.

In looking over the car, *I don't know why we stare at it when we don't know what we're either looking for or at most of the time*, I did notice that one of the connections to the alternator I had replaced last month was loose. On the off chance that that could be the problem, Daniel suggested that I take the alternator in to be tested. Like so many times of late, I had mixed feelings when Tony at the O'Reilly auto store told me that the alternator was bad.

On the one hand, I was obviously thrilled that we had solved the mystery (the loose connection caused it to short out only after the car had heated up. Then when the car cooled, it contracted back to normal size and the short was gone). On the other hand, I felt a little foolish because so many of these problems were caused because I simply missed tightening one of the bolts. And I was also bothered that I had to trouble Tony at O'Reilly when I wasn't going to be spending any money there. The alternator was still under warranty, so it was a not so quick trip in Sr.'s jeep to a different shop on the other side of town to pick up a replacement. One lesson for the day: *Always keep all of your receipts in the glove box.*

122

After double-checking to make sure that everything was tightened, the car started right up and ran for a good half-hour without so much as a hiccup. Then I gave Rob with the PRC another call…*We're back on for tomorrow!!!!*

False Alarms

September 27-29

I have been trying very hard, and think that I've done a good job of accepting life according to God's timetable here. I can even accept that by spending more time in Missouri, I was still staying with Roy Jr. when Rita hit so that I was able to help his family. Had it not taken so long to get the car fixed, I likely would have left the Dome a week earlier and been somewhere in Mississippi when Rita came ashore. However, the last few days have affected much more than just my own personal timetable.

Having replaced the alternator on Monday evening, Daniel and I were both confident that the problem had been resolved, so I called Rob and made plans to meet him and the PRC crew on Tuesday morning. Unfortunately, after I had packed everything up and left to meet them Tuesday morning, the car barely had enough juice to make it five miles. I had to call Rob again and let him know that it still wasn't fixed and I would have to meet up with them later. Even though the alternator I had bought in Colorado less then a month ago was bad, there was something else going on with the electrical system. Of course, Rob was very understanding of the problems a 15-year old car can present, cordially told me to give him a call when it was fixed and we'd move forward from there.

After hanging up with Rob, it didn't take long for me to discover that one of the main connecting wires on the starter had melted loose. Rather than my own stupidity of missing another bolt, this one wasn't my fault and was actually one of the connections soldered on at the factory. After a lengthy discussion over the phone with Daniel, much of it spent in confusion as the untrained Sunday repairman tried describing black wires and nodes over the phone, we decided that the broken wire on the back of the starter could be causing the short, even though he didn't think it could drain that much power. Daniel faxed me the receipt for warranty replacement, there was no way I was going to pay to replace a starter that was barely two weeks old, and well before noon, the car was running just as well as it ever did. I placed another call to Rob to set up to meet Wednesday morning, but that wasn't the last conversation we had.

That evening, my steering wheel was on the receiving end of yet another heavy beating as the car came to a rolling stop in a grocery store parking lot. Just like before, the radio had gone silent and the car sputtered when I tested the headlights. Then it went completely dead. Adding to the anger of my small tantrum was the fact that I might have made it back to Roy's place had it not been for the putzy car in front of me that dorked around and kept me from making it through the last stop light. Once again, I had to give Rob a call. This time though, I gave up and had to tell him that instead of more yo-yo calling, I had no idea when or if I would be able to join them. "I'll give you a call after we're sure the problem has been fixed."

Internally, I was beginning to honestly think that my car could be on its last ropes. Whatever this problem with the electrical system was, it had plagued me since the week I left Colorado and it had already made it passed one mechanic. By this point, I was beyond dejected, yet had enough hope in me that I told my mom over the phone that I thought I had one last chance to fix it myself. Maybe, although I didn't really believe it, with a continuity tester I would be able to find the short without having to spend hundreds of dollars. I went to bed running through the calculations in my head of just how much taking it to another mechanic would cost, *$100, $200, $500... there's no telling how much it'll cost before we find the one wire that's causing these problems.*

First thing Wednesday morning, I borrowed Sr.'s jeep to go and buy a continuity tester. It bothers me to be spending the money people have donated for me to be volunteering down here, but at this point, it's just as much a necessity as paying rent back home. I should also mention here that Sr. has been tremendously helpful in letting me use his jeep in order to get parts and tools as I have needed them the past few days. He's normally not the type to hand over the keys and let some young kid go driving all across town, but he hasn't hesitated even once in letting me take it as I have needed.

I started off completely lost as to what to do, even though I've done a lot of work on this car and others; as much as putting in new engines, and I have the Chilton's manual with the tester in hand. I stared at the electrical diagrams, followed strait lines across the page with my fingers and still only saw a bunch of crooked marks and little boxed shapes randomly scattered around the page. The reality of my situation, that I would have to shell out lots of other peoples' money, significantly shortening the amount of time I could work down here, was settling in when Daniel returned my call from earlier in the morning.

All I can say, and with complete sincerity is, "Thank God for Daniel!" He spent a good hour on the phone with me, much of it just as puzzled and bamboozled as I was, patiently leading me step by step through every possible line to check. We finally focused our attention on the oddity that while there was perfect continuity between the battery and the alternator, meaning that power was going from the alternator to the battery, there wasn't any power coming from the battery. The physics of it made absolutely no sense, it was like electricity traveled halfway down a wire and then inexplicably stopped. It was especially odd because I had just bought the battery a few weeks earlier when I changed the alternator. On a long shot of desperation, we decided that since I had completely drained the battery, it had not had a chance to get a good charge.

Neither of us felt very convinced that this was the problem, but everything we thought we knew for sure was having us grasp at any imaginable possibility. That, and it was virtually the last resort. If the problem wasn't somehow linked to the battery, then I had no other choice but to randomly start pulling out and replace the wiring until I happened upon the culprit; that was an ugly option. So it was with a mixture of trepidation and hope that I took the battery to the nearby O'Reilly store for them to charge it up.

I returned to the O'Reilly store an hour later and as soon as I walked in, Tony from behind the counter glanced up and started shaking his head. The three week-old battery was no good. *Had I somehow managed to not only buy a bad alternator, which isn't necessarily rare, but to also buy a bad starter and a bad battery all at the same time? How ridiculously bad could my luck be?* God or someone had to have had a hand in this and it really petirked me that there could be no reasonable reason for all of this crap. I was of course, also relieved that we had found a problem, and that once again, it was a matter of finding the right auto parts store in town to warranty replace a part that was less a month old.

I spent the better part of the rest of the day driving around enough to drain the new battery and hopefully get the car hot enough for it to die if it had not been fixed. Satisfied that three hours of looping around and through town was enough, I called Rob again and promised that I would give it one final chance, if something happened and I wasn't able to make it, then he would have to count me out for good.

Tomorrow morning, I will finally be leaving Roy's house and spend the next two weeks with the PRC, somewhere to the west where they are working on Rita recovery. I had expected to be closer to Mississippi by now, but God knows and everything that has happened might have been so that I would be able to help with the Rita recovery, even the bloody car deal. And if that's the case, then I'll gladly accept it, although, there are much cheaper, and less aggravating ways that God could have used.

The PRC

Friday, September 30

This was a complete waste of my time. I left Roy's at 7:00 this morning, my car was packed and I had said my final good-byes. I owe so much to both of them; Sr. for being such a big part of my experience down here, and to Roy Jr. for opening up his home and treating me like a long-time friend. When I last spoke with Rob, the idea was that I would be spending the next two weeks working twelve-hour days with the PRC, but that wasn't anywhere near what actually happened today. Instead, I worked for maybe two hours today and then came back home to Roy's.

All week long, the PRC has been distributing food and supplies to Rita victims in a town called Jennings, about 30 miles down the highway toward Lake Charles, where the eye of the storm hit. Despite what I saw at the farm last weekend, this gave me my first opportunity to see the actual wind damage caused by a hurricane. It was incredible, how mile by mile the trees slanted more and more. In Lafayette I had seen a few limbs and signs blown down, by the time we reached Jennings, nearly every tree and sign had been uprooted. The town itself, a decent size of 30,000 people, was beginning to look in good order. Most of the businesses were open, several windows had been boarded over, and only a few traffic lights were still out. Most houses had a fallen tree or three, in the front yard. There is certainly a lot of cleaning up yet to do and there was a feel of slothness about, but all in all, I was surprised to see things getting close to normal.

Once we arrived at the distribution sight, the first thing I learned was not to walk in the grass. The mosquitoes were monstrous, big enough that you could feel the extra wait when one landed on your arm and even with a good coating of bug spray, it was literally walking through a curtain of flying bugs. The first thing we had to do was walk around picking up the trash. It was nothing significant. We weren't clearing out a debris field. Rather, it was just like when my brother and I were kids and our dad had us pick up the trash around our house. While picking up yard trash wasn't even close to what I had in mind, but I tried to do it with an attitude that I was there to do whatever was needed, not just what my idea was.

Picking up the trash took 15 minutes and I hung out with the college kids, tossing around a football and killing time for an hour before the supply truck arrived. It may have taken us 20 minutes to unload, then start sorting and packing the mixed canned goods into shopping bags that we would hand out to people.

Their setup was good. People could drive a loop around the church, pop open their trunk and we would load the car as they drove along in a line. We had water, toilet paper, a few diapers, baby food, canned goods, pasta and several boxes of Frisbees. The line was a couple hundred feet long with about four stops, and they never had to get out of their cars.

After 30 minutes of bagging the canned stuffs, I was forced into taking a break by Teddy, the leader of the group. In contrast to my time at the Dome, he made me feel like a child who didn't know how to take care of himself. Rather than let me continue bagging, he stopped just short of grabbing me by the shirt collar and dragging me to sit down and take a break. "Trust me," he said, "you're going to be doing plenty of work later and need it." I guess it's understandable though, since he's used to working with young college students who do need someone to reign them in from time to time. We sat and had a cold drink for a bit before it was time for lunch. Fritos with chili and that was it. Not only was it far from the meals I had grown accustomed to from the Red Cross, but I also found out that this would be the only meal they would be providing each day. *A small plate of nachos is not enough to keep us going through long days of physical work.*

Lunch was finished and it was already after noon, yet we had done virtually nothing. At the same time, it was only a little after noon and I already had the feeling that two weeks of this was not going to work. I started thinking about what I would say to Teddy at the end of the day, when I told them that I needed to look for somewhere else to spend my time.

At 1:00 we opened the distribution line for business. The line of cars parked along the highway was at least a mile long, and I thought: *Maybe we will be busy and actually worn out by the end of the day.* As I've already said though, I was extremely wrong. Once we opened, from what I could tell, only about a dozen more cars joined the line. From their experience earlier in the week, everyone who needed supplies had learned to come early.

In the beginning we were doing a good job of handing out a reasonable amount of supplies, one case of water per family (some cars were picking up for several families,) one pack of toilet paper

per family, a bag or two of food, etc. The change in jobs from what I did at the Dome was wonderful. Instead of spending my time telling people what I couldn't do for them, I was actually giving them something. We also had more than enough people working so I had time to talk with some of the folks as they drove along and make a bit of a personal connection. It's just such a shame that once again, I find that I can't remember any names or the stories they shared, just pictures of their faces and the cars that they were driving. As they drove by, person after person thanked us and asked for God's blessing on us, making the bright sun fell that much brighter. For the first time down here I was really enjoying myself.

After little more than an hour, the attitude of the rest of the crew changed from giving people what they needed to one of getting everything out and be done as quickly as possible. The slowing pace of the cars meant that one person could easily handle passing out the water and I found myself throwing he football around again. By 3:15 we had cleaned everything up and one final car picked up the last case of water. We were done for the day and apparently, done here for good.

I only listened in, but the organizers had decided that they weren't needed in Jennings any longer and would have to think about whether or not to move in closer toward Lake Charles; *so much for having all I can do for the next two weeks.* I also found out that the crew drives back to Lafayette to sleep every night. Along with promising me meals, Rob had said they would have a place for me stay; *I wonder where that would have been?* Nonetheless, I ended up not having to address the issue of telling them that this wasn't what I was looking for. If they were done here, then they were done and I could just move on without any questions being asked. What bothers me even more is that no one talked to me today about my plans and the next two weeks I had signed up for. *Today was a complete waste of my time!*

Disappointed again, I came back to Roy's house tonight. Jr. gave me the number for a friend of his, Robby who can probably put me in touch with someone in Mississippi. I don't know why I didn't think of this earlier, but I also realized tonight that I could call the Diocese in Biloxi, if they're still standing, and they could surely find a place for me to work. It'll just be a matter of tracking down a phone number, made more difficult since Rita knocked out the wireless internet connection I had been using and it hasn't come back yet.

Unlike the Red Cross, I'm not angry with the PRC, just extremely disappointed. They are a new organization, established as a response to this year's storms, and they mostly use college students as volunteers. That's okay, it's their niche. I just don't fit into it right now, but I do wish that Rob would have been more honest and upfront with me. I do, however, want to be more frustrated than ever with my own situation. I've been in Louisiana for three weeks now and I'm nowhere closer to getting over to Mississippi, where I know they need the most help. Oddly though, I don't actually feel frustrated or angry, just disappointed and a little disheartened. *Maybe I'll take this extra time to go back to the Dome for a few days?*

Contact

Monday, October 3

Today was another day that I cowered at thought of going back to the Cajun Dome. I know that I have people back home supporting me financially, I should be out there doing something, and part of me does feel guilty about that. But, my head just isn't ready to go back and face such a huge unknown again. Too many things have changed: I have no idea how services around here have changed since Rita came through, virtually every one of the Red Cross volunteers I had been working with left to go back home early last week, plus when I'm there, I'm the expert who is supposed to know everything; I'm simply not ready to handle that yet. However, something did happen today that takes away all my excuses.

Since my trip began, I've been writing about the frustrations I have felt, and some that I wanted to feel, over how difficult it has been to get in touch with any organization working in Mississippi. Today was the day I made contact...well, sort of.

I have been trying to get in touch with any group or organization for almost three weeks. That is the entire reason I left Colorado, to go down and work on the front lines of the recovery efforts, not to be sitting down at a table in sunny Louisiana, answering questions and doing work that almost anyone else could do. Not to demean the work at the Cajun Dome, nor diminish the amount of help I know that I have provided. But I'm used to working twelve-hour day after twelve-hour day of physical labor and most people aren't; I'm willing to live out of my car for the next few weeks and most people aren't. This is far from arrogance and anything but an indictment on *most people*. Just a basic observation that we need people where their talents can be best utilized and these are two things that I have to offer.

All other criticisms aside, I have never felt that working with the Red Cross here is the best utilization of my talents, even though I accepted that I was doing a lot of good work and admitted that it was better that the people were able to work with me rather than some other shmoe who didn't care as much. (I realize that it sounds hypocritical, but that's how emotions often go. Maybe it means that I should have put more pressure and been more assertive with agencies to let me go help them. I think though that I should be more recognizing of the fact that God knows what He is doing better than I do…I'll have to work on that.)

For the most part though, all of these thoughts, how I decide to look back on this time as either a waste of it or as part of God's plan, only matter in retrospect now. The important thing is that I got to speak with someone from the Diocese of Biloxi this morning, I think here name was Mary, who told me to call Sherri Cox with Catholic Charities and she would know where they need help. On the surface, it sounds a lot like the response from Samaritan's Purse who was only using groups of volunteers and not individuals, Habitat for Humanity who is waiting for the rebuilding phase to start their work, or the PRC who claimed to be the only organization around that was actually sending people into the field (we know how that two week/one day experience went.) But there was a huge difference today; Sherri called me back this afternoon.

Unfortunately, I didn't get to actually talk with her. Rita made the phone system even worse down here; it now takes me a dozen tries for me to get a call through. Nonetheless she called, left a message and just as soon as we can talk, so I know where I will be going, I will finally be going to Mississippi to do the work that I set out from Colorado to do.

There was also something else wonderful that happened today, and it is helping me to better accept that there are reasons why it has taken so long to move on from here. In all honesty, if I played any part of it, this alone would be worth three weeks of my life. I have previously mentioned that Roy Sr. has been getting more and more on my nerves over the past several days.

Part of it is that he treats me like I don't know anything, whether it's fixing the car, listening to God or cooking a meal. Another part is that he's one of these people who says "Thank You Jesus!!!" at every little thing that happens, like when I bought a car battery last week that actually started my car. Thanking and praising God is a good thing, except he says it in such a way that I don't think he believes it, more like he's trying to convince himself and others that he does. Mostly though, a source of the problem has been that his overall attitude toward and his relationship with Roy Jr. reminds me of my biological father Curt. Obviously there are some significant differences. First, he's around Jr. as an adult, and second, he's still alive. But the intense similarities are there and while I've recognized that it gives me some unique insight on what they can do to improve their relationship, every time I see him, I'm also reminded of the emotions Curt stirs in me.

For the first time, Sr. was gone when I awoke this morning and he didn't return for a few hours. He had gone to talk with his sister about renting a place to live and had bumped into someone at the store who was looking for a roommate. From the sounds of it, I doubt that it would be a good rooming situation, but there is an underlying meaning here that's important. He's taking responsibility for himself and is working toward moving out. Even more, it's not out of desperation or spite, which was the direction he and Jr. were heading toward.

Later in the evening, I talked with Jr. and he confirmed what Roy had told me: They had had their first real and constructive discussion since Roy had moved in a couple of months ago. This, coming just one day after I had laid out some pretty harsh things for Sr. as gently as I could; In Roy Jr.'s eyes, Sr. wasn't around growing up and that now he was disrespecting his house and him.

Certainly the late nights listening to Roy Jr. about his frustrations and sharing my few thoughts have been a help to both of them. I don't know if anything I did provided a spark that helped edge along the beginning of the healing process, but even the chance that it did makes being stuck here longer worth it.

The last few weeks have been a strong test of frustration. Sometimes, like in trying to help people register with the Red Cross, it meant that I needed to keep pressing forward with new ideas, while at others, it's been a matter of accepting God's time table; that God does indeed know better than I do where He needs me and what He needs me to be doing. After all, it's by His grace that people have given my enough money that I'm able to volunteer and don't have to work while down here.

I think I'm getting better at accepting these things and it feels great that I can finely tell the Roys and my Mom with confidence that I'll be leaving for Mississippi soon. As for tomorrow, it may be one last chance for me to go to the Dome and say "goodbye."

Return to the Dome

Tuesday, October 4

It's been over a week now, and today was the first day I made it back to the Cajun Dome since they had evacuated for Rita. Part of me feels bad that I've spent most of the last week playing video games at Roy's, a little guilty that I didn't put my full effort into finding a way of getting down to the Dome while my car was broken down, and somewhat ashamed that I've had such a lackluster attitude when people back home have given their heartfelt money for me to be working. Whether it is because everyone I knew here had left, or too much had changed after Rita and I felt like I was clueless and knew nothing about what's going on with the different services anymore, the bottom line is that I really didn't want to come back to the Dome. When I arrived though, all of those excuses turned into more frustration and if I had been angry with the Red Cross before, I was almost immediately hair-pulling furious; and it wasn't my hair that I wanted to rip out.

The one pleasant surprise was that I did see two volunteers I knew, George and Kathy, a couple in their mid 60s. I remember them so vaguely that if George hadn't been so passionately grateful to see me, I would have passed both of them off as two seemingly familiar faces I have never actually seen before. They were bouncing back and forth between their registration duties and running the information table, which was now a complete mess of disorganized fluttering sheets of paper, randomly scattered as though they were left wherever the wind had let them fall. *I cannot believe that I felt inadequate at coming back.*

The first half-hour was a matter of putting out fires and figuring out that appearances weren't deceiving. What had looked like nothing, really was nothing. George showed me one sheet of phone numbers for a few local services. Not only was the single page, front and back, a far cry from the six-page packet we had been providing to people before the evacuation, but he had just the one copy. It was the same with all of the other *handouts*, he had only one copy, meaning that unless people came prepared to take notes, we really had nothing offer, not even a blank piece of paper for them to write on. My disgust for the Red Cross was so complete that it took me over an hour to settle down enough before I stopped to really look at the sheets and realized that it wasn't just the best pieces of information we were missing. Everything that we had had before the evac to Shreveport was gone, even the boxes we had been using to store stuff in.

Now, I could go through each and every step that I went through. I could detail the short, apathetic response I got from John, the man who is now in charge of resident registration, and go through the other people I spoke with, but the important thing is that after more than an hour and a dozen other people, no one had a clue about either the lady with the Red Cross or the van that took our box of materials up to Shreveport. From the start, I had honestly felt like it was a futile effort, but one of those things that you have to go ahead and try anyway.

I shouldn't have waited so long to come back. Perhaps, if I had not been so lazy and afraid to return, we would have all of that stuff, or at least had a shot at finding it. But it's all gone, and the best there was for me to do was spend the rest of the day making copies of what we did have and drawing maps for people to take with them.

In the middle all of that mess, I did have the chance to work with and talk to a few people, even being gone a week and clueless about the new operations, I still knew more than anyone else around here. Most people, it turned out, were from the Lake Charles area. One of them, David, had rode out the storm and stayed at home, cooking on his grill and going into town to get ice and water each day. He decided to come to the Dome after he found out yesterday that it would be another 5-6 weeks before electricity would be restored; it would be even longer for water.

Emma and her bright blue shirt is an image I will remember for years to come, if I ever forget her. She's 65, in strong health and has spent the last five weeks piecing her life together from the comfort of her back porch. She hit her breaking point today, shedding a few tears on my shoulder for a minute. Regathered, she took the small portion of papers I had compiled and set out to find some food, clothes and a little money for gas (I heard that the Salvation Army has been distributing their own debit cards.) That, of course, brings me back to the inevitable when dealing with the Red Cross here…registering for financial assistance. The current word from George is that they have finally decided to set up an on-site registration tent beginning tomorrow, nearly two weeks after Rita and over a month after Katrina. I'll believe it <u>IF</u> I see it.

This is still only *most likely* to be my last day in Louisiana. Sherri and I have continued playing phone tag. It sounds pretty certain that she has work for me, but I'm not sure that I want to leave before I know exactly where I am going. A part of me feels bad about leaving here, especially after seeing how much I was missed. But the greater part of me knows that the people in Biloxi need me more. I also think that I was able to do enough today so that they're in much better shape than when I first arrived this morning. At least, I am trying hard to remind and convince myself of that.

PART III

CATHOLIC CHARITIES BILOXI, MS

From the Wal-Mart Parking Lot

Wednesday, October 5

This is more like it!!! Biloxi and I have been playing phone tag for most of this week. Most of the messages I've been leaving have centered around my need to talk to someone before I leave here because I needed to know for sure that I had a place to go, and where I was going. (A far cry from what I felt when leaving Colorado.) This morning, however, I decided that it was time to leave a different message: "I'm on my way to Mississippi and would like to know where you want me to go?" After making the call, I finished reloading the car from my PRC flop and planned one final stop by the Cajun Dome for a few pictures and to say goodbye to anyone left that I might know.

Since cameras weren't allowed inside, which is the main reason I have kept putting off bringing my own, I thought that I could at least get a few pictures of some random people hanging around outside. That way, people back home could get some sense of life in this place. *It's a real shame that I don't have any pictures of or with the volunteers that I spent most of my time with and grew close to throughout our fight against Red Cross policies.*

When I arrived at the Dome, there was a random mix of people sitting in chairs, lounging against the brick work or along the curb of the drive; a perfect picture of everyday life here. I felt the same awkward sense of smallness that greeted me on my first few days, so I thought it would be polite, while also easing my own intrusive jitters, to ask some of the people before I started snapping pictures. By the time I had walked the twelve feet across the drive to ask if they would mind if I took their picture, eight chairs sat hastily emptied. A lone woman in her upper 40s sat on the curb smoking her cigarette. This is exactly why they don't allow cameras or television crews in the dome and I felt horrible. Just the threat of a camera sent them running for the hills (On second thought, this might be the one time when wearing one of those red vests would have been good.)

"Would it be alright if I took your picture?" I asked her.

"Why?" came her simple, worn out and tired response. Her name was Mary and I shared with her my own situation; how people back home were supporting me financially and I wanted to be able to send them at least a few pictures of the work they were allowing me to do. Mary reluctantly conceded, but it was still click and run; a few steps back, tap the zoom quickly three times, snap, wait for the digital delay and run for cover while murmuring a feeble "Thanks." It was one of the fastest pictures any photographer has ever taken.

Fortunately, George and Kathy happened to be on shift. George and I walked out to the highway so we could each take a picture of the Dome itself. No matter how desperate and frustrated I have been with trying to get away from here, I still felt the sadness of departing a close friend. This has been the most difficult job I have ever faced in my life. By far the most stressful, but it's also been one of the most rewarding on a personal level.

It took some time, but I did start believing the other volunteers I have worked with. Although anyone can sit at an information table and pass out fliers, few people could do the job I did of comforting and finding ways to help every person that walked up to us. In their own words, "I handled the stress better than the professionals did." I stepped well beyond my comfort zone in cornering that news crew and teaching people how to circumvent the system in order to get the help they need and were being promised. It was hard, but I stayed true to letting God lead my actions and followed my mom's advice not to go wandering off on my own. And even though I wasn't doing what I thought that I came down here to do, I did what I came down here for: to help people who survived, yet lost their lives.

Mixed in with this sadness was a deep feeling of concern that troubled me for its taste of arrogance. Not only was I leaving my 'home' for the past month, but I was deeply wondering: _What's going to happen to the people who aren't living inside when they come for help now?_ Once I'm gone, there really will be no one here to help the hundreds of people who I was helping. That's not just a feeling. Yesterday proved to me that the Red Cross really doesn't care to help these people.

Even though I only spent a few hours with them over two days and they weren't part of the *original* crew I worked with, George, Kathy and I traded cameras and took the traditional *tourist* pictures of each other. Then another one of the residents spotted me with my camera. She stopped in mid-step, and posed raising her arms in victory...that was a really good note to leave on, and I started driving toward Mississippi.

It was shortly before dusk and I was just an hour or so from Biloxi when the red light started blinking on my phone. Once again, I had a message from a call that never came through. It was Marlene from Catholic Charities. It took us another two hours, three calls on my part, and two more messages from ghost calls before we actually spoke with one another. By then, it was well into dark and I had managed to find the local Wal-Mart, so we both agreed that the best thing to do would be for me to get a good night's sleep and meet up with them first thing in the morning.

In saying "...it was well into dark," I'm not just referring to the hours that had passed and the sun being long gone. The town itself seems to have descended into a deeper darkness. It has that same spongy feel as home always did right after a Midwest thunderstorm had ripped through town and the few lights that are on still seem dark. I must admit, I would be scared to try finding that retreat center Marlene was talking about in this.

There is a rusty red pickup parked a couple of rows away, a lawn chair sitting in the back next to something that looks like a table. A group of guys were gathered around the steps to an RV, drinking beer and killing time. For a moment, I remembered how much I miss the time last year when I was selling my handcrafted toys; traveling to a different town, and often state, every weekend; looking for their local Wal-Mart haven for a park and sleep; working

147

with my hands to make something real, instead of punching numbers on a bank computer. Most of all, I miss spending hours watching kids, and some grown ups, run around laughing and playing with the toys that I had made. But then I remember the endless 15-hour days of working alone, being away from home and friends every weekend, and I no longer wish that I could do it all over again. It's just a fond memory that adds to the adventuresome feel.

After nearly a full month of being cramped away in Louisiana, I'm finally here on the front lines, where the action is and the real help is needed. *I wonder what I'm going to see when the sun comes up tomorrow???*

St. Louis and Dedeaux

Thursday, October 6

First thing this morning, I met Marlene from Minnesota at St. Mary's Church, where Catholic Charities has their temporary office setup. She is the person I spoke with from the parking lot at Wal-Mart last night and is in charge of coordinating things from the office. She explained to me that they have two operations that are going on right now: cleanup and debris removal, and a food distribution center in Biloxi. For now, I, along with a man named Ron from Michigan who also showed up this morning, would be helping Ed out at the Warehouse, what used to be St. Louis Church. Sometime in the next couple of days, we will work out a longer-term plan for me to help with the work crews.

It was good 30-minute drive from St. Mary's to Biloxi and signs of the hurricane were everywhere. Tree branches and random pieces of furniture lined the shoulders on either side of the interstate. There were no more billboards. At first, just the rusty painted poles, then as we got closer to Biloxi (which was further from where the eye of the storm hit) a few of the iron rectangle frames had managed to hold on, bent so they were nearly parallel with the ground. Had I not known better, I would have thought that Katrina had just moved through a couple of days ago.

In town, police officers were still directing traffic at once major intersections. Where there used to be stop lights, now there are stop signs bolted to orange construction drums or held together in a make shift 4-way stop box in the middle of the intersection. The five-lane main drag is now a two-lane slow crawl, walled in on both sides by mounds of trash ranging from five to twenty feet at the highest peaks. On nearly every street corner there is a small blue canopy overhanging a bank of a half-dozen phones (I found out later that those are for anyone to use). The grocery store, auto repair shop, gas stations and every other business are boarded up, at least half-fallen down, or otherwise just plain ghostly. In other words, nothing that's more than a half-mile from the interstate is open...*No wonder it seemed so dark last night!*

Devastation really is the truest word to describe it, and even though I've heard that same word used many times about New Orleans, not one of the pictures I've seen coming from there compares to this on any level.

The church we we're using as a warehouse was fortunate for the simple fact that it is standing, now an empty shell with the pews, decorations and all of the other furniture piled outside behind the church. The house across the street sits a good ten feet from its former deck. Next door, the roof to the patio is simply on the

150

ground, and the next house over now stands five feet tall, attic included. It is a heart-wrenching sight, especially when I realize that it's been a month now since Katrina hit.

Between all of the people I met in Louisiana and my brief time here, it turns out that Ron is the first person I've met who has one upped me, not that there's a competition going on. A painter, he was disabled a few years ago in a severe car accident and after hearing the reports of Katrina, he sold, but mostly gave, everything he owned that wouldn't fit in the back of his truck to move down here and help for as long as he is needed. The plan for Ron is that once things get to the cleanup stage, Sherri will put him in charge of the paint and dry walling crews. Until then, which looks to be weeks away, he'll be doing whatever the steel rod in his neck will allow him to do at the Warehouse...which brings me to the work that we did today.

In theory, at least, it was the exact same thing that I did with the PRC, helping to distribute food and hygiene supplies. However, in actuality today wasn't anything like working with the PRC for several reasons. First, from the moment we arrived at 9:00 am, until closing up at 5:00 pm, we actually worked. No time for throwing the football or Frisbee, and no annoying 'adult' to force me to take a break. For lunch, Ron and I took 15 minutes for some tuna, crackers and fruit from the supply of food my grandma had given me. Second, there weren't 20 energy filled college students running around like they're at summer camp. There were just five of us and I was the youngest. Third, we had at least three times as many people come in for supplies and had a lot more to give them. Fourth, NO mosquitoes. And finally, I am dog out tired, which made the last surprise for the day all the better: The retreat center we will be staying at has a cook.

151

When I met him, I first pegged Art as one of those people who moves in and naturally takes charge, which helped me feel more at home at the Dedeaux Retreat Center and more at ease about rummaging around the kitchen for something to eat, otherwise, I probably would have hit the grey totes in my car again. I also thought that he was just being nice when he asked me what kinds of things I liked to have on my burgers. Turns out, although he is that nice of a person, he and his wife Polly came from Montana for the month to cook for the volunteers staying here.

Tonight, there are five us staying in the men's dorm room and just a few women, including Marlene, in one of the women's rooms. In all, there are four rooms with bunks for about 90 people, and other wonderful amenities like private showers, laundry, and a TV lounge area. But as it's been a long day and I spent most of the night meeting and singing with the other volunteers so I'll have to save the rest and tell you about Ed, Joe, Rick & Mary, Billy Ray and the others sometime later. For now, I'm looking forward to another busy day tomorrow at the Warehouse (formerly St. Louis church.)

Dedeaux

The Tears Aren't Far Away

Friday, October 7

Today was another day of hard work at the Warehouse; unloading and shipping out more food, water and hygiene products. Their vacation was over, so Rick and Mary left last night to return to Michigan. For the last week and a half they had been playing a major role in keeping the Warehouse running. I don't remember where Rick had told me they had planned on going originally, that really wasn't very important, but once they had seen the devastation left by Katrina, they decided that working in Biloxi would be a good way to spend his two weeks of vacation time.

Despite the enormous amount of frustration I felt in taking so long to make contact with someone over here (I had wanted to spend absolutely no more than two weeks in Louisiana, which would have put me here a little more than a week ago,) I'm beginning to see that I arrived in Mississippi at just the time that I am needed here. *Ron and I had arrived at the perfect time to take the reigns from them.*

When we arrived at the Warehouse this morning, expecting Ed to already be there, Ron and I were the only people there to open operations for the day. God's sense of timing is impeccable! We were supposed to open between 8:30 and 9:00 am, but it was almost 10:00 before Ed appeared, lazily walking from his van. Even having spent several hours working with him yesterday, there's very little that I know about Ed except that he looks to be in his mid-20s, has been in charge of running the Warehouse from day one, has come from Irvine, Ca. (aka Orange County), and the company he works for, which he claims is the world's largest distributor of dairy products, is paying him and three other guys to work here for two months. From showing no concern at being over an hour late, to the fatigue in his voice when he tells us, "just do whatever," everything about him says that the last four weeks have taken a hard toll on him. As everyone kept telling me, and from what I actually experienced in Louisiana, even the hardiest of souls starts to wear down after the first two weeks.

Aside from the devastation, one of the most heartbreaking things about this work is that we have received a bunch of good clothes and toys for kids. Unfortunately, the combination of our limited facilities (we are operating out of a gutted out church) small number of volunteers, and Ed's fatigue, all mean that the clothes were all left outside overnight to get dampened by a gentle rain and then scattered by people picking through boxes in dawn-lit hours. There had been two groups of clothes when we had closed up the Warehouse last night. An enormous mess of a 50-foot wide pile of fabric that had been thrown in the field between the church and rectory, and a huddle of a dozen pallets of boxed clothing that someone was supposed to be coming to pick up. At least that's what Ed had told us yesterday.

Before leaving last night, I had heavily shrink-wrapped all of the boxes together in hopes of discouraging people from picking through, scattering them across the parking lot and essentially ruining the better part of them. This morning, there were still two separate groups of clothes outside, but the one went from organized neatly in boxes, ready for someone to pull up and load onto their truck, to a largely indiscernible mess of clothe and cardboard that mirrored the pile by the rectory. Only, this new mess wasn't pushed out of the way. It was quickly spreading across the lot, where every last parking space was being used by people coming in to pick up some food and supplies.

It was an embarrassing madhouse. Although no one was fighting, people were creating special stashes, peeking and reaching over shoulders when someone else turned their attention another direction. There were, of course, more people who were asking strangers what sizes they needed and passing each other clothes or a matching shoe. But the overall sight made my heart sink and reminded me of dogs foraging for food in a trash heap. It's physically painful to see so much good stuff lost in this time of need.

While Ed just wanted us to throw the clothes and other half-filled boxes on top of and next to the other pile on the other side of the lot, I was finding my assertive compassion and directed the other volunteers to take a few extra seconds to line up the boxes of clothes into aisles, leaving enough space so they would remain somewhat accessible for people to pick through. In the process of carrying them over, I noticed a large box of brand new teddy bears and pulled it inside so we'd have them to give out to kids. There were a few other toys and a couple of Bibles I happened to see and pull aside. Some of the volunteers held up nice coats and dresses, asking me what to do with them. All I could say was to just set them out with the rest. We were doing what we could and had to turn around, ignore and forget what we couldn't.

It's a struggle, but just like at the Dome, I'm learning to trust myself more, to stop asking another person about every little thing and just do what I think needs to be done. After all, that's what life is about down here now; no more concerns over which brand of tuna you buy, what grocery store you shop at; no more playing games of trying to keep up with the Jone's...life is about doing, figuring out what needs to get done and getting it done, however that may be.

They haven't started, but the tears are not far away. After the first few days, one might begin to accept the sight of an apparent war zone as normal, but the stories will continue to wreak a long havoc on your heart. The first night I was at Dedeaux, Joe had pulled out his guitar and we sat around singing bits of whatever songs we could remember. He left the next morning and ever since, we've taken up sharing stories about what we've seen and heard during the day as a way to cope with what we are all experiencing.

The story of destruction for tonight was about the town of Claremont, it simply isn't there anymore. Even the double-brick constructed houses, walls made of cinder blocks and covered with a layer of brick on the outside, lay in scattered piles of ruin. Then, there is always a story of survival.

Tonight's was about a family of seven and a neighbor whose life they saved. Like so many others I've met, they paid more attention to history than the weatherman and figured that riding out the storm would be no problem. As the water level rose in their house, they were forced to abandon it for a small boat and headed toward the dark silhouette of their neighbor's house that was sitting on a short knoll. Then the boat began taking on water, so while the father wrapped his arms around a nearby tree, two of the daughters swam to the house and through a window they had to break open. They were amazed at how quickly the water was continuing to rise, nearly trapping them on the bottom floor before finding and then sloshing their way to the stairs. Once upstairs, they were shocked to find their neighbor fast asleep. He was under such strong medication that he had no idea a hurricane going on outside and the first floor if his house was underwater. The girls searched the bedroom and found a long stretch of an unused bolt of fabric under the bed that they used as a rope to pull their dad and boat over to the second story window. The family, along with their neighbor, lasted out the storm in the third story attic. *The tears are not far away.*

On a bit of a lighter note, I found out tonight that I was wrong about Art and Polly, they're not married. In fact, they've only known each other for about as long as it takes to drive from Montana to Mississippi. Each one had decided on their own to do whatever they could to help. Some would say, "even if it's just to cook for other volunteers," but that way of looking at it just isn't right. It's been an amazing help to not have to get up an hour earlier to cook breakfast. For me, it probably would mean that I would skip breakfast, or settle for a quick bowl of cereal, and then pay for it the rest of the day. Then factor in the group of 55 college students we're expecting to arrive from Ohio later tonight and it's clear that Art and Polly are doing just as much as anyone else down here.

The kids will be here for four days, largely working on clearing out houses and debris removal. Thinking about it now, it would be much harder to have to actually go into your house, having to throw away everything and physically toss it to the side of the road, than it would be had the hurricane blown and washed everything away, essentially doing the cleanup for you. Most certainly, neither is good, neither is easy and there would be an empty pain of never getting to see your life again, but that might be better than having to watch it sitting in a trash heap. As I said, *the tears are not far away.*

The three houses across the street from the Warehouse

A Gift From Ni

Saturday, October 8

It goes without saying that the last couple of days have been wrought with moments of extreme sadness. Today, however, I enjoyed one the happiest moments and feelings of my life. Fifty years from now, I'll still see the smile and glint in Ni's eyes just as brilliantly as I do tonight.

Yesterday, I mentioned that while hauling the boxes of clothing to the rectory field, I noticed that one was full of brand new teddy bears, so I pulled them aside to keep in the Warehouse, where they would be protected from the weather and we could hand them out to little kids when they came in with their parents. All morning, whenever Linde, Ron or I would see a kid, we would either pull

159

them inside to pick one out, or grab one ourselves and surprise them while they where following mom around. It was right around noon when one of the cutest little girls I have seen in a long time came walking up with her mom. She was not quite two years old, wearing an orange and pink striped shirt, tan shorts and a black, woven hat. As her mom was looking around at the supplies we had today, I told her that I had a very special present for her and went inside to grab one of the bears. Like any child her age, her mouth lit up and eyes smiled as soon as she saw what I was carrying, but that wasn't the most memorable part.

As she was leaving with her mom, I stopped them to ask if I could take her picture. I wasn't sure that I wanted to bother them, so I wasn't prepared yet and Linde had barely gotten my camera out of the car, I had knelt down and before I knew it, Ni was running toward me, threw her arms around my neck and gave me a kiss on the cheek. If just seeing her happiness was incredible, the feeling of love and joy she gave me is indescribable. And, of course, Linde was still trying to figure out how to turn my camera on so we missed that 'perfect shot.' Hoping to get a shot that was in-action, I turned my head, and pointed to my other cheek...Ni's mom, was by their van, laughing the entire time. Once again though, Ni proved still to be too quick for us and we had to settle for a simple picture of me kneeling with an arm around her, and her hands clenched tightly onto that bear...*and Ed had wanted us to dump everything into one huge pile to sit in the rain at night and people to forage through during the day.*

One of the reasons that I was able to spend so much time with Ni was that most of the food that had come in yesterday was already gone. By 10:00 this morning, the five of us were spending a lot of time sitting and waiting for any one of the two trucks Dawn had told us were coming today. Occasionally, like this morning, we get a heads up that a truck is coming in, sometimes we'll even know where it's coming from and what might be on it. For the most part though, we find out that a truck is coming when the driver calls Ed for directions, or when it pulls into the Warehouse parking lot and he asks us where we want him to park. It was 1:00 and there had been no signs of any truck of any kind, which I am finding out is how things go here. So instead of sitting around doing little more than waiting, I put on a pair of gloves and breathing mask, grabbed my pry bar out of the car and joined the Dayton crew of college kids cleaning out a house next door.

When the students first arrived this morning, I was once again surprised to find out that I was the expert. Just like my first few days at the Dome, someone newer than I had arrived, so I became an instant veteran. Once again, I played the part, showing the group of twelve students over to Mimi's house, next door to the Warehouse, peering in doors and missing windows, trying to decide where to have them start.

The images were dark, wet mud coated the carpet and walls up through the ceiling. The aroma was not hard to imagine; salty, ocean water soaked into carpet and furniture, baking in Mississippi heat for a month. Of course, if you are having trouble imagining what rotting ocean water smells like, just think about spending a sweaty day running in a muddy field in your sock feet, throw that pair of socks in a bucket of pond water, let it sit outside for two weeks, then wring them out, hold both socks an inch form your nose and breathe deeply. The hardest thing, beyond the smell which the breathing masks only made bearable, was dealing with throwing Mimi's possessions to the curbside.

When I first joined the Dayton crew in the afternoon, two girls, Sarah and Jessica, were emptying a buffet cabinet that was full of photos. They came up to me holding a dripping piece of thick cardboard. Inside were photos that still looked reasonably well and the two girls were wondering if they should put them aside to save.

161

"If it got wet, it has to be thrown out." I could see the beginning of tears in Jessica, but she plugged them up and said something about the difficulty of having to go through and literally throw someone's life away. "It's hard, but what's gone is already gone, and anything we find that didn't get wet, we'll set aside to keep." *A small gift for Mimi of her own belongings.*

The rest of their questions were easier, having to do with what needed to be taken out and what needed to be left, mostly it was a matter of wrangling in the over enthusiasm and excitement that handing a sledge hammer to a 19-year old male inspires. Add together three hammers, a few crowbars and two flat head shovels (which work great for smashing out drywall) and it was amazing that we only had one near miss when a crowbar punched through a wall inches from Margaret's face as she was scooping up pieces of ceiling tile on the other side. Thinking about it now, that really was the word for the day: *Amazing*

First, there had been the experience with Ni, one that I played over and over again in my mind as I was ripping out windowsills and doorframes. There was the ever growing pile of trash outside. Even though I know better, I still can't believe all of that had been inside because the pile had to be bigger than the house itself. And then there are the kids themselves. I was amazed at how they all kept going and going; Alex, Jacob, Stephen, Jessica, Heather…motored along at a near run. Even more amazing is to think that a dozen of us working for almost nine hours, still fell just short of getting one house completely cleaned out. *How many houses are just like Mimi's?*

That thought puts things down here into a whole new perspective, but it wasn't the most amazing thing that happened today. For the first time since Katrina hit, St. Louis Church celebrated mass outside the Warehouse, conjuring images of mass being held in third world countries. The altar had been saved from the church and was placed between two oak trees. The Holy Water was held in a plastic water bottle with the label peeled off. Milk crates served as chairs for most of the half-dozen older members, while the rest of us either sat on the ground or simply stood throughout the ceremony. It was an enjoyable end to a good day.

Ni and I

Miracles

Sunday, October 9

After only a few days of working in Lafayette, I had decided that no matter what the circumstances were, I was going to take Sundays off from working. This wasn't some holy embrace of observing the Sabbath, but one of the few things that I've learned from passed mistakes. Left to my own instincts, I would work strait through 15-hour days, seven days a week, occasionally thinking to force myself to eat one meal a day, until I physically collapsed. If I were going to be here for a week or two, that would be fine, but the long-term meant that I had to take care of myself too. That means eating at least twice a day and taking one day off each week.

While Ron went to the Warehouse, Art, Polly and I drove down to Pass Christian (pronounced more like Passchristan and it took me two days to realize that Billy Ray wasn't talking about Pastor Stan.) It was our first chance to drive around and look at the destruction. Even from what I've seen in driving to the Warehouse in Biloxi, today gave me a new understanding of what *devastation* means.

For a stretch of about a mile along the beachfront, there is nothing left but scantly scattered debris and smooth building foundations. If I didn't know better, I would think that this area was actually better off. Most of the cleaning up and debris removal was already done by the storm itself. Entire houses had literally been swept away. Art mentioned that he remembered seeing pictures of floating mounds of lumber and garbage that stretched off the coast for as far as the camera could see, like a chain of mile-long barges drifting sideways out to sea. Since there's no sign of them anywhere on land, our only guess is that's where the houses we drove by today are now.

At one point we saw the under frame of a house with the words "Rebuilding. Do Not Bulldoze" written on it in neon orange spray paint. I had Art stop the car so I could take a picture and while I was setting the zoom I noticed a lady standing in the middle of where the house had been. I didn't so much feel three inches tall as I wished that I were. If I had seen her, I wouldn't have asked Art to stop because I know that people don't want to be put on spectacle by *disaster tourists*. I needed her to know that that's not what we were, that we were actually down here volunteering and just taking an afternoon to see how bad things really were down here (I know, that's what a *disaster tourist* is, but that's what I was thinking anyway.) I wanted to slink away. *Why was I afraid to even say "Hi" to this person? What should I say to her? Should I apologize for intruding?* I motioned to Art, walked toward the driveway and asked how her day was going.

Her name is Karen, she is living in Nebraska and this had been her parent's house. Her and her mother have been coming out everyday for the past three weeks, rummaging through the small bit of debris that was scattered in the sand for anything worth saving and finding "the oddest things," like a crystal pickle bowl. At first, she was excited to see that it was in perfect condition, then her smile faded after noticing that there was a small chip along one edge; so close to finding something that had made it through the storm unscathed. But her mom insisted that the chip had long since been there, so Karen was excited again, and amazed that such a fragile thing had survived. Then Karen set the pickle dish on a small plank of boards, next to a rusting rifle and a shard from a decorative plate. I believe that their searching is less a need to find things as it is to have something to do, although it certainly helps when they do find something. It will be another two to three months before power will be back, that's two to three months before they can start to rebuild.

Oddly, the thing that struck me the most today wasn't the missing house, the either half-buried or upside down car, or the Wal-Mart store with every one of its walls blown out, absolutely nothing left inside and one cart sitting in the middle of the parking lot. It was something that took awhile before I realized that I was seeing something that's not normal. There is no green; no leaves, no grass. The ground is buried in sand for at least a mile inland and all of the trees have been stripped bare. It reminded me of winter in Minnesota and that's when I realized that it's early October, 80 degrees, and we're in Mississippi. The few palms that are still standing look decapitated, just a 20-foot pole of textured wood stuck in the ground.

A couple of miles down the road from where we met Karen, we took some time to stop and look around St. Paul's Church. Behind the church is a grade school and auditorium. Unfortunately, I don't remember much about the school because my attention was drawn elsewhere. All around us, there were scattered piles of random debris heaped in piles ten feet high. They weren't like the mounding walls that neatly line the roads in Biloxi, but were scattered around parking lots, in front of businesses and in peoples' yards. They're not the tidy mounds waiting to be taken to the dumping grounds, not the creation of people cleaning up and stacking stuff to be cleared away.

Like the houses we had seen earlier, everything remains just as the storm had left it. The school auditorium/gymnasium reminded me of one of those easy open cans of spam or sardines, like someone had tugged on the metal tab, taking the middle third of the building along with it. The metal roof literally looked like a bomb had exploded inside, blowing away two thirds of it, leaving the rest punched out skyward at jagged angles. Inside are the remains of a few basketball goals, one neatly positioned in the middle of the opening as though they had opened the roof to host some outdoor ballgames. St. Paul's Church is a peaked A-frame, the angled sides nearly running to the ground. There are a few sections of tin sporadically rolled up along the sides, but for the most part the roof is intact. The bottom ten feet of the outer walls, except for a few narrow sections, are completely gone, blown out by the storm surge.

There are three amazing miracles at St. Paul's: First, each end of the church is made almost entirely of glass; twelve-foot high panes of glass staggered into three sections. The top and lower panes were clear, the middle sections are stained glass depictions of the Stations of the Cross. Most of the clear glass, all of the windows below and most of the ones above the stained glass had been busted out. Not one of the middle windows, fourteen separate panes, had even the tiniest piece missing.

The second miracle was above the spot where the altar used to stand, Jesus hanging on the cross. The bottom of the cross came down to within an inch of the waterline, the same line where walls of brick and cinder block had been blown out. Jesus and his cross were unscarred, seeming to hover over us in perfect, unharmed condition.

The third miracle stands outside the Church. Facing the ocean, a statue of Mary with a child-like angel supporting her stands without a blemish. She's less than 100 yards from a steel building with a car hanging out of what would be the second story. It's difficult to imagine anyone standing in these places and not realize that God is sending us a message.

We drove back to Dedeaux shortly after leaving St. Paul's. A chainsaw group of 20 people arrived from Florida. As I was getting ready for bed, I talked for about ten minutes with one of the guys. His name was Ahlee, and he was in New Orleans just two hours after Katrina had hit as a photographer for the AP and FEMA. Toward the end of our conversation he asked me what had impacted me the most. "I don't know," was all that I could think of to say.

A few items found and set aside for rescue (above) and the debris fields of Pass Christian (below), just as Katrina left them.

The gymnasium at St. Paul's School (above) and the unharmed Stations of the Cross in the church (below).

From Tuesday

Monday, October 10

This was by far both the hardest working and the best day I have had since leaving Colorado. I anticipate though that there are even better days to come. The Lions Club Girl Scouts from somewhere in Virginia had sent us a 24-skid semi of miscellaneous canned food, cleaning supplies, tuna, canned meat, paper towels, etc. Even after having worked at the Food Bank in Missouri, I never expected that I would be so excited to catch site of a few boxes of Tilex bathroom cleaner. I literally jumped up and shouted for joy because cleaning supplies, and especially straight mildew killer, are in high demand and extremely short supply. I remember hearing about a lady who has been bleaching the walls of her house everyday to keep the mildew at bay. She knows that ultimately it is a loosing battle, but where else is she going to live until either FEMA comes through with a trailer or she can start to rebuild?

Before I get going too far into the day, I should mention that I am actually writing this on Tuesday because Monday was such a long and tiring day that I needed the forty-five minutes of writing time to sleep (Had I not taken Sunday off, I would not have had the energy to do all the work that needed to be done.) As it was, I spent so much time saying good-bye and seeing off the Dayton University students that I didn't get to sleep until nearly 1:00 am (They left at 4:00 am on Tuesday morning.)

I really hope that Marin's ride on the bus wasn't too painful. She stepped on eleven nails Monday, and no, she didn't manage an unimaginably spectacular maneuver to step on that many nails at the same time. After the first four, Nancy, one of a group of four nurses from Florida volunteering for a few days, and I tried to get her to stop working, but Marin wouldn't have any of it. Her passion to help people is so strong that she kept going and stepping in more nails all day. I'm sure that the adrenaline rush had something to do with negating the pain so she was probably telling us the truth when she told us that it didn't hurt very much, "As long as she stayed on her feet." But there's no staying on your feet for a bus ride that's over 20 hours long and I figure the adrenaline started wearing off at about the four-hour point.

The unloading of the Lions' Truck was an incredible sight. We set up four pallets behind the back door of the trailer so we could roughly sort the boxes of repacked food-drive food onto pallets of cereals, canned veggies, meats, peanut butter and snack foods. The Girl Scouts had taken the time to mark the boxes, which meant that it didn't really take us any extra time to sort as we unloaded, plus by having them fill up four pallets at a time, I was able to keep up with the floor jack. Of course, I was keeping up until Alex, one of the

Dayton students, hollered at me, "We've got one ready to go on the other side!"

What other side? I thought. I had been so busy hauling in pallets and directing the crew at the rear that I hadn't even noticed there were doors along the sides of the trailer, not even that the kids had been unloading from the side doors as well. The next thing I knew, John was taking the pallet jack out of my hands, "We'll take care of this, they need you on the other side."

(I realize that I've been throwing out a lot of unknown names, often without much explanation about who these people are, and I know that when it comes to writing a story, some introduction is generally helpful. But then, I'm not crafty enough and don't know how to write in some of those details without breaking the flow of the stories. In reality, the confusion and abruptness that you're likely feeling may actually help you experience the story the way I have; so many volunteers, names and places who jump in and out of these days. If you're confused at time, left wondering about who people are, and maybe even a little frustrated by these unknown names, then you've fallen right into this part of the story.)

Being in charge was the other thing that really made it a busy day for me. As soon as the truck pulled up, Ed stood back and handed the reigns over to me. Something tells me it was more out of his desire to get out of work than anything else, but I was more than happy to take over. I may not be an expert at running a food pantry, but I am unexpectedly the most experienced one at this down here and with Linde's mission experience, the two of us have the table covered.

The day was a blur from that point on. I remember running back and forth, from side to side, helping with the unloading, but mostly I was watching them restack the boxes. It sounds like a very simple thing, but there is an art, so to speak, to stacking boxes on a pallet so they don't crash over as soon as the pallet is moved. Inside the Warehouse, John kept things rolling and organized, and Linde kept the distribution running smoothly on the outside. I kept trying to keep Ron grounded, literally, so that he wouldn't wear out his back, jumping in and out of the truck, or otherwise push himself too hard. Sometimes though you just have to give up on some things. From the time the truck had pulled to a stop, to when the last pallet was wheeled into the Warehouse, it was cleared in just over an hour.

Maybe that sounds unsurprising and slow, but remember, we have no forklift. Every pallet had to be unloaded and restacked by hand one box at a time. What made today even better was that normally we would have to shut down distribution at the Warehouse for a couple of hours in order to reorganize and restock the new goods. But thanks to the Dayton kids, we were able to keep things running the entire afternoon. I can't imagine what it would have been like if this truck had come in on that first day I was here, when there were only five or six of us; or any other day last week for that matter. It would have taken us hours to get that thing unloaded and we would have had to shut down for the rest of the day. Once again, I'm getting the feeling that God knows what He's doing and when.

Speaking of that first day, at that time everyone who came to pick up some supplies went inside the Warehouse. There's a short gathering area just inside the church doors where they had set up some impromptu shelving, and a rope had been tied off about fifteen feet into the Warehouse in order to keep people from wandering around the building. Throughout the day we had kept the shelves stocked with the things we had lots of: cereal, applesauce, baby supplies and peanut butter. The bulk of the canned food had been pre-bagged so that everyone who came could grab one bag of food, along with a small bag of hygiene products (shampoo, toothbrush, soap…). Not everyone took a bag of food.

At first, Ron and I had chalked that up to a sign people were starting to get back on their feet and were not in dire need, but then we paid a little closer attention and realized that it was because they knew they wouldn't use half of the stuff that was in the bags. You could also see the hurt in their eyes when they scanned the stacks of food in the back, catching sight of some canned chili, macaroni and cheese or anything else they wanted and was in easy view. That was the one thing that Ed's lazy, "whatever," didn't apply to. He was firm about them only having what was on the shelves and not picking through the bags of food. "They can take a bag or not," was his attitude.

That had been the situation on Wednesday and by Friday, at Linde's suggestion, we had started setting the supplies along the curb at the corner of the parking lot, just outside the door. Not only did this give us more room to put a larger variety of things out, but it also meant that we didn't have to keep ushering people from the other side of the rope. Even more, people could only see what they could have, not the supplies we still needed to sort through. It's one more thing that sounds trivial, but it really is a big deal. Not only did it make our jobs easier, but we got rid of the, "you can look, but don't touch" environment.

The best thing that moving things outside did was that it allowed us to give more attention to taking care of children. Instead of stocking the shelves with every kind of food we had, we turned the front corner into a baby center. Now, we ask everyone who comes up if they have kids. If they do, Linde takes them inside to *shop* around for formula, baby food, diapers and anything else they might need. On Saturday, we did a better job of how we had things organized. Mostly, that meant putting the *limited/premiere* items like toilet paper, paper towels, fruit juice, etc. closest to the Warehouse so that we could keep a better eye on them and one person wouldn't sneak off with all we had. Our primary goal is to make sure that we get as much as we can to as many people as we can reach. Today we got it all figured out.

Once again, Ed was rather late in coming in again so while we were talking about how to set things up we decided to stop the pre-bagging altogether. I don't think I need to explain all of the reasons why it was/is a bad idea, so needless to say, people were surprised and greatly appreciated it today. When they came in, we handed them a bag and let them pick out what they wanted.

Before the Girl Scout truck arrived this morning, all 50 of the Dayton students worked on moving all of the garbage from behind the Warehouse/church: the pews, furniture, empty boxes and other debris, out to the side of the road for it to be picked up and taken to the dump. They hadn't even been finished for half an hour when a backhoe with its entourage of dump trucks arrived. By lunchtime, the mounds of debris and trash had all been cleared. With the other work that we were able to do in organizing the Warehouse and some general cleaning up we did outside, it was truly a touching sight to see.

I don't know any other way to express what I felt, except to remind you of my earlier impressions of how devastated the area looked when I arrived; streets lined with trash, every store boarded up and houses that had collapsed on their own porches. When I left the Warehouse last night I began to tear up. *St. Louis may be the Warehouse now, but it looks like a church again.*

The Rectory (left) and St. Louis Church (right) on the day I arrived in Biloxi (above) and after today's cleanup (below).

A Simple Day

Tuesday, October 11

We arrived at the Warehouse a little before 8:30, set up the shop outside, gave out a lot of food and supplies, and closed up at 4:00. It was a simple day and despite an awkward start, it went by with a much slower pace than yesterday.

Ed is off to Florida for a few days of much needed rest so what was a matter of practicality yesterday, became official today; I am now in charge of running the Warehouse. As uncomfortable as it is for me to even write that, it felt a hundred times more uncomfortable for me to say it. I was even caught by complete surprise when a group of older women walked up to volunteer early this morning and asked me who was in charge. I turned my head to look around for someone else and Linde quickly pointed to me. Then a larger group of older gentlemen joined the circle. I think we're all familiar with what that gulping "Uh-oh!" feels like and the feeble "I am?" that follows. I was really in charge? And I hadn't even figured out what we were doing yet.

"We just got a truckload of stuff in over the weekend that needs to be sorted." I told them, "if you don't mind just hanging out for a couple of minutes while I figure out how we want to set things up, then we'll get you going." Then another, more comforting surprise walked up a few minutes later, John and Dawn returned.

They had originally told me that they would just be down for the one day and I had already forgotten that John had mentioned to me last night at Dedeaux that they would be back this morning. Also returning were Kelly and Mary, a couple from near Topeka, KS who were down in Mississippi to celebrate his dad's 90th birthday. Like John and Dawn, they were originally only going to be helping out for the one day and weren't going to be able to make it today because Kelly has a radio show back home that he needed to do. He decided, however, that his cell phone was good enough and he could do a *call-in* show from the Warehouse. Not only did this mean they could spend another day working here, but he also enjoyed having the opportunity to share his own story of Biloxi and encourage others to come down and work. I wish I'd had the chance to at least hear his side of the broadcast.

Sometime around noon, I stopped a lady who had started to wander inside the Warehouse. Now that we're set up outside, we try to keep people from going inside altogether because that just causes more headaches for everyone, including them. It turned out though, that she hadn't come by to pick up supplies. She had grown up and still lives in a house that's just three doors down from the church and just stopped to see how things looked. I gave her a quick tour; it doesn't take long to look at one room that has been stripped from floor to ceiling (the floor included.) Her own house was collapsed, so she was living at her daughter's place with six other family members. It's no surprise that prior to Katrina, they had all been living in their own houses, but only one survived the storm.

I helped her put together a box with plenty of tuna, canned chicken, some chips and snack cookies for the guys, a couple cases of Gatorade, some Ramon Noodles and veggies, and I asked if she needed a work crew to help with her house. She said quite simply, "I don't know because we haven't figured out where we need to start." It made me think about a story John had shared with me last night. While driving around some of the most devastated areas of the coast, his fourteen-year old daughter asked him, "Where do you start?" His answer was genius, "At your feet." I gave the woman a hug and wished her good luck (like most of the people I've met, I haven't a clue what her name is).

A couple of hours later, I saw a lady in her mid 30s pick out a couple small stuffed animals and put them in her bag. She took a third, then a fourth, dug in the box some more and pulled out a fifth before looking up and turning her head toward me. She had that unmistakable, "Is anyone looking?" appearance on her face that made me wonder what was going on. As soon as I stood up, she blindly grabbed another, stuffed it in her bag and hurriedly walked away to her car. For some reason it felt like I had just watched someone shoplift; *But how can you steal something that's already free.* Besides, if people what something that badly, we always let them have it.

It's just like I've been explaining to Ron when he gets upset over someone taking more than their *fair share.* If they don't need it, then it's on their conscience for taking from people who do. That's all beside the point here because I was more puzzled than concerned about what that lady had been up to. When I looked in the box I saw at least 30 Beanie Babies in perfect condition.

Now, I can honestly claim that I know nothing about Beanie Babies, except that some of them are worth as much as my 1972 Nolan Ryan baseball card. However, I do have my suspicions that those "born" in '95 and '96 might be among the original, more valuable ones, It's most likely that someone has given up a rather valuable collection in order to help make some kids happy, not some collector in her thirties.

Later in the afternoon a two-year old Vietnamese boy walked up the lot with his mom and I asked her if it was okay for him to follow me inside for a surprise. She said it was, so I took him by the hand and led him to the box of Beanie Babies. He quietly pointed to a Penguin. Admittedly, I was a little disappointed that he didn't jump, scream or do anything else to indicate that he was happy, but then I reminded myself that I'm a stranger and that's how most kids react around people they don't know. Not thirty seconds later, he was holding the Penguin above his head yelling, "Mommy, mommy."

Like every other day that I've been in Mississippi, I could write for hours more about the people who I met today and the two groups of volunteers that came from Florida. As it is, it's getting late and there are two more things from today that need mentioning. First, when they left today, both of the Florida groups told me how impressed they were with things now and how much better the Warehouse looked today from when they were here last Tuesday.

Under Ed, they had spent a lot of time sitting and doing nothing. In fact, they had come thinking that today would probably be their last day since it had seemed like their help wasn't needed, but things were completely different. I kept them moving around and working hard enough that they'll be back next week. Linde also commented today that she had noticed a lot of different people coming in that she had not seen before and everyone seemed to be feeling a lot more comfortable about coming in for *handouts*. So even though my throat catches and I have to concentrate in order to say, "I'm in charge." I am beginning to realize some of my own qualities, and must admit that there's a reason Bill asked *me* to take things over.

Second, the national news focused on New Orleans once again. Every night at Dedeaux we gather to watch the news. All of us were upset at hearing how the so horribly destroyed city is closer to being back up and running with college courses resuming, the Kid's Hospital reopening and the Army Corp of Engineers proclaiming the city "Dry." I know that New Orleans isn't really anywhere close to back to normal and that the media is just trying to put out a feel-good story, but thanks to our *award winning media coverage*, almost nobody outside of Mississippi has any idea just how bad things are here.

The milestones that we reached yesterday included reopening the first stores within miles of the coast, the only grocery store for five miles and a hardware store that's being run out of their warehouse. What upset me even more is that I've watched the local news every night and seen their coverage, Waveland and Bay St. Louis were hit harder than us. If CNN, or any other network, would take half an hour every night and run the local news nationally, then people around the country would see that New Orleans is the smaller part of a bigger story and tragedy.

Routine

Wednesday, October 12

For the most part, today was what has become a typical day at the Warehouse: We opened, gave out lots of food, unloaded two moving vans, gave out more food and closed down.

The distribution is going beautifully. Linde and I have noticed a couple of things happening since Ed's been gone. First, the people have started talking about coming here like it's their daily trip to the grocery store, rather than going to some charity service and asking for help. When it comes to things like tuna, canned chicken or toilet paper (probably the most valuable commodity down here) they'll kindly ask how many and we'll tell them two or four, depending on how much we have.

Second, and this is something that Linde began pointing out yesterday, we're seeing more non-Vietnamese people coming in. The first few days that I was here, close to 90% of the people I saw were Vietnamese. Every day this week though, more and more black and white people have been coming, so now it's about 50/50, non-Vietnamese and Vietnamese. I should admit that I am having a difficult time writing this without feeling prejudiced, but it's an important part of what I've experienced.

There are significant racial tensions down here, and it's not just between black people and white people. For example, a black lady mentioned to me that one of the reasons she had previously been coming just once a week was that the Vietnamese are "pushy and like to grab anything they can get their hands on." She just didn't feel comfortable. There was clearly a racist tone to her voice that made me feel uncomfortable, but I realized later that there was still something important in what she was saying. The problem isn't that these people are extremely rude, but that there are some very strong cultural differences and they have to be accounted for in delivering aid. What we consider extremely pushy is a normal way of life in Vietnam. By reorganizing the operations here in a way that people who are aggressive and those who aren't can get the same amount of supplies, we've created a friendlier environment that is bringing in and reaching more people.

We also had enough volunteers today that we had time to put together several dozen bags of food for an outreach program. Mary Ann and Ron, a couple who just arrived from Michigan, spent a couple of hours this afternoon driving around the area and delivering the bags to people who either couldn't come to the Warehouse, or didn't know about it. In complete contrast to my time in Louisiana, I feel like I'm making a huge difference here.

We had two deliveries come today. The second one came from an Orthodox Christian Cooperation group (I'm not sure about their name.) They brought us heavy rakes, brooms, mops, scoop shovels, hoses, camping chairs, cleaning supplies, laundry detergent and (dramatic pause for growing anticipation) 18'x9', 4-room tents. They were literally bringing in our wish list that Marlene had given them.

The hardest part was unloading all of these things in front of the people coming in. Not because they were fighting to get to it, but to see the light in their eyes shift as I dashed their hope, "No, we're not giving any of this out yet." If nothing else, we needed to at least get the truck unloaded and see what we had before figuring out how to use and distribute it fairly. It was hard telling people that they couldn't have things that we need, but I kept reminding myself that there was a good reason why we didn't just start passing the tents and chairs out to whomever was waiting at hand. A few hours later, after having given away four of the chairs, I realized that it would be best to save them for the church whose building we were using. This way, the parishioners would have something more than a few milk crates to sit on for mass.

Steve also wanted to keep the scoop shovels and most of the rakes so we would have plenty for the volunteer work crews to use when clearing out houses and cleaning up yards. If we had given them all away, our crews would be nearly worthless. As for the tents, Steve found that the East Biloxi Crisis Recovery Center has a waiting list of people who need tents and they gave him a list of the next 14 people. *It's one thing for someone to take a few cans of chicken they don't need, but something entirely different when there have been people patiently waiting for a tent that will help give their family shelter.* Unfortunately, I wasn't the one who got to make the phone calls and give people the good news, but I will at least be the one who gets to hand it to them.

For a change of pace at Dedeaux tonight, we went to a local place called the Broke Spoke…a good ole country bar that in Art's words, "looks like a hurricane hit it, but it was that way before the hurricane came." There's family friendly writing in permanent marker over every inch inside the building and like many other local, hole-in-the-wall treasures, the Broke Spoke has it's own unique tradition; hanging souvenir bras and underwear from the ceiling and stapling them all over the walls. Some had been signed by the people who had left them, others by someone who couldn't find anywhere else to write. Its big claim to notoriety though, is that it used to be a regular hang out of NFL Quarterback Brett Favre.

The Lord Provides

Thursday, October 13

This is another entry that I had to write a day later due to sheer tiredness and my need for sleep. Therefore, it's another short one as well.

Since both Linde and Marlene are going back home to Minnesota tomorrow, this was the last day that they worked with us. Marlene always reminded me of Sharon from back home in Missouri. Sharon worked in the church office and was that person who knew everyone and everything that was going on. She exuded joy and compassion, was always laughing and only seemed sad when she wasn't able to help someone in need. Seven years later, I can still hear her echoing encouragement. Marlene mostly worked in the office down at St. Mary's, scheduling the work groups and talking with people who need assistance. She was the first person from Catholic Charities I spoke with and is also the one responsible for giving the incredible shopping list to the Orthodox Christian Charities. Even though I only saw her in the evenings at the retreat center, or for brief moments at breakfast, I will greatly miss her presence.

When it comes to Linde, I almost hate to see her go. She has worked with mission efforts in Cambodia, Vietnam, and Albania. She not only knows how to help people, but also has an endless desire to do whatever it takes to help them. She was the rock that I've depended on at the Warehouse. Without her, aside from her experience and knowledge, I wouldn't have had the courage or confidence to step up to the plate. I think the best way to express how I am feeling is that I am more than a little concerned about how things are going to go at the Warehouse without her. But it wasn't just Linde.

The reason that I have been so successful in running things is that we have had an extraordinary crew of volunteers. First thing this morning, while I was running around loading an empty pallet with all of the food we needed to open up with, Randy stepped right in front of me and took what I had out of my hands, "Just tell us what to do and we'll do it." Jon went to the Home Dept, which is half an hour down the interstate, bought a plumbing snake and spent two hours trying to clear the main sewer line so we can use the bathroom again. John reorganized the Warehouse to open more space and make it easier for me to figure out how much and exactly what we have. In short, all I've had to do is indicate to people what we wanted to do, sometimes not even that much, and they've done it.

With both Linde and Marlene leaving, I received a clear lesson in trusting in God to provide whatever I need; maybe I should be making a connection that I'm not making with the extreme differences between when people leave here, versus when I left the Dome back in Louisiana. On Monday, Linde told me that Compassion Center, the place where we had been able to get ice so I could have cold drinks for the volunteers and work crews, was not going to have any more ice for an unknown time. The grocery store down the street, the only one in the area that's open now, received their first shipment of ice on Tuesday. On Wednesday, when she went back to get ice, they didn't have any left and she was told that Friday would be the earliest that they would be getting any more in. Fortunately, the ice left over from the previous day had been enough to hold us over. *But what we were going to do for ice today?*

There is no question about it, our crews need to have something cold to drink, it almost seems like the least that we can be doing for them. I was extremely worried and after a few minutes of brainstorming over dinner, Mary Ann remembered that we had a restaurant style icemaker at the retreat center. We would just have to make sure to bag a couple of garbage bags worth to bring with us in the morning. Of course, I was 10 miles down the road this morning before I remembered that the bags had been left sitting in the hallway. All of that trouble blew up into more stress and frustration. I was lost and felt minuscule. Then, shortly after 10:00 am, a truck pulled into the Warehouse parking lot. I joyfully threw my arms in the air to welcome a truck of food before a man leaned out the window and asked me if we needed any ice. It was the first time that I had seen or even heard of the Red Cross making ice deliveries.

The Lord knows what we need and He provides.

Stairway to Heaven

Friday, October 14

Today was one of those days that I don't know whether it was a good day or a very bad one. Every experience I've had with a volunteer organization speaks to the fact that you have what you have and have to do the best you can with what you have. What we had at the start of the day was myself, Ron, a line of people waiting for us to go at 9:00 am and a moving van to unload. Normally, in these circumstances, I go into a super-panic mode, frantically trying to do and worry about the dozen things that are impossible for me to get done. For whatever reason though, that didn't happen this morning; maybe I am really starting to take and accept things as God presents them. Ron asked me about helping parents and getting stuff for babies. I calmly told him that while the driver and I

190

unloaded the truck, he needed to keep an eye on things outside. "I would let them go in and help themselves, just keep an eye and only let one person go in at a time."

"But you know how they are." He told me. "Once you let one in, they all want to go and the next thing you know they're running around the entire Warehouse."

"You're going to have be firm Ron. Only let one person in at a time."

"What about bringing more stuff outside. I can't keep an eye on the door while I'm trying to keep up with bringing out toilet paper and tuna. I mean, I'd like to, but I can't do it. It's just too much."

"Don't worry about restocking stuff. Hopefully Polly or someone else will show up before we start running out of things. If not, then don't worry about it. We have what we have and we'll do what we can. But don't worry about trying to do everything." He added another halfly protest about having too much to do and I tried to impress on him not to worry. If we did run out of stuff then once the truck was unloaded I'd start restocking, but I needed him to stay outside to keep an eye on things. After all, up until this week, Ed's automatic policy was to shut down the Warehouse as soon as a truck arrived, regardless of how many volunteers he had. Anything the two of us were able to do was already more than what had been done before.

Fortunately though, it didn't take long for help to arrive. Before the truck had come to a complete stop in front of the Warehouse doors, Ed and Jake came strolling up the parking lot. Then John and Dawn arrived. I gave John a shout, excited that I wouldn't have to unload the entire truck myself, glad that Dawn could take care of the parents who were already lined up. But then the driver rolled up the back gate on the truck. For the first time, I felt disappointment.

Not only was the short box van half empty, but half of what there was less than useless, including a pallet of Magic Mix-Ins Applesauce. Had this been the food bank in Missouri, or just about anywhere else, I would be jumping for joy. Applesauce is nutritious, there's no cooking required and the Mix-Ins would be something that kids would enjoy playing with before eating. However, one of the first things I learned last week is that applesauce doesn't exactly have a very prominent place in the traditional Vietnamese diet. We've had three pallets of the stuff sitting in the Warehouse for over a week now. Inside the van was also a pallet of yogurt smoothies, REFRIGERATION REQUIRED.

Even if we had a real warehouse, with cold storage facilities, there is no electricity down here. *What in the blazes is anyone down here supposed to do with something that needs to be refrigerated? Who sends yogurt to a place that doesn't have any power, and what idiot told them to send us more applesauce?*

I don't know what whoever was thinking when they loaded this truck up, but it couldn't have been much. I was even half tempted to shut the gate and tell the driver just to take it all back, we have no use for it here. But my better sense knew that any food was better than nothing and I should still be grateful for getting whatever we can get. Besides, this was one of the two trucks that the Alabama Food Bank is sending us every week, and I worked in a food bank office, I know the banter and words that fly around. If we send stuff back, regardless of our reasoning, it's likely to be the last one that they send us, period.

My disappointment, however, still churned. And as for what to do with the yogurt, we set the EZ-Up tent at a cockeyed angel, raising the front legs and leaving the rear legs completely lowered, to stretch out the shade as much as possible. We encouraged everyone to take at least one case and by 4:00 the pallet was empty.

I mentioned that Ed was one of the people who arrived this morning as the truck was backing in. While I was at St. Mary's last night, using their wireless internet to upload a new batch of journal entries onto my web-site, I had seen him for the first time since he left for Florida. It always bothered me that despite working together for a few days, he's one of the very few people here in Mississippi that I never connected with, so I had tried to make up for that.

The trip had been exactly what he needed, a chance to get away from the every day stress down here and truly relax for a few days, but it hadn't been enough. His voice held that same vacant sound and he still had that *"whatever"* attitude, not sure about when he was going to make it back to the Warehouse or what he was going to do when he did come back. In other words, he didn't know if/when he would be back in charge of things and if he did come to the Warehouse, it would likely be just for a couple of hours to help out with whatever is going on. Aside from a little sports talk about the Angels and how they're going to get walloped by the White Sox (yet another thing we couldn't agree on,) that was about all he said, which is why I was surprised to see him this morning. I was even more surprised, and angry, that without so much as a "good morning" he started taking things over, ignored all of the changes we had made over the past week and had the entire Warehouse crew in a fever pitched, although quiet, uproar within the hour.

As soon as John, the driver Mark, and I were finished unloading the truck, I could tell that something had Ron heated up. I asked him what was going on and he waved a pointed finger toward Ed, who was setting a random box of mixed food in the middle of the parking lot. Understandably, Ed was doing things like they had been done before he left for his mini-vacation. Had he talked to me, or anyone else for that matter, we could have explained how things had changed, but I know Ron well enough to know that he doesn't like being the bad guy to approach and reprimand someone.

I gladly went to Ed, grabbed one of the four boxes he had scattered around and gently explained to him how we had been setting things up, grouping stuff like pasta, canned veggies, cereal, etc. together so that people had an easier time getting what they needed and it had helped them feel more like they were making their daily trip to the grocery store instead of scrounging for handouts. He said nothing, which I took to be his typical, lazy, *"whatever,"* response. I also thought that he was just hanging out for a couple of hours and told the rest of the crew not to worry over him, but just let him do his own thing and he'd be gone in a little while. I didn't realize how much and how quickly one person can screw things up.

Within 15 minutes, the people coming in had gone from a spontaneously smooth flowing line to darting toward every new box that came outside. Kathy was nearly having to fight people off her back before she had a chance to even set the boxes down. More times than not, someone else would ply the lid off trying to get to the good stuff before anyone else had a chance. I spent another ten minutes trying to move things around, keeping some sort of organization, but finally gave up as I yelled at everyone that was not working to get on the other side of the food line. Even though the *system* had completely blown up, we still needed to be able to get in to keep things stocked, not to mention a small area for the volunteers. They had the entire parking lot to use, all I was asking was that they we had one side of a 30' L reserved for the volunteers. Besides, I had already had to kick a dozen people away from our supply cart and a half dozen others out of the drink coolers. I needed cold drinks for the Warehouse volunteers and work crews.

On the way back into the Warehouse I had to kick out four people who had slipped in and had started picking through the pallets. It was complete mayhem and I needed time to gather my thoughts. How had it gotten so bad so quickly? It wasn't even 10:30 yet.

Inside, Polly asked me what was going on, if Ed was back in charge. "I don't know. He hasn't said anything to me at all this morning," was all I could think of to say. While we were complaining about how bad Ed had made things and trying to figure out what we needed to do, I frequently caught Dawn's eye up at the front of the Warehouse. She had that "What's going on?" look. After several minutes someone, I think it might have been Ron, called back that they needed more toilet paper. We hadn't come up with any answers, but keeping the Warehouse going is by far the most important thing, especially since I felt like I had already caused a mess of turmoil. *Ed may have been the one causing the problems, but I should be handling it better.* I think you know by now that normally I would have jumped right in with a load of toilet paper, nearly beating Ron to the door, but I still didn't know what to do so I asked if Polly wouldn't mind taking care of it for me.

Just then, John was coming in to fill the hand truck with another load of Gatorade and, seeing that I was no longer in a deep whisper with someone, stopped to ask me who Ed was.

I was so used to John being around that it shocked me for a moment to realize that the only other time he had seen Ed was on Monday, the day I actually took over the Warehouse because Ed wasn't doing anything. Keeping things to a whisper, I explained the situation to him briefly and asked him point blank, "What do you think I should do?" Before he had a chance to answer though, Roger showed up to grab the hand truck for a load of tea drinks. He also told us that we had run completely out of Gatorade, so I had John stack me up with a few cases and headed out front.

As I was walking out, I heard Kathy tell someone that they should take as many cans of the chicken meat as they wanted. I felt bad that things had already been so busy that when they first arrived I didn't have a chance to greet them and give them a quick rundown on what was going on. Instead, I had simply pointed them toward Ron and Dawn. *They would be able to get them started.* I told her that we only had one pallet so were only letting each person take two, but that they could take as much tuna as they wanted. "That's what Ron had told me to do, but that other guy," pointing toward Ed, "told me not to and let them take as much as they wanted of everything."

"Ed's been out of town for a few days and probably doesn't know that we don't have very much of the chicken. I'll talk to him, but we do only want them to take a couple of cans so that everyone can get at least some. But make sure you tell them that they can have as much tuna as they want though. We've got plenty of that." I quickly went over the numbers on the few things we had to limit with her, Roger and a few other new people that were standing intently: toilet paper, paper towels, bleach and chili. I also reinforced that they could take as much of anything else as they needed. Then I went to talk to Ed for a fourth time.

I don't know why I was still trying to give him the benefit of the doubt, maybe I was still hoping that any minute he would decide that he'd had his fill for the day and leave, or I still felt sorry for him, knowing how hard the stress has been, that he is worn down to the bone. Once again, I gently went over how we were trying to sort and group things together and then explained why we were placing limits on a few things that we didn't have very much of. All he said was "Okay,"

By the time it took me to take one of the eight boxes he had placed in the middle of the lot, set it with the rest of the cereal and walk 15 feet to the Warehouse door, Ed had told Kathy not to put limits on anything. I give her a lot of credit for putting up with the two of us. She wasn't angry, but frustrated, completely confused, and on the verge of giving up. She tugged me aside, "We don't care what it is. Just tell us what to do and we'll do it. But we can't take any more of being told to do things one way, turn around and have someone else tell us to do it differently. Who is in charge?" That was the question.

"I'll be right back." I held up a finger in that "just a minute," gesture, turned around and walked strait over to Ed, who was setting yet another box out in the middle of the parking lot. "Are you back in charge?"

"Yeah." That was the entire conversation, although I may have added something in about how he should have at least let me know after what he had told me last night. After telling everyone to do whatever Ed said, I tried to disappear into the Warehouse to sweep and sulk. It wasn't that I felt like I had just been fired, after all, I knew this was coming and it had taken me two days to really believe that Bill had asked me to take things over. Rather to look outside and see what had become of our hard work, to see everything we had accomplished in the past week simply hurt...it really hurt!

The issue was finally resolved, yet the mood in the Warehouse continued to weigh heavily. Ron and others would periodically ask me about setting things out front, if I wanted to go through and sort some things first or to go ahead and take it outside. I literally threw up my hands, "Whatever Ed says. He's in charge now." I knew they didn't like how things were going any more than I did and it felt good that they still considered me to be the one who knew what to do and should still be in charge. I could also tell that they were looking for me to give them a way to go around Ed, like Ron, Linde and I had done the first few days we were here, but I wasn't going to do it anymore. Ed would have to be responsible for his own crap. Maybe then Sherri (Director of Catholic Charities and Ed's direct boss) could see what he was really doing and change things.

Then, within a few minutes, my attitude had completely turned around. And no, it wasn't because Ed had changed his mind and left for the day. The International Orthodox Christian Charities were back with their bright yellow Penske trucks. Last time they had brought us tents, rakes, hoses…literally our wish list. Today they brought us pillows, bedding, inflatable beds with built-in, battery powered air pumps, chili, dishes, pots and pans, pasta and laundry detergent.

Once again, it was hard telling people that they couldn't have anything before we had it unloaded, especially since not everything was ours. From here, they were going to Bay St. Louis and as greedy as I've gotten over getting the most and best for my people here, I reminded myself that it's all going to people in need and to be grateful for everything that we get. After all, it takes a lot of goodness to go into Wal-Mart and write a $1,500 check for other people. Unfortunately though, Fr. Nicholas informed me that it was the last of the money they had, and this would be the last time I would see them. So once again, I wasn't sure whether to feel good or bad.

More good things happened while we were unloading the truck. Mr. Phan showed up asking about his tent. I still had the list of people that were coming to pick up tents and Steve had specifically told them to ask for me, so even if he had tried, this was one job that Ed wasn't taking away from me. Being able to introduce him to the men who had donated his new tent made it an even more incredible experience.

Throughout the late morning and early afternoon more people came to pick up their tents. Of course, all of them were extremely grateful and it was a welcomed surprise when we added in a bed, lantern and some batteries. Needless to say, I was the recipient of a lot of warm hugs, none more memorable than Ti. She lives near Pass Christian and on her way out of the door, her five-year old son was curious as to why she was coming to Biloxi. "I'm going to pick up our new house." She told him. *Wow!!!* After everything I had to do and all of the bad news I had to give at the Cajun Dome, I am so glad that I get to be the person who gets to pass out the good stuff here.

An hour or so after Ti, Steve caught me in mid-tantrum as I threw the clipboard back onto the front supply cart, spun toward the Warehouse doors and plowed my way inside. *Where the hell is my bloody camera? I knew I shouldn't have left it out here where someone could easily take it.*

Steve followed me in and asked plainly what was going on. I briefly explained what had been going on today with Ed. About the conversation we'd had last night and then how he showed up this morning and didn't say a word to me. "It wasn't until I went to him and asked him point blank that I found out he was running things again. But what's got me upset right now is that my camera's gone. And all of the pictures I've taken down here along with it. Even the ones from back in Louisiana."

The few pictures I took at the Cajun Dome, that first day in Biloxi, pictures of people here at St. Louis, of the Warehouse, our trip to Pass Christian on Sunday, all of them were gone. I could put up with Ed and the crap he was pulling. Maybe even keep on working here, doing things the crappy way he wanted them done, but if that camera was gone, I was done.

It was no small accomplishment on his part, but Steve was able to calm me down enough that I was able to let him help me look for the camera, which turned out to be exactly where I thought I had put it and right were I looked the first time; sitting on the cart, buried under a few pairs of work gloves. With everything that had happened and my present mood, it was a very good thing that John and Dawn were taking me to lunch, which is why I had been looking for the camera in the first place. They were going to treat me to a real, good-ole' Southern Po'boy (it's like getting a Philly Cheese Steak in Philly) and then show me around the damage in Ocean Springs.

Part of me still wanted to feel bad about leaving for such a long time, but the bigger part reminded me that it was Ed's show now and I am back to being an ordinary volunteer. After lunch, they took me on a tour of Ocean Springs, I came so close to crying that I could feel the tears going down my cheek, even though they weren't really there. Whereas last weekend, when Art, Polly, and I had driven around Pass Christian and could only imagine how things might have looked before Katrina, John grew up here and his stories, like one about the house that used to be the oldest one in town, brought the destruction to a whole new level for me, one that I can't describe. Every time I close my eyes tonight I see an iron staircase attached to a vague image of a two-story apartment complex, roughly the size of a football field. In reality, the complex is completely gone, it's just a staircase leading into nothing now; a stairway to Heaven.

That image seems like a very good place to end for the day, but unfortunately, the day kept going. After the rest of the volunteers had left, except for Polly who was riding back to Dedeaux with me, Ed and I had it out.

What was at issue was whether or not to leave stuff setting outside overnight. For my part, I really didn't think that going ahead and taking my time and energy to put them inside at the end of the night would be any big concern for Ed. I was wrong. Some of the details of the argument are probably important, but I don't feel up to going into them. What it really came down to was I had my experience, he had his and they didn't agree with one another. There was, for me though, the most important thing, which was the fact that no matter how many times we refer to this place as the Warehouse, it is still St. Louis Catholic Church and it should be treated like a church whenever possible, even after a hurricane of described biblical proportions. Leaving pallets of water and stray boxes of food outside because we're too lazy isn't a part of that treatment.

Back at Dedeaux, Steve and I had a long discussion about the day at the Warehouse. For one thing, he wanted to follow up from the short talk we had had earlier in the day. For another, I felt like he should know about the fight between Ed and I; if for no other reason than that he'd be pre-warned when fire came his way. Surprisingly, not only did he have his own questions about what Ed was doing, but Ed hadn't talked to anyone in the office about his plans. Before leaving for Florida, the word had been that he would take as much time as he needed before returning and no new word had been given. For the time being though, we'll just assume that he's in charge and running things, and I'll go along with what he says, except when it comes to taking care of the church.

While the tenseness of the situation bothers me, and I do feel a little responsible for creating a bad air at the Warehouse, I am proud of what I did, stepping up to do what needs to be done, regardless of who might be offended, or whose toe's I would be stepping on. Two months ago, that's something I would have only thought about doing. Even last week, I would have asked Polly what she thought and then tentatively suggested to Ed that we had been moving everything in at the end of the day. Had it been in Louisiana, I probably would have talked with the mental health workers about what *should be done* and left it there. The bottom line, whether or not I was justified and it was worth the fight, I saw something that I believed was important to get done and I made sure it got done (of course, it helps that Polly, Ron, Art and Steve thought it was important too).

The Warehouse parking lot with Ed in charge.

FEMA

Saturday, October 15

I didn't know what to expect at the Warehouse today. Ed had continued to be the topic of conversation for most of last night. Steve, Polly and I where trying to figure out what to do. On the one hand, he simply doesn't know what he's doing and doesn't care. As I told him after we closed yesterday, he doesn't understand that there's more to helping people than just getting out as much food as you can as quickly as possible. It's about respect, dignity and trying to reach as many people as we can, not just the lucky few who live closer, are more aggressive, greedier or have bigger cars. I understand that he has never done anything remotely like this, but the bottom line remains, and we all agreed, that Ed isn't doing a very good job. That's the one hand, but Sherri's on the other. She is the boss and Ed is her man. No one wants to question her on that. This morning began where we left our discussion last night, Steve was going to talk with her first to get some handle on at least what Ed is thinking: Is he really back for good, or just going to randomly show up? Then we'll figure out where to go from there.

Admittedly, I was still fuming this morning over yesterday's events and how Ed had largely ignored me and the other volunteers. That continued today. By 11:00 everyone was sitting down waiting for something to do. Roger, who had arrived from Florida yesterday, and Jon were taking off to help with a chainsaw crew since they clearly had nothing to do at the Warehouse. *Barely a half-dozen people and there really was nothing for us to do.*

I could have kept 30 people busy, bagging food, delivering packages out into the community...any one of a dozen things so that, if nothing else, the volunteers at least felt useful, like they were accomplishing something. But Ed doesn't think there's a need to do anything for the volunteers, not even make sure everyone has lunch and a cold drink. Yesterday, when John, Dawn and I returned from our long lunch, the first words from Ron were, "Where did you all take off to? We thought you had gone to pick up lunch." Ed had done nothing, not even get a tally of how many lunches were needed and send someone down to the Relief Center Tent. Polly, Ron and the others were left to make do with whatever snacks they could find in the Warehouse.

Nonetheless, Ed is in charge of the volunteers and everything else around here. I was committed to doing things however Ed wanted them done and like I said, I really wanted to get away from the tension and upheaval of yesterday, but I also wanted him to fall flat on his face. If we continued to pick up his slack then nothing will change, there would be no reason for Sherri to change up the mix. I also wanted Ed to fall flat on his face so that she could see who was causing the problems and fix them accordingly. It was 11:00 and we were sitting around with absolutely nothing to do because it doesn't take long to pick up a box and dump it wherever seems most convenient. But I wasn't going to sit around all day and do nothing, if Ed wanted to be a lazy bum, that's his prerogative, not mine.

Fr. Steve was going to be celebrating mass again tonight and all of the work that the Dayton kids did last week was wonderful, but it had been on the other side of the church. Nothing had been done to clean up the side where they've set up the outdoor chapel. The ground people sit on is still covered by a mixture of crushed leaves and ocean silt left when the floodwaters receded. Five weeks of weather dried trash is caught up in the fence and there's still a scattering of fallen branches, though it does look like someone may have thrown a few into the hibiscus bush that's directly behind the altar.

With nothing for a half-dozen people to do, I decided that it would be nice if when Fr. Steve arrived for mass tonight, that the area was at least cleaned up. I grabbed a rake, along with Ron and whoever else wanted to work and started clearing out the brush, trash and leafy mud. That's when Jerry from the Catholic Charities main office in D.C. walked up to me. "Why are you cleaning up over here?" He asked me. I don't know if it was actually in his voice or not, but it sounded more like, "What the blazes are you doing wasting your time on the yard instead of working on that house right behind you?"

I answered him, "Ed doesn't have anything for us to do." My voice got softer and softer with each word. All confidence was gone. "They're holding mass here tonight so I figured that it would be nice if it was cleaned up for them when they get here."

"How about I take you to lunch?" Jerry and Jayne arrived yesterday, they came in separately, but are both from the national office and are here to see what we're doing and get a first hand feel for what the national office can do to help us out.

I quickly found out that Jerry didn't simply want to take me to lunch, he also wanted to introduce me to the VAL office at FEMA. The purpose of VAL, the Volunteer Action Liaison Office, is to facilitate the works of local relief agencies by establishing a central office for them to communicate directly with each other. This way, we could do a better job sharing our efforts and providing our services to people down here. It's not as complicated as having each organization set up their main offices right next to each other, with FEMA breathing down their neck, but a simple matter of sending one representative to VAL who can keep in touch with the main office. This way, everyone knows what each other is doing. When someone comes to the Warehouse looking for clothes, we would *know* exactly where to send them or who to call to come and pick up a load of clothes before they sit out in the rain all night.

Just the other day, a man brought us a bag with several pairs of good dress shoes. It sounds horrible, but I didn't want to even take them because I didn't want word to spread around that we were accepting clothes and then be drowned by donations we could do nothing with. Had we had a person at the VAL office a couple weeks ago, then I could have made one phone call and immediately known where to send him. If the Salvation Army ran out of baby food, they would *know* to send them to us.

There wouldn't be such a swarm of uncertainty and it would really help us stem the flow of rumors because we would literally be in the same room talking with each other and they would *know* what we're telling the people at the Warehouse instead of guessing all of the time. In the long term, as things move from emergency recovery to case work, the VAL office will help to coordinate those efforts so we can sit down with each family case, talk about who can offer what services and have their needs taken care of in a matter of minutes, rather than leaving them to drive, or otherwise be tossed around from agency to agency, finding out more about who doesn't have what, than who can really help them. People still come up to me everyday and ask when we're going to be open again, or tell me strait out that they had no idea we were even here. VAL would help us get the word out. And according to Jerry, there's a slew of financial assistance and other services that Catholic Charities is missing out on because we don't know it's out there. Lunch was Jerry's way of encouraging me to be the VAL representative for Catholic Charities.

Those who have known me for very long know that this is very similar to an idea that I've had for many years, trying to create a central network for charities to work together on a broader scale. I even wrote a paper for a public policy class in college about how the government could/should create this, only on a much larger scale. I had absolutely no idea that FEMA was trying to do this, much less that this is one of their central functions; to help the local community to do its own disaster recovery work.

I've heard the same things you have, about how late they were in bringing in relief supplies, how much trouble people are having in getting their trailers and how their debit cards have been used at strip clubs and to buy jewelry. (As far as I'm concerned, as long as there's no fraud involved, these people lost nearly everything they owned so they should be able to buy whatever they want.) It's just another sign that our major media sources aren't doing their job. It seems to me that three weeks ago a story on CNN about how FEMA's VAL office sat empty and unused is just as news worthy and would have accomplished a lot more than continued complaints about how few trailers have been delivered. Even on that, they've done an absolutely horrible job of reporting.

I've discovered first hand that the county governments are causing just as much trouble for people and one of the biggest reasons why people are getting denied by FEMA is that they filled the form out wrong. There is a box where the applicant is to indicate whether or not they are willing to relocate. Marking "yes" doesn't mean moving hundreds of miles, it means that you are willing to *relocate* out of your house and into a trailer placed in your driveway. But most people don't realize what it's really asking, so they mark "No." Their application is immediately rejected and they have to go through weeks of appeals and writing letters.

In all fairness, this is a problem with the form and that is FEMA's fault, but that message isn't getting through to our crack shot media reporters. Don't you think they could actually be doing some good if they started reporting why claims were being denied so people could stop making the same mistake over and over again? Does it not seem likely that a lot more good things would be happening down here if they paid more attention to reporting the news rather than drawing in ratings? I do, but I also digressed considerably and got away from what was really important about today.

Today's lunch wasn't about slamming the news coverage, it was about possibly getting a new job with Catholic Charities, one that might even be paid through a FEMA grant. It's amazing how impeccable God's timing can be. Not only would this take care of the brewing conflict between me and Ed, but it would also mean that I would be able to stay down here through the end of the year, as I had originally planned.

I know that a lot of people are upset with the government's response, mainly FEMA, and this in no way makes up for their earlier failures, but it's nothing short of exciting to have found out that they are providing such a tremendous resource and very disconcerting that organizations, like the local Catholic Charities, are not taking the least bit of advantage of it. As Jerry put it, his job isn't to show up after a disaster hits to get people caught up, but to get someone to work with FEMA during "peace-time" so that when a storm like Katrina hits, they are able to jump right into the recovery effort (Admittedly, Biloxi would still be in trouble because there wasn't a Catholic Charities organization here prior to Katrina.) We didn't just talk about FEMA though.

Jerry has been involved with disaster recovery for decades. Most recently in Africa and last year with the tsunami in Southeast Asia. I remembered how I felt the first day I arrived in Biloxi. How I thought it looked more like the day after a hurricane than four weeks later. And despite how good I felt that night when the trucks came to remove all of the debris from in front of the church, it seems like the debris removal is taking way too long. So I asked him strait out, "From everything you've experienced, should they be a lot further along in getting rid of the debris, or is it really that bad." Here's a good place to remind you that Jerry works for Catholic Charities and not FEMA or any other government organization, so there's no reason for him to naturally take sides.

Without the slightest hesitation, he said that they should be much further along. "There's no reason for it to be taking this long to clear the debris from the streets." According to Jerry, the problem is that the local governments are responsible for debris removal, your typical weekly trash pickup, and there's no system in place for either the State or Federal government to jump in and take over in times of major disaster. These small counties simply don't know how to handle a situation this big and haven't asked the State for help.

In short, there's probably a lot of turf fighting going on and offering assistance to remove debris isn't as politically advantageous as signing millions of dollars for recovery aid, but it's needed just as much as anything else. If they wanted to, and been allowed, the State could have sent a fleet of equipment down here and had everything cleared off the side of the road in a matter of a few weeks.

As for me taking the new position, it's up to Sherri now. One of Jerry's primary goals today was to get me on board with the idea so that he can approach her, already having someone who is ready to slide into the job.

Even after yesterday and the way that this morning started out with Ed, I have to go ahead and say that today was a very good day. When I got back from lunch, the Warehouse was shut down because the parking lot was filled with dozens of three-foot tall watermelon bins filled with canned goods, toiletries, baby supplies, sheets and pillows. A little of everything that people need, and I do mean everything. At the back of the truck, which was from the Diocese in Orlando, were four pallets of brand new small appliances: microwaves, toaster ovens, toasters, coffee makers, crock pots, dish sets and more.

Like always, it was difficult to have to shut things down and not let anyone take supplies before we got organized and sorted through what we actually had. We also had to figure out how to distribute the appliances in a way that was fair and did the most to ensure that they ended up with people who really needed them. Ed had a very good idea. As a show of our appreciation for using their building, and because most of them had lost their homes too, we would surprise the parishioners who came to church tonight with the opportunity to each take two of the small appliances home.

210

The problem for Ed though, was that he would have to stick around until after mass to pass them out and he was ready to leave. Naturally, he asked if I would take care of it. I know that it's more from his laziness than anything else, but the reason doesn't really matter. The bottom line for me was that I would get the smiles and hugs from handing people a brand new microwave oven. There weren't enough microwaves for everyone, of course, but with such a small parish, most of whom haven't come back yet, we were able to get everyone taken care of and stayed around a little longer so they could put together a box of food too.

This would be a good place to stop for the day, but there's one more story that needs to be shared. In fact, it's the most important story to come out of the day: A woman in her mid 30s stopped by the Warehouse just before lunchwho . She was digging in a box of snack crackers and at first, since she was still wearing a breathing mask and heavy work gloves, I thought that she was with one of our crews looking for something to take back out to the worksite. We had already pulled out a lot of things, like the pre-packed chicken salad and crackers, for them to come and get without having to spend a lot of time looking. I already knew the answer, but asked her if she was with one of the crews as a way to start up conversation. I was wrong.

This lady had been working on her own house for the last several days. The reason for the breathing mask is that her throat has been worn raw with all of the chemicals and foul air she's been breathing in. Her hands are much the same way, worn raw from scrubbing with bleach and other heavy-duty chemicals. The real story, however, was held in the bruises running up the inside of her legs, from the bottom of her shins all the way under her shorts. This woman, yet another one whose name I didn't get, had stayed to weather out Katrina. As the water level was rising, she walked across her living room to prop the front door open, letting the water

211

flow freely into the house instead of bashing into the side and eventually knocking the whole house off its foundation.

The initial rush of water pouring in was so strong that she was afraid to leave the door without being swept away. She started hugging the doorframe, but by the time the flow had calmed enough that she thought she could move safely back into the house, the water had risen so much and so quickly that she was afraid she'd end up trapped and drown before making it to the stairs.

She did the only thing she could do, continue holding onto the doorframe as tightly as she could for almost ten hours. That's where the bruises came from. She was literally holding on for her life by squeezing her thighs around the frame of the door. She stood there for ten hours, watching her life float by right in front of her face as the waves pulled in and out. Her desk, coffee table, chairs, dishes, everything that would float washed by. For ten hours, the water level continued to rise slowly. When it was up to her neck, she saw a bottle of holy water floating out the door, grabbed it out of the water, kissed it and said a short, profound prayer, "Lord, take this water you are about to drown me in and save me with it." Two minutes later, she was standing on her dry porch.

Ocean Springs

Sunday, October 16

Sunday has become the traditional day for me, Art and Polly to go for a drive and look around at some of the damaged areas. Ron was also around Dedeaux this morning and I wanted to invite him along, but Art would be driving Polly's car. No matter how much more assertive I've become these past few weeks, some things are a matter of respect and I didn't feel like it was my place to add people to someone else's car. I was so glad that Art spoke up and Ron was able to join us as well.

Ever since the trip with John and Dawn to Ocean Springs on Friday, I knew that I needed to bring Art and Polly back there. Part of the feeling was that I wanted to get back there with my camera, but it had also been such a powerful experience for me, that I knew they needed to see as well. Of course, I once again found myself directing things without really knowing what I was doing, remembering far less about the drive earlier in the week than I thought possible; I knew that we needed to turn right until we hit the ocean and not much else after that; I couldn't remember where to turn left, where the oldest house had been, or how to get to the neighborhood John had grown up in.

Our first stop was at the Highway that used to lead across the bay to Biloxi, we spent a good half-hour there. The first day Ron and I were at the Warehouse, we took some time after work to drive around part of Biloxi and had ended up at the beach, looking at the same highway from the other side. The sights were completely different. From there we could see nothing, only the top few feet of the cement support columns sticking out of the water. It felt a lot like we had stopped by to check out the progress on a new highway construction project, like they were getting ready to start laying down the slabs of pavement.

On this side, however, there was no way of confusing things for being under construction. The 50-foot sections of highway looked like a child had taken his bucket of grey lego blocks and dumped them in three scattered lines. Some blocks were completely upended, the butt end toward us, sticking up 25 feet in the air. Others lay on their side at a 30-degree angle. The one or two sections closest to the beach had been lucky. They were still lying flat on the ground, simply pushed aside a good ten feet so that the white line marking the shoulder was perfectly lined up with the dotted center lane marker. And there was a 12-year old kid climbing on one of the slabs, like the pile was a massive jungle gym. He stopped jumping around long enough for to pose for a picture.

The most striking site at the highway though, was the top four feet of a streetlight sticking out of the water. It looks like it's still sinking and made me feel as though I was watching the tail end of the hurricane passing through. I know it was just a trick of the sharp angle between the light pole and shallow waves, that the concrete slab has been firmly packed against the ocean floor for several weeks now, but it still causes me to blink. As for the road leading from the beach up to the bridge, the top two inches of pavement had been peeled away from its earlier versions. Much of it strewn around in torn pieces, curled against the concrete median, bent and folded in such a soft way that I had to keep reminding myself it wasn't tar paper used for roofing, but rock-hard pavement.

Art and Polly spoke with a couple who I think lived just a bit north of here and had just now come down to look at things. Ron walked around for several minutes before having a seat at the edge where, the first bridge section had connected to solid ground. Not a tall man, his short legs dangled a couple of feet from the bottom lip of the steel frame used to adjoin each section. It was time to move along, so I asked Art to drive along the beach road.

Just as we had seen last week in Pass Christian, the houses along the beach were simply gone, leaving barren foundation pillars to stand alone and empty. The difference though was that the homeless stretch here went on for a few miles, not just one. We stopped by the apartment complex John and Dawn had shown me, where 31 people had died. From what we could tell, it looked like there had been three football-field sized apartment buildings there. Of the front building, only steel I-beam supports remained; another naked steel frame stuck out from the half-building standing off to the side; behind that stood a third building. Although it's front half is sagging enough to put the second floor nearly in line with the first floor, it's still all there.

From the top of an iron stairway, still upright and leading into open air, I watched Ron stroll around the field of debris. Most of it was a mass of indiscernible junk (bricks, cinder blocks, stoves, splintered lumber, dry crusted clothes, plastic bags...) but there was a red wagon sitting in the middle of a clear stretch of the parking lot and what can only be described as a decapitated four wheeler parked at the base of one corner stairwell. It had four wheels and a frame, nothing else. The kiddy pool had an inch of water still in it, along with a dented water heater and several crumbling cinder blocks. As close as I had been to crying Friday, able to feel invisible tears running down my cheeks, I had expected them to come loose today. I guess it was too much though because as I stood from a perch on one of the staircases, watching Ron wander through the debris field, I didn't feel the slightest temptation to cry.

We drove around the small bay where the shrimp boats are parked. Most of it looked close to normal, although there was a small, one man sailer that had settled on top of the wooden pier posts as the water receded. An easy eight feet above the water, now it almost looks like an airplane. Most of the boats had been scattered sporadically on dry land. One was parked neatly in the front yard of a house that was minimally bigger than the boat. Across the street, three more had come to rest on a flat mound of broken lumber. Unfortunately though, I wasn't able to find our way to the 130 year old house John had pointed out to me. More than anyone else, I think that Art would have appreciated its story of surviving hurricane after hurricane, but not Katrina. Still standing, it had been moved 20 feet off its foundation and looked like a toothpick would make it collapse.

We did see two good signs before heading back to Dedeaux, and I mean that more literally than I intend. The first one was a 3'x 6' piece of particle board that had been painted white with the words "Thank You All So Much" sprayed in black. A few minutes later, we

216

drove by the ubiquitous "Trailer Here" sign written in bright orange and propped next to their neatly manicured dirt plot. Ron said something about the trailer that had once been there, but most likely it's waiting for a delivery guy to park their new FEMA home. We also had a wonderful surprise at Dedeaux tonight.

Jane from the National office treated the core volunteers to dinner at Applebee's. Once again, I felt terrible for Ron, but if I had felt out of bounds inviting him to ride along in Polly's car with us this morning, I was way off the map when it comes to someone else paying for a meal. This time though, the right person didn't step up to invite him along. Fortunately, he was already in bed, reading his Bible nightcap before we left, so it didn't seem like he was being completely left out. I still feel really bad for him though, he deserved it as much as anyone. *I should have talked to Jane and asked if I could invite him with us.*

The dinner itself was nothing extraordinary. The menu was limited, otherwise, it was a normal party at Applebee's. Of course, that was only until Jane felt the need to share her confession with us. Like the rest of the country, she had been under the impression that New Orleans needed all of the help that it could get. *Isn't our media coverage great?!* Now, having seen the devastation in both places first hand, she's changed her mind. "...you guys need the volunteers here much worse than they do."

She told us that when she gets back to the office in D.C. tomorrow, her first priority is to start getting us more help down here. Thank You Jane!!!! and I'm not talking about the dinner (of course, that was great too!)

I don't know how, gut I almost forgot one more extraordinary thing that happened after dinner. Before loading up to drive back to Dedeaux, Ed pulled me aside to talk briefly. After the fight we had

217

Friday over leaving stuff out front, I didn't know what to expect and had spent the night staying as far away from him as possible. As it turned out though, I had nothing to worry about. He told me that Sherri has some work for him to do in the office for the next several days, meaning that I'm back in charge of things at the Warehouse.

Even though several of us can't stand how Ed likes to run things, it is nothing personally against him. His well-to-do, Orange County heritage is catching up with him and he is far beyond burnt out, much further than a few days in Florida will cure. Most of us have at least had some exposure to poverty or a harder than Orange County life. Not Ed. There's a lot more down here that he has never seen before, that his eyes are being opened to for the first time. I am sincere in my hope that the experience hasn't been too overpowering for him and that once he has had some distance and time back home, he will be able to sift through and process everything that he's seen and witnessed down here.

Highway 20 from the Ocean Springs shoreline.

Ron sitting on the edge of Highway 20.

The harbor in Ocean Springs.

Beachfront home.

We Need Help

Monday, October 17

Our numbers of volunteers are dwindling to dangerously low numbers. We were previously running the Warehouse with no fewer than ten people, and keeping as many as 18 busy on a daily basis. Today, we only had three people who were here for the entire day, six others who were here for just a few hours. To make things more difficult, a truckload of food, hygiene and household products was delivered over the weekend and it needs to be sorted through before we can distribute it. No matter how good the stuff is inside, there's just not very much we can do with it until we've gone through everything. I could easily keep 20 full day volunteers busy and need at least 30 in order to put together, then deliver some outreach packs.

Hui Nguyen became yet another face to the long list of those that I will never forget. Just as Polly and I were leaving the Warehouse this evening a young woman around 18-years old jumped out of a car and ran across the parking lot to talk to me. She needed to sign her family up to get help with cleaning out their house and yard. As always, I took her information and explained to her that it might be quite some time before we will be able to get to her house. I had to tell her simply, "There are about a hundred houses already on the list."

Her face dropped instantly, "One hundred ahead of us?" I nodded as quietly as I could. As of last night we had 113 requests for assistance from our work crews, a stack of at least 30 more to be entered into the computer, and Hui was the sixth person I had taken information from today.

"It may be a few weeks or a couple of months. It all depends on how many people we get to volunteer." Is all I could tell her. "The best thing I can say is that we will call you when we get ready to come out, but do keep looking and asking around for help."

There's nothing more for me to say: *We need help.*

Answered Prayers

Tuesday, October 18

I arrived at the Warehouse this morning to a small throng of volunteers standing in the parking lot. It was more like eight or nine people, but after yesterday, it felt like a throng. After a few minutes of getting the basics set outside to open and twirling the wheels in my head, we had a crew of eleven volunteers passing out supplies and sorting through more totes of the food from Saturday's truck. A little more than an hour later, another group of nine showed up from Florida, followed by yet another couple, also from Florida and who will be staying with us at the retreat for several days. There were enough people to wear me ragged. From the Warehouse, to the makeshift sorting area we had set up in the corner of the parking lot, to the distribution area next to the Warehouse; I could see myself running in circles. But it was great to see so much getting don, especially after the way things had been yesterday.

Aside from directing the sorting and repacking work today, I focused on spending some time comforting people and handing out some of the more rare supplies we have, things like sheets, towels, socks and dishes. Shelly, one of the volunteers from Florida, brought my attention to a woman in her 60s who was noticeably upset. She asked me if we had any kind of clothes whatsoever that we could give her. Again, my thoughts jumped back to the pile of clothes that Ed had us dump out in the rain. I barely had the chance to say we didn't have anything before the tears started to pour out.

This lady had hit such a hard breaking point that I couldn't even ask if some socks would help out. Her daughter tried and failed to calm her enough to find out if she needed anything else, but all either of us could catch were tear choked mumblings of how she's always been able to take care of herself. "Now I can't even find a couple pairs of jeans." The only clothing we had was a few packs of socks and the box of tee-shirts the Wawas had brought for the work crews.

Of course, I would have been more than happy to give her the whole box if it would help, but she needed a pair of pants and I don't think it would have mattered much if I had a winning lottery ticket to offer her. She couldn't find the one, simple thing she needed. Katrina had reduced this once strong woman into the temper tantrum of a five-year old kid who didn't get her chocolate ice cream. "Just forget about it. Let's go." She said with the exasperation of complete surrender and started to turn back toward their white pickup. I managed to get in a comforting hug, then asked her daughter to pull around to a drive along the side street. I wasn't about to let her leave empty handed and I've been down here long enough to be able to put together a few things that I knew she could certainly use.

Having her pull over to the side did two things, first, it gave me some time to gather up a set of dishes, some flatware, a toaster and pack of socks. Second, I had to be a little discreet, otherwise we'd have to endure a few dozen "Why didn't I's?" and have to either lie or find a nice way of saying, "We only have a few and I don't think you need them as bad as she does."

Some things are hard, but as I keep telling Ron; *Don't think about it like you're refusing to help someone, but saving it to help someone who really needs it.* I know that everyone down here needs these things, but there's no question that this lady needed something today more than almost every one of the people who come to the Warehouse each day. The saddest part is, she's not the only one hitting the hard breaks, who still thinks that they are strong enough to stand up to a hurricane as powerful and destructive as Katrina. No one is, without the help and support of others. That's one thing that makes us human, our unity, dependence on one another and incredible strength we have when we lean with one another.

On the other hand, there was another lady who came in today who I wanted to throttle over a box of chocolate pudding. Since there wasn't nearly enough room inside the Warehouse, we had used some of the unused watermelon bins to wall off the corner of the parking lot where we could sort through the stuff that had come in on Saturday. Even with the wall, people kept trying to squeeze between the three-foot high barricade to get stuff, "Oh, sorry. I didn't know..."

One lady spotted a box of chocolate pudding and kindly asked if she could have it. Like the dozens of people who had tried to get stuff earlier, I explained to her that everything that was ready for us to give out was over on the other side of the parking lot and she could help herself to whatever was over there. She replied that they didn't have any pudding. "I'm sorry." I told her, pointing toward Ron who was standing by the Warehouse door, "You can ask Ron over there if he has anymore boxes inside, but to be fair to everyone, we can't pick stuff out while we're still sorting through it."

She jumped into an instant tirade. "Don't you tell me about being fair!" Her arms were flying, yelling and screaming about just wanting a box of pudding. I kept telling her I was sorry and encouraged her to come back tomorrow until she eventually turned around and stormed off. Aside from wanting to knock her head off, I did/do understand where she was coming from. I know that a seemingly menial thing, like a box of chocolate pudding, can be the one thing to tip someone over the edge. But there are two things that kept me from giving her that box.

First and foremost, the situation isn't fair, but we're doing the best we can do to be as fair as we can for everyone. As I mentioned, I had already told dozens of people the same thing and everyone else had understood. There also really are reasons why we need to sort through everything first. I'm not stressing over that just so I can make people wait a couple of days to get some food; that's not why I quite my job and came down here. Second, her hateful attitude was completely out of line. I wasn't about to *reward* her for yelling at me and flying off the handle. Had she reacted more reasonably, and I have done this on many occasions, I would have grabbed the box and discreetly followed her to her car with it so that other people wouldn't feel like they were being cheated.

Last Thursday night, Ed mentioned that the original plan for the Warehouse had been for it to only be open for two months, meaning it would be closing within another week or two. It's safe to say that very little along the coast has gone according to the original plans, especially considering that the same plan had been for the Warehouse to be strictly a storage facility only and all of the food/supplies would be delivered.

Over the past few days though, there have been growing whispers that the diocese might decide to shut it down by as early as this Friday. I don't think I need to even point out how shutting down in three days would really change how we need to run things this week. It was late in the day when Steve, Bill's replacement and coordinator for all of the volunteer projects, let me know that we won't be closing shop. Catholic Charities has decided to keep the Warehouse distribution going for as long as it is needed, however long that might be. My first words to Steve were, "So when's my next truck coming in?"

Unfortunately, the other news we received today isn't as good. Another hurricane is on its way through the Gulf, and the way things are looking, it doesn't matter where Wilma hits, she's going to make life and recovery much more difficult for Mississippi. Current projections show her going to south Florida, but even if they're right and it doesn't hit here, we will loose one of our largest pipelines of volunteer help. The people from Florida have been tremendous, an invaluable resource in helping Mississippi recover, but now it looks like they will be needed in their home state.

Ben, his mom, grandmother and I.
photo by Linde Gassman

Role Reversal

Wednesday, October 19

This morning started off as one of the busiest days we've had for awhile, even though nothing spectacular had been going on. I can't even say for sure that more people were coming in, it was just one of those mornings when I took one blink and it jumped from 8:30 to 11:00. I hadn't had a chance to do anything about getting ice for the day and Polly called me on it, wanting to know who I should send and where. Before I could even confuse myself over whether or not we had enough in the coolers left from yesterday, or where we could track some down at, a couple of ladies spoke up. "We can go grab some from the Salvation Army if you need some." The two ladies had been in to get supplies a few times since the end of last week. I think I remember talking with the younger one, in her early thirties, last Thursday. She was one of the people who had commented about how uncomfortable she had felt coming to pick up supplies earlier, with people grabbing for any snippit of morsel. Now, she is coming back more since things were calmer, people were less pushy and, as she said, "I don't feel like I'm begging for a handout."

I was still in the *helper* mode, *I am supposed to be the one helping them*, and didn't want them to have to go through any trouble for us. They both insisted; taking a few minutes to run down and get free ice seemed to them to be the least they could do. After all, they were just getting ready to leave with a large box packed full of free food. Sure enough, twenty minutes later, their SUV pulled up and one of them jumped out with a bag of ice in each hand. I quickly passed the ice to Ron so I could stop her from jumping right back in and leaving too quickly. She already had one foot in the cab when I made her stop and back up. I told her, "It's been a long time since I've gotten to give my own *Thank You* hug."

A little later in the day Ben, one of my favorite people, stopped by today to ask if we had anymore Gatorade. He's a young man around my own age who only comes as a last resort, he only asks for what he needs, and never takes anything more. The first time I met him, he was looking for some packing boxes. There are now fifteen people living with him on his parents' shrimp boat and with the weather turning cooler, they needed to start packing up most of the stuff in the boat in order to make enough room for everyone to sleep inside.

The next time Ben came in, he had been looking for dog food and a couple days ago, he was in the Warehouse talking with Fr. Chang when his grandmother made him take a couple jugs of Gatorade. It amazes me that he's supporting so many people, and yet, continues to turn down our offers to take more home. Today, his grandmother had sent him back for more. I knew that that was all he needed, and all he wanted to leave here with. But today, however, I was convinced that I wasn't going to let him leave empty handed.

When Ben asked for the Gatorade, I told him, "Of course. But I need you to help me with something inside for a couple of minutes." I knew there wouldn't be any real question as to whether or not he would help us out. That's his strong character, which made me feel all the better about what I was getting him into. Ben paused long enough to ask his grandmother if she minded waiting in the car for a few minutes, then followed me into the Warehouse.

Several large bags of rice had come in with the load from the Montgomery Food Bank yesterday. It would be nothing for a family to go through a 20-pound bag down here in very short order, but we also had two 50-pounders. That was what I needed Ben to help me with, to carry one of the 50-pound bags outside, and preferably to put it in the back of his truck. I knew that even if they wouldn't be able to use it all, he was a person who would share it with his neighbors, people who we most likely never see coming to the Warehouse. Needless to say, Ben was extremely gracious and we talked for several minutes before his grandmother finally ushered him along.

Ben's is a traditional Vietnamese family and as I mentioned, his parents own their own shrimp boat. Just like all of the other shrimpers, it will be next May before there'll even be the chance for them to go back out (I didn't know that there is an actual shrimp season. Katrina wiping out the shrimp beds is like a deep frost hitting the orange groves of Florida in mid-June. There is only one crop a year.) Like all of his friends, shrimping is the only job that Ben has ever known, but unlike them, he's not going to wait around for the industry to come back and is taking on a job with one of the labor crews for the casinos. After that, he's looking at getting his certification to be an electrician. He told me, "Shrimping is just too undependable, but there's always work as an electrician."

The rest of his family though, doesn't have that option and he is deeply concerned about their future. Even if they didn't owe so much on the boat, which they just bought a few years ago, they're simply too old to start a new career. It's plain ridiculous to expect people in their 50s to spend two years retraining for a brand new career. Besides, good years and bad years are a part of shrimping culture, this is just a very bad year.

As the discussion continued, we got to where I was from and how it was that I had the opportunity to take time off work (i.e. I voluntarily fired myself.) That's when Ben began trying to comfort me in the decision to leave the bank because they didn't want to reasonably discuss allowing me time off. "God will always take care of those who are faithful to Him. Whether it be here or after, in Heaven. He will lead you into something better than working at the bank." At first, I honestly felt like, *Yeah, ok. I already know all of this.* Then I found myself listening to him more intently than I have to anyone else for years, and feeling extremely fortunate to have met Ben.

I hope that I have the chance to see him again before I leave, which will be next Wednesday. Physically, I'm in great shape, working a lot less than the dawn to dusk hours I had envisioned when I was on the road to Louisiana. In the last few days though, I've begun to feel the mental weight of being down here for so long. I'm also about to run out of money. I thought about making another hard push for more donations, but it seems more like God did His job the first time around.

One of the things I had committed myself to doing was to only ask people one time. I know that's generally not the *smart* way to raise funds. Minds are slippery and you have to remind them of things they don't want to forget, but part of my test was to have faith that God knew what I needed and He would either encourage or let slip according to His plan. A year ago I probably wouldn't have accepted it this way. My original plan had been to work here through the end of the year and I would have been mad at anything that didn't turn out according to that plan. A year ago, I probably would not have accepted it this way. Now, I'm beginning to see that He gave me just the right amount of money I needed to stay down here for the right amount of time. *It's time for me to head on next week and if God wants me to continue either here or somewhere else, the money will come.*

PS—I just reminded myself about the VAL position Jerry was trying to get me into. The last I knew, he was talking with Sherri and she would talk to me if he was able to convince her to send somebody. It's been long enough now that it doesn't look like it's going to happen. That's a real shame; *Too many turf wars and egos, even in the world of nonprofits.*

Closing the Warehouse

Thursday, October 20

One of the hardest challenges down here is finding that balance between making sure people get what they need without letting people take advantage of the situation. For the most part, we've tried to put mild limits on a few things that everybody needs and that we have limited supply of: canned chicken, Chef-Boy-R-Dee, rice, bleach, paper towels, fruit juice, and some vacuum sealed smoked salmon that came in a couple of days. If people try to sneak in an extra can of chicken we'll remind them a couple of times to take only two. Even then, if they seem to be insisting, we're pretty lenient; we're not going to go pulling stuff out of people's bags. It's only on things like the garden hoses or Mr. Clean Magic Wands that we stand absolutely firm.

We're trying to find that balance where we do as much as we can for each individual, but also help as many people as possible. Yet there are still those people we see everyday, sometimes two or three times in one day, trying to get as much as they can get away with each time. For myself, there have been a couple of times when I've been absolutely sure someone has been in for their third or fourth time. Only then have I said something, that they can't take anymore today, but they can always come back tomorrow. It's a frustration that's been eating on Ron more and more each day and today, just about the entire crew was up in arms over the families living right across he street.

I had just finished loading a car when I heard Ron complaining, "That old lady's been here four or five times already today. She comes up, grabs a case of Gatorade, takes it across the street and then comes right back and takes more." I explained to him that if he knows for sure that she's been in once already today that he can and should ask her not to come back again until tomorrow. "Yeah, but you know, I hate being the mean bad guy." He's right. It's not in Ron to not help people.

I suggested to him, "Instead of thinking about it like you're refusing to let them have something, think about it like you're saving it for someone who doesn't have any. I mean, that's what we're really doing anyway. We're trying to make sure there's plenty here for everyone who comes in later today. But if you don't want to, just point them out to me and I'll talk to them. That's why I'm here. So you guys don't have to deal with it." It didn't work.

As the day went on, Ron, Paul and Jacque talked more and more about the family across the street and people who just come in here and take as much as they want without any consideration for all the other people who don't have anything. I tried everything I could think of to say something to calm them down, to ease their worry.

"We do what we can, but if a few people get more than their share, then that's something they'll have to live with. I would much rather let someone who doesn't need it take too much. Then turn anyone away who does need it." I reminded them about one of Jesus' parables. The one where the owner of a vineyard needed more workers, so throughout the day, he went into the city and hired people. At the end of the day the workers came for their pay and when the ones who had been hired in the afternoon received the same amount as everyone else, the workers who had been hired earlier in the morning grew upset and angry, thinking that they should get paid more for working longer. Like so many of His parables, there are a lot of lessons in this one, but as I told Ron today, one of the messages here is to not worry so much about what other people are doing. "Take care of yourself. As long as we're doing our job the best we can, then that's all we should worry about. As for whatever people decide to do with the stuff we give them, they'll have to live with that."

Even Sherri had heard their rumblings when she stopped by to give a couple people a tour of the place. She said something to the volunteers about how large the families are around here and even if it seems like they're taking a lot, you need a lot to feed a family of 15 or 20 people. That seemed to settle them down for a little while. That is, until an older guy pulled into the parking lot in a rusty 1980s pickup. Before he was even parked, I heard Jacque mumbling something about him having already been here today and the back of the truck had been packed full when he left. She was complaining, "Now he's back for more." Actually, he wasn't.

After lowering the tailgate, he started sliding out boxes of soup, canned vegetables and rice. True, he had been in earlier today, but he wasn't back to get more stuff. Rather, he was bringing back the things that he wouldn't use, four boxes worth. "I think the message," I pointed out, "is clear." I didn't have to say anything else about that family across the street and was able to spend more time enjoying the afternoon when I met two good hearted and hard working gentlemen: Franklin Brown and Jimmy Lee, who is retired from the Army and whose son just returned from Kuwait.

Pressed hard, I would guess they're both in their later 50s, though Franklin looks to have weathered the years better. One of the best things about them is that they love black-eyed peas. That sounds odd, but considering it's the one thing that's less popular down here than applesauce and we have a couple hundred cases, it is a very good thing. I literally filled up the back seat of his 1987 Chrysler with canned black-eyed peas.

We began talking and the conversation quickly turned toward God's message in this disaster. I thought about the conversation I had with Ben yesterday, so I focused on listening. Franklin's big concern is over how bad people are in this part of the country. As he put it, "...with the robbing, the beating and stuff they do in New Orleans. Especially all that stuff that goes on during Mardi Gras..." I somewhat agreed. I was in New Orleans for a conference just as Carnival was kicking into gear, and the things that go on there are horrible. But do I think that God nearly wiped New Orleans off the face of the Earth because of its moralistic depravity? Absolutely not! And as I continued to listen, neither did Franklin or Jimmy Lee. They just couldn't believe some of the things they were seeing on TV, like the snipers shooting at the National Guard helicopter. The message that both of them have taken up to this point is not that God is punishing us, but that there are more and more bad people in this country every day. "Evil is taking over." This is why I only *somewhat* agreed.

"I don't see that at all." I told them and then started listing off states, "...Washington, Connecticut, Montana, New Jersey, Ohio, Florida, Michigan, North Dakota, Colorado and more others that I

236

can't remember. People have come from all over the country to lend a helping hand. And even the people who aren't able to take time away from their jobs or families have given an incredible amount. I wouldn't have anything to pass out if it weren't for them."

This, I told them, is the face of people coming together to help one another, the face of good in the world and it's the face that people need to see. It's not that there are more people that are bad in this country, but I think people are choosing sides, choosing to follow good or evil." This wasn't just a line I was feeding them to help them feel better, to offer them a more positive outlook. It's one of those things I used to believe and talk about all of the time. It had just gotten lost in the mix of school, D.C., and politics and I just remembered it today.

Before they left, I made sure Jimmy Lee had my phone number. His son is coincidently stationed at Fort Collins, just a short stone's throw from where I live in the Springs. So I made him promise to give me a call if he had the chance to visit his son this year. If nothing else, I want to buy them both a thank you dinner, for their sacrifice and dedication to the people of this country (I think it's important for all of our serviceman to hear that.) As they rolled out, Franklin and Jimmy Lee were both smiling, laughing and yelling something about coming back tomorrow to get some more black-eyed peas, but I think I was feeling better than the two of them put together. Unfortunately, those good feelings didn't last very long for me.

Some of the worst news that I have heard for a long time came toward the end of the day. The Warehouse is going to be closed down after all. To be entirely fair to my ranting and raving over how the Red Cross was handling things back in Lafayette, I have to confess that I was very upset when Sherri told me this afternoon that there won't be any more trucks coming in. From now on, anything that does come will be diverted to other centers, in other cities and ran by other organizations. After more than two weeks of being with these people, talking to them, hugging them and offering a shoulder of support, I can say with a rare conviction that these people still need our help. To loose the full-time operations of the Warehouse will unquestionably hurt the community.

I feel betrayed. Just a few days ago we were worried about this very thing happened and Sherri assured Steve that the Warehouse would be open as long as it is needed. *What has happened in the past three days to change things so significantly down here? What about the families who are so big that they have to make several trips, who Sherri had just been trying to convince our volunteers needed so much food?*

Even if Sherri thinks that they don't need food anymore, there are still thousands of people still waiting for tents, and that's no exaggeration. On Tuesday night, Steve and I were talking when it came up in the conversation that the East Biloxi Crisis Recovery Center told him they still need over 2,000 tents. I hadn't seriously thought about that before.

Since Katrina, we have been blessed with incredibly good weather. It's rained only three or four days and remained comfortably warm. But winter is coming and in the last week the nights have started cooling off enough that I've had to borrow a sweatshirt from Billy Ray. He loves to give me a hard time about my cool weather wussiness, but the changing weather is suddenly making new priorities for life down here. We spent about half an hour Tuesday night brainstorming ways to come up with the 2,000 tents and were supposed to get back together last night to share ideas. After Sherri's announcement, I almost feel like: *What's the point now?*

I had thought of calling Tristen from the Mountain Chalet camping store back home in the Springs. They're all great, down to earth people and I'm sure they could come up with a few. More importantly, I figure that we could come up with a nifty email chain to pass the need along to their camping friends and end up getting more than enough...that's how big things get done, friends talking with friends. But like I said; *Is there any point to it now?*

I know there is a point to it, and that is my point for needing the Warehouse. One of the reasons why this area is in particular need is that most of the people in these neighborhoods had been working on the shrimp boats. *How is it that anyone can imagine that they're back on their feet?* Putting aside all liberal and conservative politics, you can't reasonably tell a 65-year old man that he needs to take classes in the evening so he can work a different job, not when he knows 50 years worth of shrimping. Does she expect four generation families to retrain and find new careers? This is a shrimping community with generations living together who are connected by this culture just as tightly as they are by blood.

With the season over and this year's crop lost, how do we expect them to get through until next year? The worst part though is that people have been asking us all along just how long we were going to be open. After the decision we had been given last week I had been telling them not to worry, that they could depend on us to be here for the foreseeable future. *I guess they can't.*

14 Houses and a Bucket of Chicken

Friday, October 21

I want to say that today was a day of rumors, but the way they fly around here, realistically speaking, there weren't anymore today than any other day. Maybe, it would be better to say that it was a day of surprises.

First, at about 9:00 this morning I was surprised to discover that we are handing out kitchen appliances. Not the microwave and toaster oven variety, but of the stove and refrigerator kind. I probably shouldn't have to tell you, mostly because I would have shouted it by now that we had such incredible stuff to give out: We are not giving out refrigerators.

Nonetheless, dozens of people who were standing outside thought we were, and as I found out, there wasn't anything I could say or do to convince them otherwise. Just like at the Cajun Dome, everyone who lives here has been tossed through the run around so many times that unless you are the person doing the actual handing out, or not handing something out, as the case may be, most people won't believe a word you say. Ben stopped by to see what all of the commotion and line of people was about. Since he can speak Vietnamese, and is a face from the neighborhood that they know, I asked if he would explain to them what the real story was: "We have two social workers who are here to sit down and talk with people in order find out what they need. They aren't actually giving anything out today, just finding out what people need so we can go back and figure out what we need to do." That's when Ben told me there was no point to it.

"It doesn't matter what I say," he told me, "they'll just assume I'm trying to get them to leave so I can get more." It was one of those situations when I just had to shake my head and accept that there was nothing I could do, except wait and hope that our social workers arrived soon, so they could set the story strait.

In the midst of yesterday's dismal news about the Warehouse closing I forgot to share the good news about Lucy and Mahkti. They were the reason behind the crowd waiting for us this morning and why I wasn't surprised to see it. It's been awhile since I mentioned the problems we have with the language barrier, mostly since it's become one of those things that we've just accepted as a part of life; you get used to speaking in simple words and using your fingers to count to people. Anyway, because so many of the people in this area speak either broken or no English, Catholic Charities arranged for a two Vietnamese social workers to come in from California to talk with people and figure out what they need most.

It's a great idea and we've only been a little disappointed that it took them so long to get them here. Lucy and Mahkti arrived yesterday afternoon and had planned on staying for several hours. However, within a little over an hour, they had used up all of the interview forms they had thought would be enough for two days. What was even more surprising was that they had been that busy without any more notice than setting out the EZ-Up tent, a couple of make shift tables, and chairs. After a full night for the word to spread around, it was no surprise that they talked with well over a hundred families today.

The social workers' presence also brought out another reminder of the racial tensions down here. I had several people ask me if Lucy and Mahkti were just there to talk with the Vietnamese. Again, I understand where this comes from. A line with well over a hundred people in it, every one of them Vietnamese, becomes intimidating, but no more so than if everyone in line had been white or black. Certain thoughts that normally might be unthinkable, become more reasonable. Add the fact that our social workers are Asian and speak Vietnamese, and most people assumed they were Vietnamese. It becomes a legitimate, albeit disheartening question to ask. "Is this just for the Vietnamese or can anyone sign up?"

"Absolutely not." I told them, "It's just that since so many people down here are Vietnamese, we brought in social workers who can speak the language too. They are here to help everyone." Sometimes I got the polite "Thank you. We just wanted to check before waiting in line for a couple of hours." But there were a few times that I got a harsher, "We'll come back later. We don't want to mess with all of this." The racial tension was something I hadn't been prepared to experience down here. It's not what I would consider true racism, these same people are just as willing to help one another out as anyone else, but what one culture sees as normal, another takes as rude and offensive. It's our cultural challenge we face in the 21st century and just one more thing that I knew years ago, had forgotten, and am reminded of down here.

Although this morning was one of the busiest days we have had, as one might expect with what has become the famous attraction of *The Social Workers from California*, the afternoon slowed enough that we had more time to look through the Warehouse and give more personal attention to everyone who came in. One man, I think he said his name was Tom, came in looking for some white bandage tape that he needed to tape his fingers together because one of them had been broken in the storm. At least, he thought it was broken and he will finally be going to see a doctor next week. There was also a young girl, I would guess about two years old. Her face simply beamed when I handed her a stuffed, purple turtle. Even though she became infatuated with a box of crackers moments later, that's still one of the hundreds of images that'll stick with me for years. Then came another surprise for lunch: a bucket of chicken and fourteen houses.

You don't have to be at the Warehouse for more than a couple of days before you start recognizing the *regulars* who come everyday. Some people may be inclined to think that this is a bad thing, that these people should have more consideration by coming in only two or three times a week, but I expect and want them to come back nearly everyday. For one thing, we know that we aren't giving them enough food to feed a family for the entire week. For another and just as importantly, what we have changes on a daily basis. I want a mom with four kids to come back tomorrow to get the box of salmon, pudding, or juice that we didn't have today, or a family of twelve to come back tomorrow for two more jugs of Gatorade.

Among the regulars has been one particular group of five or six ladies who admittedly, has started to raise a bit of stir among some of the volunteers because they always leave with a couple cars filled with stuff. There's also a mentally handicapped man with them who draws in a lot of sympathy and seems to get a lot of the better stuff we have. In fact, they've gotten so much stuff over the last couple of days that I've even started keeping a close eye on what goes in their cars. Today though, one of the ladies, all of whom are in their late 50s and 60s, stopped in just to bring us lunch; a bucket of fried chicken with mashed potatoes and gravy, and biscuits.

Not only did she want to express her gratitude for everything we've done for them, but she wanted to let us know why and that she had noticed they'd been taking a lot of stuff. Altogether, their family lost fourteen houses to Katrina: five sisters, their brother who had suffered severe brain damage from a stroke last year, their children and grandchildren. Out of fifteen houses, just one had survived, where the entire family has literally been camping out. Even hearing the stories and seeing complete devastation, imagining one family loosing fourteen houses develops the picture of devastation here to a whole new level of understanding.

One final note that I want to pass along before calling it a night. I began by talking about rumors and generally the last thing I want to do is add to the flurry of bees that are already buzzing around, but one came in today that I need to share. Not only does it make my physically sick to think that people would do such a thing, but from the cruel things that have happened in similar disasters, I don't have much doubt that it's true. The word is that when some of the contractors deliver the FEMA trailers they are demanding payment of $300-$600 in order to hook up the utilities. If the person starts to balk, they get told it will be several weeks before someone else will be able to come out and hook them up. Since it's not like the average person can call up to speak to someone with FEMA on a moments notice and the entire process is a whittled mess, these drivers almost always get their money.

Once again, what FEMA is doing and getting credit for aren't the same. I remember a mess of confusion in Louisiana over what people needed to do in order to have FEMA cover their hotel room costs. The simple truth was that there was actually very little a person needed to do. If a person could find a room and provide proof of residence in one of the affected counties, then the hotel would bill FEMA directly; it was that simple and this case is too. FEMA has already paid for everything. These people are running their own scam, stealing from the homeless. I know these people aren't the real face of this nation, and my point isn't to sicken you, but to help spread the word so this doesn't happen to anyone else. It's also another sign that our news media is asleep on the stories that really matter.

My Last Day at the Warehouse

Saturday, October 22

I should have known it was going to be a rough day when the Salvation Army refused to give me three bags of ice so we could keep the drinks cold for our volunteers. The lady I was speaking with claimed that I wasn't eligible to receive any of their assistance because I didn't have a Mississippi driver's license. I just couldn't believe it. After everything I have done for the past several weeks and all of the people I have done my best to help, even those who I felt where trying pull some scheme, she wasn't going to let me have three lousy bags of ice. I mean, what kind of horrific evil did she think I was planning, or did she think I was a greedy bastard who drove all the way from Colorado just to cheat them out of three bags of ice. Even while I was sitting in the car, halfway wishing I could clock her over the head, the situation made me think about Mark back at the Cajun Dome:

Just like nearly everyone else there, Mark had lost his driver's license in the storm and didn't have the money to pay for a duplicate. But unlike everyone else, he had just moved into Jefferson Parrish a couple of weeks before Katrina hit and hadn't changed the address on his license. Normally, that would have been no big deal, but in this case, it meant that when it came time to getting a replacement license from the state, he was simply out of luck.

The license bureau was refusing to give him a free duplicate because his address on the license didn't show that he had been living in one of the affected counties. Even worse, without an I.D. the Red Cross flatly refused to let him stay at the shelter. Eventually, and after several minutes of hard pressing, I was able to convince the registration boss to concede to let Mark stay, so long as the police department would do a background check on the guy. *I don't know why they would need a check on this one person.* The concession really didn't amount to much help for Mark, but it was the best that I could get this guy to tell me. I am pretty sure he knew what the police officer was going say... *There was no chance, no way, and no how that they would run a check on someone who didn't have any kind of identification whatsoever,* and that is exactly what the police officer told me.

I was quietly irate. I couldn't recall them ever demanding a background check on any one of the 10,000 people who have stayed at the Dome. Besides, what difference does it make whether or not his name really is Mark, or if he really had been living in New Orleans? He needed a place to sleep and there was plenty of room inside. Even at that time, I could easily understand Mark's frustration, but it wasn't until this morning that I really understood how he must have felt.

As the Salvation Army lady stood there, I am sure that the anger-brewing helplessness was clearly showing on my face and I think that it was the honest combination of *what am I supposed to do?* and pummeling anger that I was feeling which eventually won her over. Either that, or the 18-year old kid who nudged her to let me go ahead and have them. Still, my steering wheel took a hard beating on the way back to the Warehouse. This was my last day at the Warehouse, and it was looking to be a bad one.

I had expected, since Saturday has regularly been our slowest day, that today would be relaxing, with more time to enjoy the day and talk with more people as they came in. Once I returned with the ice, things quickly turned into complete confusion when Sherri stopped by and started taking stuff out of the Warehouse, throwing it outside wherever she felt like dropping it. I know that I sound like an old prude when I complain about how she didn't pay any attention to the way we had organized things, but I'll take that hit because, as I've said many times before, having the food and supplies arranged in groups (soups, pastas, fruit, vegetables, cereals, snacks, etc.) has made a huge difference for the people who come here. Not only in how they feel about having to depend on taking charity, but in how they act and who comes in for help.

Over the last couple of weeks, people had started using words like 'shopping' and 'store' instead of 'handing out' and 'taking'. The Warehouse had become a place where more people looked forward to coming to, a place that restored a little more of their dignity as they pieced their lives back together. Unfortunately, all of those feelings were gone today in what became an instant free for all. Just yesterday, you could set aside your box and continue shopping without much worry, today you could barely blink without something jumping out. As soon as someone would set a box down in the parking lot, a dozen hands would jump in and strip out the best items.

While I was trying to talk with Jimmy Lee, he had to fend off at least a half dozen people from taking stuff out of his own box. I had thought that things had blown up when Ed came back from vacation, but this was ten times worse. With Sherri doing her thing and directing the new volunteers to do the same, it was a completely lost cause. This was my final day, all of our hard work and improvements we had made over the last two weeks had been undone and there was absolutely nothing I could do about it. It was all Polly could do to get me to accept things as they were and toss my hands up in resignation. I wanted to cry.

I spent most of the day gazing at the new volunteers blankly watching them do as Sherri had instructed. Aside from talking with some of the regular people I have come to know, and trying to ignore the frenzy that had become of our parking lot, I tried to remember very little about the day. At 3:30, nearly two hours earlier than when we had been closing down before, we started moving everything back inside, shut the door to the Warehouse and I left. So much for a final, enjoyable day at the Warehouse. Fortunately, the night at Dedeaux went much better.

What do you do when you have a group of Miami doctors who want to play poker and no one brought poker chips? Raid the nearest convenience store of M&Ms. It would be nice if I could begin here with a grand soliloquy on my unstoppable skills at Texas Hold'em, but I was the second person out, and MaryAnn, who claimed to have never played poker, was the big winner. So rather than introducing profound insights into my character and talents, the gambling for candy-coated chocolates works better as a segway to introducing this crew of doctors.

249

A.J., Brooke, Frank, Marisella, Rosa and José came from Miami to both help and experience the side of being a doctor that goes beyond the knowledge and diagnosing. Of the six, only three are practicing physicians, two are residents and one is in her third year of med school. They had all come to Biloxi with grand expectations of being drowned with patients from sun up to sun down, not the single digits they've had for each of the last couple of days. Much like I had felt that day working with the PRC in Louisiana, most everyone in the group was feeling underused and that their time had been a complete waste. Brooke, the third year student, had seemed particularly disappointed and teetered on being disillusioned by the experience.

The difficult truth is that people just didn't know they were down here and since most people still don't have access to a TV or radio, it's nearly impossible to get the word out quickly. They had began this morning down in Waveland, but after seeing only six people all morning, AJ, José and Brooke gave up and came to the Warehouse, the one place where they knew they could find some people. Brooke sat and talked with a large, middle-aged lady for over two hours. She had been in a few times and from talking to her a couple of days ago, I know that if nothing else, she needed the time to talk with someone.

Watching Brooke and her talk though, I got the feeling that this was exactly what Brooke came down here for; to be able to spend some quality time with people, and not just rush the hordes in and out as quickly as she could. She got to experience the side of medicine that José and Marisella had wanted her and the others to see. Just like there's more to running the Warehouse than getting out as much food as fast as possible, there's more to being a doctor than diagnosing a patient and handing them a prescription.

Brooke may have already known that, I don't know, but I could tell that whatever her experience was, she's never going to forget the time she spent with this lady. Watching her and A.J. talk with some of the people was the one bright spot in my final day at the Warehouse. Tomorrow is Sunday, my day off, and on Monday I'll go out with one of the cleanup crews.

Poker night at Dedeaux.

Mama Sau

Sunday, October 23

Art, Polly and I had originally planned on taking the day to drive over to New Orleans and get a look at just how bad (or how not so bad) that place really is compared to over here. Not only would Art be able to visit some of his old stomping grounds, but it would also give me the chance to finally catch up with my brother Kevin. He lives in Texas and a few weeks ago, about the time I was getting settled in at the Cajun Dome, he got into one of the training seminars for FEMA inspectors and was dispatched to New Orleans just three days after I left Louisiana.

Had things not been so up and down with finding a place to help in Mississippi, I would have hung around the extra few days to see him, especially since we haven't seen each other since last Christmas. As it was though, I felt like it was time to leave and being just sixty miles away, one of us would surely have the time to get down and see the other. With my time running toward its end, this weekend was going to be the last, best chance for us to spend some time together. But like I said, that had been the original plan for today, and as so often happens down here, plans get slightly altered before being completely turned on their head.

The plan first changed yesterday when, Mama Sau, "Sow like the pig," she told me, invited me to join her for lunch today. Since we had already made the New Orleans plans for the day, I figured that it would work out for the three of us to meet Mama Sau for lunch and then head to New Orleans from there. It had also sounded as though she was planning on doing the cooking, so I felt comfortable asking her if Art and Polly could join us. Even though Polly has only been at the Warehouse for a few days and Art just the one, they have put just as much time and energy into helping out as anyone else; but they haven't gotten the perks of meeting people and getting treated to dinner like most of the work crews have been.

Of course, Mama Sau was more than happy to host the extra guests. Unfortunately, by the time we got back though, I was so tired that New Orleans and visiting my brother got pushed aside for a good couch nap.

Mama Sau came to the U.S. with her blue-eyed Marine husband in 1969, arriving in Mississippi just a couple of months before hurricane Camille hit. She is one of the older ladies wbo Ron has been criticizing for hording and hanging out at the Warehouse everyday for hours.

As I said, I had thought that Mama Sau was going to cook for us and we were ready for a deliciously authentic Vietnamese meal, but this is one of those moments I wish I could plug my brain into something; Mama Sau doesn't have anywhere to cook. She treated the three of us to a Chinese buffet, and I felt about three inches tall for adding two more people to her bill.

I am still a little confused as to where she is living now. I think that she's staying with her son, but it could be her stepdaughter. Barely a month before Katrina hit, she sold her house and had been placed on a waiting list to move into a beachfront complex in Ocean Springs. In the meantime, she rented a room from a lady just two blocks from the Warehouse. A few weeks after that, her friend decided that she wanted the extra room back. Mama Sau had to move into a loft space above the shop where she was working. That was when Katrina came and believe it or not, she was planning on riding out the storm in a building that looks to be barely six feet off the ocean's edge. "I been through Camille and that didn't do anything." She told us. "So I figured, if I was fine with Camille, then I be fine now. My son kept telling me 'No Mom, this is much worse and a lot bigger than Camille. You have to leave.' I only left because he wouldn't shut up."

Needless to say, I was so glad that he wouldn't shut up and even Mama Sau admitted that she would have died if she had stayed. Having no idea of the connection, the store had actually been one of the most startling pictures I had taken last week. Sitting on a short piece of beach jutting out into the ocean, it was a two-story iron skeleton that looked like very a short, pudgy lookout tower. I am not exaggerating when I say that when she pointed the building out to us, I could see images of her throwing her hands up in front of her face as water crashed through the walls and sent her tumbling limply into scattered furniture and other debris. *Thank God her son had been so stubborn and she eventually listened to him.*

From the remains of that building, it was just a couple of hundred yards to the complex that she was waiting to move into. If her son had been a blessing, then I don't know what word to use to describe how good it was that she hadn't been able to move into this place right away. This was the place where I had come closest to crying when I had been with John and Dawn; where Ron did cry as he walked around the rubble and naked I-beams; where I first saw the *Stairway to Heaven*; where three apartment buildings, each the size of a football field, had been reduced to one, plus a fragment of the second; and where 31 people had died. As Mama Sau said, with a smile on her face, "Had I been livin' there, there would have been 32."

Before dropping us off at Polly's car, which we had left at the Warehouse, Mama Sau drove by and pointed out the roof to the house she lived in right after selling hers. Ten minutes later, she slowed down to point out where the house had been. I unbuckled my seat belt so I could twist around and look out the rear window. Sure enough, almost a half-mile across the field, I could just make out the black top of the roof poking out above the other side of the bridge.

Although I said "Wow." it felt like "Ok, seen that before." Seeing a roof that far from where the house once stood just doesn't have the same impact it did two weeks ago. Even at that, there was still the heartache that the two places she had lived in the month leading up to Katrina, and the home she was going to move into where all gone. The saddest part of the day though was when we drove by the actual house that she had sold.

It had taken some prodding from Art and I to get her to drive there. She told us, "It's nothing special. Nothing there to see." It really wasn't anything special. Except for a small patch of the blue roof that covers spots where shingles had blown off and is now on

255

about every house that's still standing, it was in perfect condition. I don't know how I could have handled that, but Mama Sau was just as spunky as ever; teasing me with the picture of her daughter; thirty years old, absolutely gorgeous, and completely married; talking to an unseen truck that was holding up traffic, "What is he doing holding up traffic? Don't he know where he's going..." Had I said it, Art surely would have punched me, but that's one of the differences between a 29-year old guy and a Vietnamese lady in her sixties. We were all cracking up as she carried on, her hands flying around, "Did you see what his problem was. I don't know what he thinking stopping in the middle of the road..."

In addition to having a wonderful time, I learned something from Mama Sau about the Warehouse today that I had not even thought of before. More than being a place for people to come and get some supplies, it's become a community center. Wherever they had previously gotten together at, whether it was at each other's houses, the boats, or some other community center, those places are gone. Mama Sau spends so much time at the Warehouse because she's bored. She has no job, no house, and that's where everybody is. It may have started out as waiting to see what comes in on the next truck, but it has turned into a place where they can see and catch up with everyone. *It is going to hurt so many people when that place closes up.*

After lunch, and our tour of Mam Sau's homes, we met up with the Miami doctors again who had set up shop at the Warehouse. Actually, I'm being far too generous in saying, *set up.* In reality, they where scattered all around. Some were standing, Frank was sitting on the edge of the flower box while talking to a lady. Brooke had pulled out a couple of the camping chairs and made a table out of stacked boxes. I could hardly believe that Ed hadn't even bothered to put out the EZ-Up tent to give people a little shade. It really was a mess that I struggled to ignore...my time working there was done and if Sherri really wanted to ship out as much food as quickly as possible, with as little work as possible, then she was getting what she wanted. But I'm getting too far off on a ramble of stuff you've already heard, so back to the doctors.

The doctors still had a couple of hours to kill before catching their flight back to Miami, so A.J. and I took some time to drive around East Biloxi. Even though we didn't go much more than a mile from the Warehouse, I couldn't believe what I was seeing. In some areas, houses are still in the street, blocks of homes that had collapsed and been thrown into one another looked like they hadn't been touched since the storm. We walked around a wall-less shrimp factory that was a long mile inland and had been reduced to a twenty-foot, sloped conveyor belt on a concrete slab. A.J. pointed out that there were minnow-sized fish swimming in a pool of water along the side of the factory and several quarter-sized crab skittered along the edge. As recently as yesterday, I had thought that I was getting used to seeing these things day in and day out. And even today, I was unimpressed at the roof that had been blown over a half-mile from its house. But I guess that's another lessen for the day, some things you don't get used to seeing, you just stop seeing them. Today my eyes were opened.

After the short tour, it was a very odd feeling driving the doctors to the airport. They where literally racing to get back to Miami before hurricane Wilma hit. Frank's mom was by herself and when Brooke told him that Dade County was under mandatory evacuation his response was simply, "Okay." The *so what, I don't care* kind of okay. Mandatory evacuation or not, as long as the plane was able to land in Miami, he was going to get back and take care of his mom.

The main reason for most of them, I think, is that when they had left home a week ago, there was no reasonable concern that Wilma would hit South Florida. José has a wife and three children who he needed to get back to. And if the others didn't have family, they simply needed to get back and get their homes ready for the oncoming storm. It wasn't mentioned, but I think that another significant reason why they were so intent on getting back was for the basic fact that they are doctors. If the storm hits hard, that's where they'll need to be.

When I left the group at the airport, it was still uncertain whether or not the Miami airport would close before their flight arrived, meaning that it is likely they will be spending the night in Atlanta. Hopefully I'll be able to find out tomorrow if they beat the storm and how they fared through Wilma. These six doctors were some of the best people who I have been working with in Mississippi. I was sorry to see them leave so soon, hurricane Wilma notwithstanding, and despite what Art says; *it's not entirely because of the blonde med student.*

On a separate note about something that didn't necessarily happen today, but that I've noticed is an interesting part of my time in Mississippi. When I was working at the bank in Colorado I was fortunate to have the late morning shift, meaning that I didn't have to be in before 8:45 and could usually push my getting out of bed time to 7:30 and even squeeze out an 8:00 wake-up time once a week. Almost everyone who has known me for very long knows that I am not a morning person and I don't get up a single minute earlier than I have to. It will come as a shock to many then that on a Sunday morning, when I am not working and I'm so tired that my goal is to spend as much time on the couch as possible, that I was out of bed and eating breakfast with the rest of the crew by 7:15.

This anomaly is one of the many enjoyably unique features about my time down here. During the week a 6:00 a.m. wake up is standard and if you're not out by 6:30 you open your eyes to see a big bald guy singing "Rise and Shine," that would be Art. Only once was I still in bed for his morning greeting. Yet through all of this, I am neither groggy-eyed, nor wishing the slightest thought that I could crawl back into bed. There is simply an energy down here that gets all of us up and moving, regardless of how late a few of us stay up at night.

The shrimp factory

A Letter for Oprah

Monday, October 24

Dear Oprah:

Given normal odds, I know that there is very little chance that this prayer will even get so far as your desk. But through faith, I know that we are not dealing with normal odds and this is a prayer, not just a letter. It is my prayer to God for a man named Rodney Carter, his fiancé, his dad, and her daughter. Amidst the endless sea of faces of need I have seen in the wake of Katrina, my heart was drawn to his. My hope is that God will lead it into your hands the same way he led it to my heart.

I met Rodney while working with Catholic Charities in Biloxi, Mississippi, cleaning out houses that had been flooded by hurricane Katrina. He's in his late 30s and along with his fiancé and her daughter, had bought his first house just over a year ago. They are among the few fortunate people who did not completely lose their house, yet like the rest of their neighbors, they lost everything else they owned. Now, they're going through the taxing labor of physically throwing everything away, stripping their house down to the studs and stuck fighting the insurance company because their damage was caused by flood, not the hurricane itself. There is more to Rodney's story.

If not for Katrina, Rodney would be married now and I would be talking about his wife and not fiancé. But all of the money that had been saved for the wedding is now going into rebuilding their home. Together, Katrina and the insurance company's refusal to pay have stopped the wedding. Rodney told me, "It's going to be at least several more months from now before we can even start saving again for the wedding." Not only is the money gone, but they had both worked overtime hours to build the savings and now every extra minute outside of regular working hours is being spent on getting the house back to a point where they can at least live in it again. Rodney's pain goes deeper.

As if loosing everything he owned, his home and his wedding weren't enough, Rodney found out last month that he will likely be loosing his father as well. He was diagnosed with an inoperable, terminal brain tumor. In my heart I pray that God's hand heals Mr. Carter (I know that He can do that.) This prayer is that he will be able to see his son get married and share a dance with his daughter in-law.

Given normal odds, there is no chance of this possibly happening before Rodney's father runs out of the time that his doctors have given him to live, just six months. We know, however, that God is more concerned about our prayers and caring for His faithful than He is about following doctor's orders. I pray that He leads this story to someone who can help God answer this prayer.

Yours most sincerely,

Kendall Ketterlin

POSTSCRIPT: I wrote this letter as my journal entry for Monday night. Art and I had spent the day removing nails from studs and ripping up the wood flooring at Rodney's house, just a few blocks from the Warehouse.

I did not do my part for Rodney. The letter never got sent. I didn't get the rest of the information from Steve: Rodney's address or the names of his father and fiancé.

I failed, and yet, I wonder what God may still have done. While I do not doubt that I had been asked to send the letter, playing a small part in Rodney's life, I also know that his wedding and future was not solely dependent on my actions. There are others who God calls into to action. I hope and wonder who, if anyone, eventually said "yes," stepping up to take the banner that I left laying on the ground. Of course, all of us could have failed and Rodney's dad may not have enjoyed a first dance with his new daughter-in-law. That is the price we pay for free will. The price that I paid is that I don't know and I never will. I did not get to share in the celebration.

What an amazing vision their wedding must have been and I could have been a part of; Rodney standing in the front of the church; his fiancé slowly walking down the aisle, with Mr, Carter draping her arm. So this letter became another item in the long list of things that I failed to finish up on during that last week; *We had run out of the forms for signing people up for the work crews and there's a list of four families somewhere that never got handed over to Steve...including Li's family.*

The Most Difficult Day

Tuesday, October 25

Today was the most difficult day I have had since leaving home nearly two months ago. Before I go into the day's events though, I want to stress that this experience was entirely different from all of the problems and road blocks that I had with the Red Cross back in Louisiana. That was an issue with the organization, its disorganization and misdirected ambitions. What transpired today was strictly between myself and another individual and should in no way be taken as anything against Catholic Charities.

Early last week, I wrote about the possibility of the Warehouse closing down. We were concerned that it was still needed and all of us were confused for a few days, uncertain as to what was going to happen. You may remember the ecstatic joy I felt when Steve told me that Sherri had said it would remain open for as long as its services were needed. Last Thursday, we were told that the Warehouse would be closing sometime in the near future, and yesterday the word filtered down that the final decision had been made. The Warehouse will be closing its doors just as quickly as everything inside can be cleared out.

For the better part of yesterday, I was visibly frustrated and my heart sank deeply when I thought about the prospect of the distribution no longer taking place, about how just four days earlier I was telling people, "Don't worry, we're going to stay open for at least several more weeks." (Perhaps it was my own fault. Sherri had only said that it would be here, "as long as it was needed." Steve and I both assumed that meant weeks rather than a few days.)

As the day wore on, my frustration settled into a solid foundation of anger. Not the flash breed of anger when you're looking for someone's jaw to break with a good right hook, but the type of anger that the Bible speaks of when it says that love is slow to anger. I was frustrated at how I was played the fool and taken advantage of; but angry at how for the past couple of days the people living here had been treated like animals, boxes and crates of goods just thrown out in the parking lot for them to forage through like a pack of stray dogs. I was frustrated at how my volunteers had just been given an hour long speech on letting people take however much food they wanted because they are in so much need, and now, just two days later, they're being told that there is no longer any need; but angry because I know there are thousands here still without a tent over their heads, blankets to keep them warm or the faintest outlook of returning to work. I was frustrated because I had put the last two weeks of my life into a place that was about to simply disappear as if it had never been; but angry that everyone of the volunteers who ran this distribution center, the people who have been there everyday, still believe in its need and no one has given us any comfort or attempted to explain to us why that's no longer the case.

I have always been oversensitive about following command structures. Concerned about stepping on people's toes and being respectful not to inadvertently jump over anyone's head. Before I left Colorado, that's the biggest reason why I often failed to act a lot of times. I would always defer to the appropriate person because it was their job. But even though in these past few weeks I've become more assertive in my own actions, ensuring that the job gets done, I still hold onto a fundamental concern for treating people with the respect and dignity that their position deserves. That is what I tried to do today.

I was too angry to let the issue of closing the Warehouse drop without so much as asking for some explanation, and the feel I got from others, Polly, Art, Ron, Deacon Art, Mary Ann, Billy Ray... was that it was too important to let drop (even though I am planning on leaving Dedeaux on Thursday.) So, as the coordinator of all the volunteers and work crews, I asked Steve what he thought I should do. He was, like the rest of us, at a complete loss as to why the Warehouse was getting shut down and suggested that I take it up directly with the person who made the decision, Sherri. That was last night.

I think you know by now that I am not a fan of either questioning authority, neither do I jump head first into direct confrontations. Back in Louisiana, I didn't corner the news media on day one, but took small steps each day to try and find new ways for people to register with the Red Cross. Here, I didn't jump right into a fifteen-minute argument with Ed on the first day. Linde helped encourage me to ask less, do more and before he went on vacation, we all tiptoed into consulting with Ed less and less about things that needed to be done differently. I can still clearly see the dozens of times I've stepped out of my normal boundaries, each one leading to a bigger test, and as difficult as each of those have been for me, I knew that what I was about to face this morning was going to be the big one. Following Steve's advice, I was going to talk to Sherri.

It was a nerve racking, 30-minute drive to St. Mary's, one that we've all made at some point in our lives. *Was there really anything I could say to convince Sherri to change her mind?* No, that wasn't going to be possible. Perhaps if I was going to be down here for several more weeks, then I could offer to run it and she wouldn't have to worry about how to keep it staffed. But I'm not staying and it's time for me to head back home. I'm too exhausted, worn down and stressed out to be of much good anymore. I even thought about using God's authority. Telling her that His desire is for the people down here to be helped, that by shutting the Warehouse down she is abandoning them, and worse than simply not helping, she is standing in God's way, preventing others from doing His work. So I prayed for calm, for peace, for Him to give me wisdom, to guide my words and to give me strength to stand firm and not back down from what's right.

In my prayer, I ran through the discussion dozens of times. Like a dream, it only took a few seconds to go through a twenty-minute conversation. Honing my arguments, rearranging the order, figuring out which ones to throw out first and which to hold back and use as a response to her own points. Thinking about what's happened in the last week, how we went from closing to saying open to closing again, and about all of the rumors I've heard, trying to guess everything that she might possibly say. By the time I pulled into the parking lot at St. Mary's, I had accepted that it really wasn't my place to try changing her mind. *My job is to say what's in my heart and let her decide what to do with it.* I started the conversation. "I was hoping you could help me to understand why the Warehouse is being shut down?"

267

In response, Sherri did an excellent job of making me question and then feel as though I have wasted the last three weeks of my life. Even worse, that I had even caused a lot more harm than good. More than directly, Sherri told me that she had removed me from running the Warehouse for many reasons, but largely because of how poorly I had treated the volunteers. The last thing I knew was that Ed had not planned on returning until Wednesday and it was only after my asking that he took over the Warehouse on Monday so that I could spend a couple of days cleaning houses before leaving. As I tried telling everyone later at Dedeaux, it's only fair that the rest of details of the conversation stay between Sherri and myself. What was important was the overall feel of the discussion, that she had verbally thrashed everything I had come down here to do and made me question all of the positive changes I had made. She made me feel, and begin to believe that I had helped no one and wasted all of my time down here.

I was proud that throughout the conversation I maintained my course and did not let my own comments match hers, degenerating into a personal assault. I tried everything I could think of to get some reasonable, consistent explanation and treaded carefully not to make any personal attacks against her. More than anything else, that had been my goal from the beginning, to say my piece and let Sherri decide what to do with it. I believe that those were the last words I said to her before turning around and hurrying out to the car. Then it was time to cry.

Needless to say, that talk with Sherri had not gone anything like I had planned, but just because one thing doesn't go the way it's supposed too, doesn't mean that my plans for the rest of the day had to suffer. It was barely ten o'clock and I was on my way to meet up with Jenny, Deacon Art, Brandon and Tom. Aside from having time to recompose myself so as not to disrupt their day, it was probably good to have forty minutes of driving to let the nerves settle before starting up a chainsaw.

I had been looking forward to spending the day with this crew. They all arrived separately a few days ago and, like Ron, Polly, Art and I, it's another one of those groups that hadn't known each other before coming to Mississippi, yet had become close friends in just a couple of days. Jenny is one of those people who I haven't seen very much and otherwise, I don't know why I haven't had the chance to get to know her very well. I know that she grew up near here and is working at a convent in South Dakota.

Brandon recently graduated from one of the colleges in D.C. with a degree in marketing. He's at that new grad point in life where he's trying to find a job, not sure what he wants to do, and figured he might as well drive down and help for a week since he had the time.

Tom is a deacon from New Jersey, I think. Aside from the fact that he's been working with and is a huge fan of the Red Cross, that's all I know about him (and that may have something to do with why I haven't spent much time talking with him.)

Deacon Art from Connecticut is the one I've spoken with the most. He has that father to all, friend to everyone character and a passionate faith that resonates in his voice whenever he talks about God. It came as a bit of a shock when I found out that he had been an investment banker. The idea of being a Deacon wasn't something new for him. It had been in his mind for several years, but there just wasn't the time. Then he retired and there weren't any more excuses not to do it. As he told me, "I enjoy finally being able to do something that I truly believe in." The most important thing to know about Deacon Art though, is that for a 200-pound, 50-year old Deacon, the man can still move pretty fast.

Something will inevitably go wrong when you put together four men in a group of five amateur tree cutters. Add an older brother from across the street and your pretty well guaranteed that something bad is going to happen. Only, when you're working with chainsaws and 70-foot tree limbs, bad is usually serious and almost never a laughing matter.

When we first arrived at the house, the backyard simply looked like the densest parts of the Appalachian forest. The only difference being that none of the trees here were actually standing upright and two months ago, there had been only two trees in the yard. Deacon Art and I used the pair of week-ender chainsaws to cut the limbs into pieces small enough for the others to carry to a burn pile in the front yard. The main trunk that was over three feet thick, however, would have to wait for some industrial boys to come along. Even had we stopped there, the yard was pretty well clear except for one last monster branch that had been hung up and rested in the nook of another tree, 40 feet off the ground. Brandon and I tried pushing, rolling and twisting the branch, but although it seemed on the verge of falling for fifteen minutes, we weren't going to be able to get it done. That's when the lady's brother showed up from across the street. He quickly left to get his truck and I went to get the bag of rope from my car.

The plan was very simple, tie one end of the rope as high as we could reach on the tree limb, and the other end to the back of the truck. It truly was a simple, basic plan, yet everyone was worried about me. I wanted to get a picture of the limb as it was falling and the best place to get a good shot just happened to be right where the truck would be going. I knew what I was doing. There was a good twenty feet between me and the truck, plenty of time for me to take the picture and move out of the way.

The brother started to pull forward and the first ropes snapped. After tying a heavier duty tow-rope around the branch, he eased his truck forward more slowly. I focused and zoomed in the picture, then caught the high squeal of tires spinning in the mud. He put the truck in reverse, backed up several feet and Brandon yelled for me to watch out one last time before the brother gunned it. All I remember is hitting the button on my camera, running clear of the truck's path (which had stopped twenty feet from where I was standing,) then a blurry image of Deacon Art crashing into the side of the truck.

In my picture you could see a rush of grassy streaks, the bottom half of Brandon and, in the upper corner, a pair of legs in running motion. The limb landed inches from where Deacon Art had been standing. It was one of those rare times when something had gone wrong, but we were already laughing, admiring the dent he had put into the side of the truck. Then Brandon announced he had caught the whole thing on video: Deacon Art leaning casually against the fallen tree, looking in my direction, then up at the branch, the truck spinning its tires, backing up, Deacon Art looking my direction again, the truck jumping forward, limb starts to move, then twists; Deacon Art still looking up casually at the top end of the branch as it begins to slide and lean forward before easing over toward his direction, then a leap around the wheel barrow, three steps and two crashes: the branch hitting the ground and Deacon Art putting a basketball size dent in the side of the truck.

On the way to grab lunch at a camp that had been set up to feed volunteers and whoever else needs it, I heard that Rosa Parks had died. The importance of this news, aside from her being a person whose actions shaped American history, is that it showed me another side of Deacon Art. Growing up, he had been good friends with a boy who had been killed, Emitt Till. I do not recall hearing his name prior to today, but apparently, his death had made a significant impact on the civil rights movement. Deacon Art had written a book about growing up with Emitt and his death, so he spent most of the time over lunch on the phone with a reporter talking about Rosa and Emitt.

After lunch, we went to a second house that needed to be ripped down to the studs. I had managed to keep my emotions from earlier in the morning in check, but still looked forward to some much needed, and safer, stress relief in tearing apart a house. That stress relief was needed even more once my car door closed and I realized the keys were locked inside. Ten minutes later, I had popped open the lock and joined the crew in mid-demolition.

From 10:00 am, when we started up the first chain saw, until we called it quits about 5:00, this had been a good final day of work, but the whole day wasn't over and if I had thought things had gotten off to a rough start with Sherri this morning, I was headed into a real nightmare. Sherri showed up to have dinner with us tonight because she wanted to talk to all of the volunteers.

I thought, *This could be it, maybe something I had said did get through to her and she was going to explain to us why she thought the Warehouse was no longer needed.* Personally, it didn't matter to me what she said anymore, I had already gotten a good piece of what was on her mind, but at least it would do some good for the rest of the group to have some understanding of what was going on. It seemed as though she started the discussion pointed in that direction, before it turned into an hour-long monologue on her experience before working with Catholic Charities and everything else that she has done to help people these past few months. It was such a waste of time and spouting of horse snot that someone later taped a note on the TV, "Sherri's a bad manager." By that time, enough word of our encounter had spread around that I'm sure most people assumed I had been the one who had left it. For what it's worth, I didn't. But I did take some comfort in knowing that other people felt the same way I did.

A few minutes later, I finally caught up with Steve to go over how my talk with Sherri had gone. We had planned on meeting, just a report on what I was able to find out. Once again though, I was completely unprepared for what actually happened.

After I left St. Mary's this morning, and went to do a near full day's work, Sherri had contacted Steve and asked him to have me pack up my things and leave Dedeaux immediately. She didn't even want me to finish out the day's work. In her opinion, I was too exhausted and suffering from such a severe case of *Compassion Fatigue Syndrome* that I needed to leave immediately, for my own good. Apparently I was in such bad shape that it would be better for me to start a thousand mile road trip after a full day of physical labor, than for me to eat a good meal and get a full night's sleep at Dedeaux. Fortunately though, Steve was able to talk her into letting me spend one last night here so long as I do leave tomorrow. There wasn't much more to say to Steve and nothing for me to argue about since I knew his sincerity and sympathy. This was something forced by Sherri.

I want to make a very important distinction here. Sherri only made me feel utterly worthless. If I have not written too long of an entry tonight, then you recall that I introduced this entry by saying it was the most difficult day I have had and not the worst. As hurt and upset as I am tonight, there is still a nugget down deep in me that knows Sherri is wrong, that I have helped an enormous number of people during the three weeks I have been in Mississippi. I know this because results speak louder than any other words, no matter how sharp they were intended.

273

I have gone back and read these journal entries, reminding myself of the conversations I've had, the images of children hugging their stuffed animals, the personal responses from the volunteers who have actually worked at the Warehouse, how I didn't have to eat lunch out of a styrofoam box for four days because people had wanted to either take me out to lunch, or bring it for all of us working at the Warehouse. Much more, I know this thanks to the words and deeds of encouragement I have received from the other volunteers staying here at the retreat center. In accordance with Sherri's wishes, I will be leaving the retreat center tomorrow, but not returning home just yet. Billy Ray Dedeaux is letting me spend the night at his house (His family owns the land all around the church and there's a reason why the retreat center bears the same last name.) He was actually the first person I wanted to speak with as soon as Steve and I had finished talking.

There had been a reason why I had already planned that today would be my last working, yet that I would not be leaving until Thrusday. I need another day here. Despite what the "expert counselor" says, I've known for days now that I need one day of time alone down here to walk around and begin to process what's gone on down here and everything that I've experienced since leaving Colorado nearly two months ago. I need a day to catch up on sleep, to say good-bye to the close friends I've met and mentally get myself ready to move on to the next phase of my life. There is also the big dinner that Polly has told me they're planning on having in my honor tomorrow.

I also pulled Deacon Art aside. Tomorrow may be a personal day for me, and his last day working, but I need his help. No matter what I *know*, Sherri did a tremendous job of making me feel horrible and tiny. I keep thinking that I'm worthless and I have truly wasted my time by coming here. After breakfast tomorrow, he's going to take time out of his day for us to talk…again, he wouldn't do that for someone that was as bad as Sherri had made me feel.

Steve has also made it clear that he is happy for me to stay around as late as I want to tomorrow night, so long as he can keep his word to Sherri that I will be leaving the retreat center tomorrow. The rest of the gang, Mary Ann, her Ron, the other Art, and Polly, made me promise that I would be their *invited guest* for breakfast before heading home Thursday morning. And it tried to be comforting that they are nearly as upset over the situation (ie at Sherri) as I am. Like Billy Ray and Deacon Art, I know that there wouldn't be such the uproar had I really done the things and been the horrible person that Sherri has made me feel like tonight. But that's where concern over my day ends and my worries over Michigan Ron's day begins.

I have written a little about Ron, not nearly as much as he deserves. He is a man of staggering character. Whereas I left everything at home in Colorado, he moved out of his apartment and either sold or gave away everything he owned that wouldn't comfortably fit in his pickup. The original idea had been for him to help wherever he could manage until the paint crews were up and going. He physically wouldn't be able to do much of the actual painting, but after 30 years in the business he knows the craft and would be the perfect person to oversee and coordinate all of the crews. But Ron didn't have the grace of financial support from people that I have had and, due to a serious car wreck and a six-inch metal rod in his neck, he has only the limited income that permanent disability provides. So he asked Sherri if Catholic Charities could help him out with some gas money since it's a 30-mile drive to the worksites, each way. His response from Sherri wasn't a simple "No." Rather, she told him that she did not want anybody down here who could not support themselves. Ron was the second person today who was asked to leave immediately.

275

I am nervous about including these events in the journal because of the negative impact on Catholic Charities as an organization that it might have. My purpose isn't even to complain about and make this person look bad. I included them for two reasons only. First, this is supposed to be an honest, strait forward account of my experiences. As difficult as it is for me to recount and write about what has happened, today has been a major event in my experiences down here and will have a major impact on how they affect me for some time to come. Not writing about today, would be like not writing about anything that I did at the Cajun Dome.

Second, and more importantly, something needs to be said for Ron's faith and generosity. Absolutely no one deserves to be treated the way he has been, especially not Ron. He literally gave up almost everything he owned to help people down here and tonight, as he put it, "They don't want my help because I'm poor!" There is nothing more I can say to describe his mood and how he felt.

For my part, I was/am afraid that Sherri's attitude is going to cloud over his entire experience down here. That he wouldn't be able to see all of the good that he's done. That God did bring him down here for a reason. Maybe it was simply to help hundreds of people; maybe to find the answers he's looking for in his life; maybe it was to show him that he still has a lot to offer people, even though he can't work any more; or maybe there's something completely different God is looking to do for Ron. Whatever it is though, I know that if Ron listens to what Sherri had to say, he will never find it, and I told him as much. Other than that, there wasn't much else for either Polly or I to do. Just get ready to say *goodbye* in the morning and let him know that he would be sorely missed.

Ron is a part of the lesson that we should all be taking to heart. Forget about the sheer devastation and the upheaval of lives that

Katrina caused, even the people here understand that all of that will be restored. But remember the love that has sent people from New Jersey, California, Montana, Washington, Ohio, Iowa, Pennsylvania, Florida, Massachusetts, Colorado...and Michigan to care for their brothers in need. *God still dwells in the hearts of the people of this nation.*

The house we cleaned in Waveland when we arrived (above) and Jenny working a few hours later (below).

277

Solitude

Wednesday, October 26

After my encounter with Sherri, and her demand to have me leave Dedeaux, I desperately needed someone to talk to and was in bad enough shape that I actually pulled the Deacon aside last night and told him I needed someone to talk to. I'm almost never that strait forward, but I guess it's like all of my other work down here and I'm learning not to second guess myself. Before, I would have waited until I calmed down, and then most likely decide that I'd be okay because I had clamed down. I would have thought, *I'll just keep my eye out for an opportunity to present itself to talk with someone.* And when it did, I would come with another good reason to coward out, so I would end up not talking to anyone and be even more upset because I had been abandoned with no one to lean on. But last night was very different than normal, and I have already grown so much from my first day at the Dome. Despite the bad circumstances, that's one more thing I can chalk up as something that I've gained from this trip.

Deacon Art had planned on meeting Tom and Bob at the Warehouse first thing this morning to pick up some tools before working on one of the neighborhood houses. Since it's still a half-hour drive from Dedeaux, he suggested that I follow in my own car, that way, both of us wouldn't have to come back and he could get started on his final day of working down here.

After leaving my car parked along the street, Deacon Art and I drove around some of the East Biloxi neighborhoods. This way, he could see some of the damage while we talked. I didn't know what to expect from him, but like I wrote last night, I didn't know what I needed to hear, just that I needed someone to talk to.

Throughout our conversation, he wasn't as supportive of my arguments toward Sherri as I wanted him to be, not that he was supportive of Sherri either, just very careful not to take anyone's side. Nonetheless, he never undermined the pain that I was going through and his words will remain vivid in my mind for a long time to come. We were a few hundred yards from the ocean's edge, a small shrimp boat was actually on it's way out of the harbor, giving us a small comfort that some forms of life are starting to reappear. I was halfway leaning against the inside of the door, Deacon had his left hand resting high along the steering wheel, and I had finally reached the point where I didn't know if I needed to cry again. "How could she do that to me? I just don't understand why she would turn around and say such horrible things to me. It was like she was trying to make me feel like I had done nothing but hurt people down here."

He looked at me with a fatherly ease and said quite simply. "No Cross, No Crown."

He had me repeat it a half-dozen times. I felt a little bit like I was back in 9th grade French class, only repeating in English felt even more absurd. Yet it worked and each time I said the words, I caught a vision of Christ's head hanging limply in the air, blood seeping down the sides of his head, and then his full body raising in Glory toward heaven. Deacon Art didn't know why. He didn't even offer an attempted guess. He led me into remembering that all of the time I have volunteered, both here and in Louisiana, is a gift to God, to everyone I have helped, to the other volunteers and to myself. Whatever God wants to give me, his entire plan for my experience down here, the business with Sherri is a part of that. Because it's a part of the gift, it will be a part of the reward as well. In Deacon Art's words, "How much greater will that reward be since you've had to go through this to get it?"

"No Cross, No Crown!" (I guess I believe it, but I'm not all that sure.) He also suggested that after I get home I should write Sherri a simple letter thanking her for the opportunity to work with Catholic Charities and not to mention anything else. It does encourage me not to write her a letter trying to further defend myself. Beyond that, I doubt I'll even give it any more consideration. *Sherri won't be getting any letters from me.*

On a separate note, there was one small thing that I felt I was able to give Deacon Art this morning. After we had dealt with the issues concerning Sherri, we talked a little more about his life, how he came to being a Deacon, my thoughts about considering the priesthood. At one point he told said very simply, "It's nothing as high as becoming a priest." And that's when I corrected him.

It has always bothered my when people compare jobs as one being more important, or better than another. As though being a doctor is fundamentally better than being a woodworker, a lawyer better than a teacher, or a priest *higher* than a deacon. I told him with as much quiet honesty as I had, "Not higher, just different." The highest calling that we can achieve is the one which God is calling us toward, to use the gifts He has given us. If we aren't doing that, then we are failing and doing less than what we should be. So a woodworker raising his family can be much *higher* than a doctor, or a priest can be failing if God had called him to be a doctor. "Not higher, just different."

Deacon Art gave me another look, "Thank you. That means a lot." I could feel that his sincerity matched mine and soon thereafter, he started the car. It was time for both of us to move on with our days.

One of the reasons that Sherri's demand for me to leave Dedeaux hurt me so much was that I had I set aside today as a day to spend quietly alone, driving and walking around the area according to whim so that I could begin my own process of healing and processing everything I've seen and witnessed over the last couple of months; struggling to work with the Red Cross; rescuing Tiny; wasting a week trying to fix my car; wasting a day with the PRC; being asked to take charge of the Warehouse; seeing the empty staircases; leaving the Warehouse the night it started to look like a church again; and all of the people I have met throughout it all. Despite all that I know, have learned and how much growth I've already seen in myself, I haven't even begun to realize what all has happened.

Although it will take much more than a day to figure it out, I don't think it would ever happen without taking a day for myself. This is what I told both Steve and Billy Ray last night. Unlike Sherri, they understood and thought it was a good idea. If for no other reason, I do have another 1,700-mile trip in front of me and it wouldn't be good to start that long of a drive already exhausted. Today was the first day in two months that I faithfully put everyone else second and dedicated it for myself. The tears finally came.

Several days ago, I wrote that "The tears are not far away." That night, as I wrote those words, I could feel them swelling behind my eyes. I was sure that it was only a short matter of time, a day, maybe two, before they came all of the way through. They never did come. Along with the confusion and uncertainty around here, there's the added pressure of having to stay strong. I think that this is the one thing that is harder on the volunteers than it is for people living here. We came down here to help, with the expectation of providing a shoulder to cry on and the least desire to need one. We have burned in us an image of people looking directly at our faces, asking and expecting that we can help them. It's hurt all of us when we've had to say, "No," or the softer, "I don't know," no matter how compassionately we said it. But we fight those emotions off so that we are able to move forward and be ready for the next person who we can do something for and help.

I knew what I was doing, understood the mental image of turning my back and walking away from someone that I couldn't do anything for. There was no point in troubling over things I couldn't do, just worry about doing as much as I could for whomever I could. That's good wisdom, and it was certainly exactly what needed to be done these past few weeks. Today was much different though. I was alone, walking the streets in former neighborhoods where Katrina's eye hit when I realized more of what it means to be living in a *War Zone*.

We have all heard the news reports describing this area as a *War Zone*. The pictures told the story and I agreed; it really does look like bombs have torn through the area. Absent the gunfire, sporadic mortar blasts and roadside explosions, living here feels a lot like living in a *War Zone*. The mental trauma of seeing your life destroyed; the uncertainty of where, how and even if you can start to rebuild; not being able to do anything about the mounds of trash heaped along the streets and the challenge of simple things: mail delivery, grocery shopping, finding a place to go to the bathroom, to make a phone call…all weigh on the soul. Where do you go if you step on a nail, or you husband is having a heart attack? (I actually heard a horrific story of an ambulance from North Carolina that was lost for nearly an hour before finding someone who knew the area and they could follow to the hospital.)

If the Salvation Army runs out of ice, where do I go to get some so I can keep my food cold? Do I have enough water for the day? When will we start getting running water back? Where's the nearest working bathroom? Questions that we never have to consider, have suddenly become our greatest concerns. If not the violence, we are surrounded by the uncertainty of war. (This should also open our eyes to just how bad war really is.) There's also the added burden of staying strong, for our children, our spouse, our neighbors, for everyone except ourselves. As I walked around, I finally allowed myself to really see the devastation around me. I had already understood it, seeing and embracing their faces, but today I realized a new appreciation for the spontaneous breakdown I first witnessed back at the Cajun Dome.

Both sides of the street were lined with mounds of broken down houses. Nothing had been left standing, just heaps of splintered wood, half-walls and bricks scattered throughout. Small coves had been dug out where people had started setting aside piles of rescued memories. Various statues of angels and Mary had been gathered together in one pocket. The driveway across the street had been mostly cleared. At the end was a grey plastic tub sitting next to a wooden antique rocker with the American flag draped over the back.

It's a sign that I have seen many times, our flag picked up off the ground and hung on the nearest point of rescue: on a chain link fence, next to a front door, or hung from a tree to mark where a house had once been.

Before today, those empty staircases leading to nothing had touched me deeper than anything else. At the time I had come closest to crying, I was in the van with Jon and Dawn, staring at the site where I later found out over 30 people had been killed. Their presence is probably what held the tears inside, but no one was standing in the street with me today. Except for a few banging sounds of a hammer beating on metal, I was alone. I saw a simple sign, standing about six feet high in the middle of one mound of broken lumber and everything flooded into the present. My strength broke.

"The Bailey's 312 Nicholson"

This just wasn't their house, it still IS their home. Everything simply wasn't destroyed be Katrina, it IS destroyed. Entire houses *ARE* gone...only a few sparse pillars stand. Churches *ARE* empty...there *IS* no electricity...people *A R E* living off generators...they *ARE* sleeping outside, waiting for someone with a tent to call. Katrina isn't something that simply happened, she's not a historical story, but is happening in the present.

I fought the temptation to remind myself of all of the good things. Grocery stores are opening, help wanted signs hang in almost every business window, the Home Depot is packed to the roof with people who have started rebuilding, and fewer people are going hungry now than had been before the storm hit. I don't need to feel better or happy staring at that sign and the rubble it marks. I need to feel the sadness and heart wrenching that I've been turning my back on for weeks. Unlike the person who needs a tent that we don't have, I can't send them down to the East Biloxi Crisis Recovery Center. After a couple more hours of driving, walking and taking pictures, I was ready to leave. I know that it will take a few weeks to fully process all of this, but whatever it was that I needed to do to get myself ready to move on was done. It was back to Dedeaux where the word was that I spent the next four hours passed out on the couch.

****

Last night I had mentioned that there was another reason, aside from the need for personal time, that Sherri's order for me to leave was problematic. Polly, Art and a few others had planned on making a special dinner for me. Tonight was Thanksgiving at Dedeaux. I am so blessed to have these amazing people in my life right now. How could I question whether or not I've done any good these last few weeks when I have a plate full of turkey, stuffing, mashed potatoes...and fresh baked pumpkin pie waiting for dessert? While I was still working on my first piece of that pie, Polly presented those of us leaving in the next couple of days, Steve, Jenny and myself, with special gifts pulled from the supplies at the Warehouse. *Ron should have been here for the dinner too, he deserves it more than anyone else who has been down here, myself included.*

Because of how I've been feeling it's worth noting that this is the first time there's been any type of a going away celebration. My haul included some snack size boxes of Lucky Charms (since I had spent several days looking for a box at the Warehouse to bring back to Dedeaux for breakfast,) 1 can of chicken, a pack of Oreos...and one 4 lb. can of tuna. We all laughed.

Deacon Art shared what he had written in his daily journal for yesterday, which has been picked up by a few small papers around the country. Naturally, it included almost getting killed by the tree and us gathering around Brandon's camera to laugh at the video of the entire thing.

I still have that backward feeling that wants to nag me that I was terrible at running the Warehouse, a hindrance to their work and every other terrible thing that Sherri had said to me. But there's no way Ron, Mary Ann, Polly, Art, Billy Ray, Steve, Deacon Art and all of the others would have been so supportive if they had felt the same way...and these were the people who have actually worked with me day in and day out. I can confidently say that despite Sherri's attempts to the contrary, I've never felt more loved and valued than I do tonight. Thank you! With all of my heart, Thank You!

I'm ready to go back home.

Art and Ron cooking our 'Thanksgiving' dinner.

Six weeks after Katrina. A small cabin that had come to rest against a utility pole (above), and one of the neighborhoods a half-mile from the coast (below).

One of the small coves of statues that had been pulled out of the rubble (above) and the rocking chair that sat on the foundation across the street (below).

A New Orleans Drive By

Thursday, October 27

One of the things that upset us the most at Dedeaux, was the constant attention that the news media kept giving to New Orleans. Not that we didn't feel a modicum of sorrow for the people who used to live there, we knew that life had to be difficult and understood the shear numbers of people driven from their homes, after all 80% of the people I dealt with in Louisiana had been living in or around New Orleans. But Mississippi feels forgotten and from everything we were seeing, it was. In addition to getting to spend some time with my brother, who I haven't seen since last Christmas, today was my chance to see just how bad this city really is.

After the cataclysmic media reports, I was very surprised to see that much of the downtown area was untouched. That doesn't mean, however, that lunch offered the typical New Orleans flare. Both supplies and people are significantly limited, so it was a burger and fries served on paper plates with plastic knives and forks. They have running water, but it's not enough for the luxury of washing dishes. Business hours are limited to daylight; not enough electricity, and there's still a standing curfew in order. Of the few people about, no one was wearing their weekday business suit or *I'm a tourist* tee. It's a city of fireman, police officers, relief workers and a few residents just trying to piece their lives back together. It's the cars though, that tell the story here, not the Sunday quietness in the middle of the week.

I was driving in from the highway when it struck me that the dealership lots are still filled with the same cars that had been there before Katrina rolled through. All of them are covered with a dirty brown film of lake bottom mud. The side streets looked the same. Cars are parked in driveways and along the side of the road; they haven't moved in weeks and are sealed in the same mustard brown shell of a western ghost town. A few small tree limbs were scattered around and a front door rested open here and there. Except for one car, overturned with the trunk upended on top of a six-foot high wooden gate, everything else seemed to be abandoned in its normal place. There were no people, only quiet neighborhoods. I could see the evacuation, people looking back at the house they were leaving or taking another hopeful look for the dog who was going to be left behind. Or maybe that was a porch where someone had waited to be rescued after the flood came, teary eyed as a neighbor paddled the canoe around a submerged car.

It doesn't just feel like it, this town really has slumbered with its people trapped in scattered shelters with nothing to do but wait for the waters to recede so it can wake up again. It's as if the two places were in a serious car wreck, while Mississippi broke nearly every bone in its body, New Orleans suffered only a broken arm and possibly a hair line fracture in the leg, but otherwise escaped serious injury, before falling into an unconscious coma, from which it's just beginning to wake up. Which is the worse for wear?

I for one have always gravitated toward the lonely patient who all of the visitors rush past, that, and once New Orleans gets back on her feet, the recovery is going to be much faster here. My heart does feel for the people of New Orleans. Yet, despite the ghostly sadness, I'm not heart broken. They're getting the bull's share of attention, money and help, and from what I have seen, Katrina didn't leave them in nearly as bad of shape as Ocean Springs, Biloxi, Waveland, and everywhere in between.

Putting aside all of the talk about Katrina wreaking destruction of Biblical proportions, few of us have been able to get a realistic handle on just how much of an impact she's going to have on this country. We've all heard stories about separated families, some reunited, others are still searching for each other and wondered how many people are going to return to New Orleans. In Biloxi, there's reason for concern over developers scalping land from residents so they can build condo societies and questions linger over the future of the shrimping industry. The acadocrats talk about social dispersion on a scale never before seen in this country. There really is no way of predicting just how Katrina is going to change things in the long term, but the fact that both Kevin and I were caught up in the relief efforts is a good sign that indicates she will have a greater impact than any other disaster that has already occurred in my lifetime.

I'm sure that there are thousands of close friends and families who have pitched in their combined efforts to help out, but my brother and I have never before been involved in disaster recovery.

291

We are further apart than the distance between Colorado and Texas, and made completely separate decisions to come down here.

I was at home putting a new alternator in my car when I realized I could ask for a leave of absence to come down here and work. Kevin had just ended a summer promotional job when a friend of his told him about the training seminars to become a licensed FEMA inspector. I was a banker preparing for a run into politics, he is a writer. He is staunchly liberal, I am so conservative that people sometimes confuse me for being liberal. I actively talk about Christ, he treasures Him quietly in his heart. I think President Clinton should be tarred and feathered (for lying to the courts), he thinks President Bush should be wiped from the face of existence. I run six miles a day, he may have jogged six miles in his entire life and would do better at swimming six miles. Aside from having the same parents, there's very little we have in common. That we now share an experience with Katrina will surely help to bring us closer, the bigger story, however, is that Katrina's impact is big enough to pull both of us into her wake.

I don't know how it has affected him yet, part of that is it feels like I never know how anything effects Kevin, mostly though, a two-hour lunch is barely enough time to catch up on what we've been doing, much less to get into any deep emotional details. One thing that I did pick up on is that there is a tremendous trade off for the large amount of money he's making right now. Although I've been living off the generosity of others for the past several weeks, I've had the comforts of a bed, indoor heating and real bathrooms. He has a cot, drafty tent flaps and access to forty Port-A-Potties. More so than enjoying the luxury accommodations at Roy's house and Dedeaux, I've also had the benefit of meeting dozens of extraordinary people and have made friendships that will be around for years to come.

I feel bad for Kevin because he doesn't have the chance to meet the same caliber of people that I have had. He doesn't have the circle we had at Dedeaux where we'd sit on the porch after dinner, some drinking a glass of wine, sharing stories about our day. And aside from the one person who he had already known before coming to Louisiana, there's no one for him to talk to. I wonder how he's going to be able to handle the stress of being down here after a couple more weeks of this.

After lunch, we headed back to the FEMA camp so Kevin could check to see if his next list of assignments had come in. Of the twenty houses on the list, there might be five that he will actually inspect today. For some of them, it would be later in the week before he would be able to make contact and schedule the appointment, nothing more than the usual difficulty one could expect in trying to make an appointment; several of the families are still scattered across 48 states, living in shelters or staying with family members and have no way of getting back; The last five or six are addresses that don't even exist, the cases of fraud, people signing up just so they could scam FEMA out of the initial $2,000 check.

For the many who aren't able to get back to their house, there are a few that can be done with a quick drive by; the homes that are clearly destroyed or would be too dangerous to enter (simply opening the door to a brick house, mortar dissolving after being underwater for nearly a month, could cause it to collapse.) But for the rest, if Kevin needs to go inside the house, they'll go back into the pool and show up on someone else's list a couple months down the road. Like so many things, that's a tough problem. While FEMA needs to have someone at the house to witness the inspection and answer any questions the inspector might have, it's a bit ridiculous to expect someone staying at a shelter in Baton Rouge or Lafayette, likely without a car, to come back to a house they can't live in, or don't even know whether or not is still standing, just to meet with a FEMA representative for ten, maybe fifteen minutes.

With the day half gone, it was time to let my brother get some work in before dark. Even though he's getting paid, it's more important to the five families whose homes he can inspect tonight, than for us to spend a few more catching up. As for my own opportunity to drive around and get a better look at the city, I don't have any more desire to see more damage. I'm anxious to get back home, first to Missouri and then to Colorado so I can start looking for a new job.

PART IV

AFTER MISSISSIPPI

Loose Ends

Sherri

Probably the most important, and immediate question at this point is: *How did my encounter with Sherri paint my Katrina experience?* The night after our confrontation, I wrote about how horrible she had made me feel about the time and efforts I had put into helping people in Biloxi. That was before finding out that she had asked Steve to have me leave immediately, and before I found out she had asked the same thing of Ron that. That evening, very few minutes passed by when I wasn't on the verge of tears, questioning if I had done any good for anyone in Biloxi, or even all of the way back at the Cajun Dome. Even worse, Sherri had done her job so well that I was wondering whether or not I had done more harm by being there than if I had stayed home in Colorado. I have never doubted that she knew what she was doing, trying to tear me down as a person and everything good that I had done. Even now, I can feel the tears welling up inside as I relive that night, but in part, also because I just now noticed a song playing on the radio that goes along with exactly what I was about to write:

296

"When I find myself in times of trouble
Mother Mary comes to me
Speaking words of wisdom,
Let it be."

Almost as soon as I had finished talking with Steve that night, I was on the phone with my mom. We both knew that there was nothing for her to say that would make the pain go away, that wasn't her job…true pain needs to be felt and I had rarely been hurt so deeply as I was that night. But just like it has happened so many times before in my life, she was there, offering a consoling ear and speaking her own words of wisdom. When such horrific events break into our lives, like a hurricane, tornado or an earthquake, it's easy for us to recognize the devil's hand in the pain, grief and destruction, the looting and chaos that seemed to take control of New Orleans. Then we stand in awe and wonder at God's work, at the one house that's left standing in an entire neighborhood, or the statue of Mary, still standing outside without the slightest scratch. It's as though God is saying to each of us, "I am here."

We often forget that long after the storm, Satan continues his own fight against God, humanity and life itself. That night, my mom reminded me that while God gathers workers from all over the country, Satan is just as hard at work, blocking the hands of human compassion, trying to increase the pain and suffering we feel. Just as God calls us to provide volunteers and supplies, Satan uses people to discourage us from lending that helping hand. My encounter with Sherri was one of those times.

I am not in any way trying or meaning to say that Sherri is an evil and wicked person. There is no way that she would have given so much of her own life and time to running disaster relief efforts if she were. In my own humble and untrained opinion, I felt like she was fighting her own struggle over closing the Warehouse, that her own instinct and desire was to keep it open, but logic and her education told her otherwise. I think that I became the outlet for the turmoil that was going on inside her as she tried to convince herself that she was making the right decision. For whatever reason, she opened herself and allowed herself to be used to breed discouragement and chaos. She was the one Satan sent into my life to destroy everything good that Katrina had changed in me.

Next to the day I first decided to leave home and help with the recovery effort, that night was the most critical moment of my entire Katrina experience. God responded to the challenge by sending not just one person, but by giving me an entire army of compassion and support. Where Sherri's comments stood alone in one corner, Polly, Steve, Art, Ron, Mary Ann, Billy Ray, Deacon Art, Jenny, and many others stood behind me in the other, reminding me of all of the good things that we had accomplished together and not letting me believe for one moment that I had done more harm than good. There is no way that I can fully express to them how grateful I am for supporting me. The only thing that can compare with the enormous warmth I felt from them, is the confidence in knowing that it really is like Ben said, "God will always take care of those who remain faithful to Him." For every one that Satan sends against us, God responds with an army to defend us.

No matter how many times we repeat the old saying, "Sticks and stones may break my bones, but words will never hurt me," words do hurt, and sometimes they can hurt more than taking a baseball bat squarely to the head. It is impossible for us to go through such an experience without a mark being left and although I didn't fully believe it at the time, it is exactly like Deacon Art had me repeat over and over again in the car: "No Cross! No Crown!" Thanks to their support, Sherri's rumbling didn't tear me down or destroy everything positive that had come out of my time in Biloxi, but served to strengthen my faith and reinforce what I discovered about my character. That doesn't mean, of course, that I gave any more consideration to writing the letter to Sherri that Deacon Art suggested, thanking her for the opportunity to help and giving me a place to stay at Dedeaux.

As much as I am convinced that what she said to me was a result of her own *Compassion Fatigue*, I felt that in sending the letter, I would be acting like the encounter never happened, and something about that has never felt right. My hope is that this book finds its way into her hands and we can both remember what really happened and that God knew what He was doing, in both our lives.

Following Through, or Not

I didn't do my part for Rodney. The thoughts were there and the letter was written, but it does little good to write a letter that never gets mailed. It stood no chance of making it's way to Oprah's desk, and even less of a chance at getting him a wedding. I've felt the cutting failure of not taking five minutes to sit down with Steve and get the final bits of information that I needed: Rodney's last name, his address, or even the name of his fiancé. I failed, and he wasn't the only person who I let down. There were also the names of several families that had come to the Warehouse looking for help. Out of registration forms, their names were written on loose pieces of scratch paper that I never passed on to Steve. There was the plan to call Tristen with the Mountain Chalet back in the Springs in order to start up a donation tree of tents to help a few of the thousands of shelterless people. And I have never been able to forget about the totes of clothes that continued to sit toward the back of the Warehouse because I didn't have *enough* volunteers to sort through them properly. As much as I did in Mississippi, I also left a lot of things undone.

I've wanted to berate myself for not knowing as much as I could, for not taking a few minutes in Louisiana to call other agencies directly; find out the real scoop on what assistance they were providing for people; for wasting several days playing video games at Roy Jr.'s after Rita had come through; and for not using Lafayette's public transportation when my car was broken down. I had driven 2,000 miles without a clue as to what I would be doing to help, but it was too much for me to track down a bus schedule so I could get to the Dome, where I was clearly needed. Sitting inside me is a nearly endless list of things that I didn't do, wanting to grow into a festering guilt. But I found out that Faith isn't entirely about the future and what's going to happen, it's also about the past and accepting that God knew what He was doing and what I was doing too. As Bernadette, one of the college students from Dayton pointed out, sometimes we can see it, and sometimes we can't.

Sometimes Faith could be like my slow return to the Cajun Dome after Rita; I could have kicked myself in the butt and forced myself to go back to the Dome the day after we got back from the Farm, but after I had been in Mississippi for a few days I realized that had I done that, had I taken the harder road and walked the quarter mile to catch a bus, I would have been in the exact same condition that Ed was in, burnt out and exhausted far beyond what a few days on a Florida beach could cure.

On another hand, Faith could be like my letter for Rodney; I have no idea what happened to him, if his father is still alive or where he and his fiancé stand in their wedding plans. Maybe they're married, maybe a date has been set for next month, or maybe they're still spending so much of their time and money repairing the house that it's still a distant thought. I don't know, and what Bernadette told me is that I don't need to know. Besides, am I so arrogant to think that by not mailing a letter I am able to thwart God's plan for

Rodney's life? Maybe God had decided that Rodney's father would live long enough to share that dance with his daughter-in-law, and no one would argue against that reason for waiting another year or two before having the wedding.

It's also possible that Rodney's father died just a few days after I left, and the last thing they needed was for Oprah's staff to call two days later with news about giving them a wedding; or maybe God had put that letter in my heart as a way to give Rodney and his fiancé a wedding beyond anything they had ever imagined and I did fail. If that's the case, then I have no doubt God simply took a pencil, drew a line through my name and continued down the list for the next person to step up and take care of the job. I've imagined dozens of different things that could have happened, and the only thing that I can be absolutely sure of is that, as for letting these failures tear me up inside, the letter and those loose sheets of scratch paper don't matter anymore.

A Mystery of Faith in Christ is that He didn't promise accepting Him into our lives would make us perfect. He will change us profoundly, but He actually promised just the opposite. We will fail, Peter would deny Christ and his most loved disciples would scatter in fright. But God, and other people, will always be there to lift us up again. So long as we are faithful and continue our struggle to follow Him, nothing that we do is indestructible.

Of course, this is not to say that I should shrug off any mistake I made as a part of God's master plan, but if He can work through the betrayal of Judas, He can handle my lazy moments. I am confident that He called someone to step out of the shadows and get whatever it was that Rodney and his father needed. What's important through Faith is that I remind myself that I did everything I was capable of doing and that every night I pray for God's help in becoming a better servant, which is one more thing that I learned. There is a difference between loving God and wanting to serve Him.

I have always loved God and often said that all I wanted to do in life was to serve His Will, but buried within that promise, there was always a taint of my own ambitions. I think that John from Mississippi is the one who helped me see the difference. Love and service is like the college girlfriend who I serenaded, painted a Sylvester the cat on a flower pot for, and spent hours preparing romantic dinners for. I did everything I could think of that a *boyfriend* was supposed to do, but none of that could have saved our relationship. It's been ten years and I still know that there is no one I have ever loved half as much as her, but I lost her because I was caught up in that list of things that you're *supposed* to do when you're in love, rather then first seeking to serve and do the things that she actually wanted.

Certainly, true love entails a character of the desire to serve, but by not recognizing that the two are different, I wasn't able to allow our love to grow. Our relationship with God is the same. It's the difference between ourselves deciding what it is that He wants us to do with our lives and the desire to let Him tell us what He is asking us to do. I discovered that we serve God, and others, through our actions, not theoretical and formless emotions hidden away in our brains or hearts. We serve Him best by living and being who we are, even in times when those actions aren't for the best...we then show our love for Him, not by surrendering to those shortcomings, but in asking for His help and seeking to change those parts of us which aren't beneficial.

I accept and do not punish myself for needing a week of video games to recover from the stress of working alongside the Red Cross, but I also struggle to keep a heart that doesn't need that time...as a good friend of mine Brent just recently expressed, being a Christian is not about claiming to be perfect, that we can do no wrong, but admitting that we are not perfect, that we are going to make mistakes and we seek reconciliation with others, to continually improve ourselves and become more like Christ. Part of being Christian is about confessing that through God all things are both not yet and possible.

On the Priesthood

Often times, when we go through such a powerful experience, our life immediately takes on major changes, then slowly settles down to something that closely resembles the way things were before. This means that one of the most popular questions remains: *How did this experience really change the direction of my life?*

A lot of issues and questions jumped in and out of my mind for the two months that I was down there. In fact, one of the reasons for this book is that there were so many things jumping in and out of my head. But one of the overriding questions that hung over everything I did was the thought about the priesthood which entered my head 40 miles after leaving my parents' home in Missouri.

After I left New Orleans, I returned to Missouri for several days, and spent some time with Fr. Mike, a close family friend who has been a part of my journey in faith since he baptize me as a child. Even though I had received several answers to that question from my time at the Warehouse and at Dedeaux, I still needed time in focused reflection to decide what God was calling me to do with my life. The following is the email that I sent to my friends and family shortly after I returned home to Colorado Springs:

****

Dear Friends:

I normally do not send mass emails, however, there are so many of you who have shown an interest in my recent consideration of the priesthood that I have to make an exception in this case.

First, let me say that I am extremely grateful for the large number of people who have leant words of encouragement and provided some guidance. Every bit of it has been helpful.

I have reached a decision with regard to the priesthood. As most of you are aware, I had scheduled a few days with our family priest that included some time with the Vocations Director for this Diocese. One of the main things that I had hoped to get from this meeting was to get a firm idea of the logistics and steps that I would take and what I would need to do to get into the seminary, should that be what I decided to do. The most important thing that I found is that regardless of what decision I made now, it would be next fall before I would actually begin seminary.

At this time, I have chosen not to pursue the priesthood for the basic reason that I do not feel this is a calling from God. I will remain open to the possibility and should something change, I will let you know.

For now, the plan is to go back home to Colorado this weekend and check with the school district about a substitute teaching position so I can get some money coming in immediately. The long-term goal is to find a job in campus ministry, which likely means that I will have to move from the Springs. If anyone hears of an open campus ministry position, or knows of a site that lists such positions, please let me know.

FINAL THOUGHTS

I think that this is the hardest part in writing any story, one last chance to write everything that I missed along the way, to answer questions that I left hanging the day that I left Dedeaux; one last chance to convey to all of you the incredible things that I learned about life and convince you just how powerful of an impact Katrina, and then Rita, had on my life. Not only do I have hundreds of ideas swirling around my head, but there are just as many questions, as well. *How do I do it? What's the best way to pass on everything that I learned, everything that Katrina meant to my life?*

It feels as though I'm having to put together a eulogy for my wife, putting into words how much her life meant to me, how she changed me. I feel the pressure of having to do justice in fully describing her love and the pain of coming to an end. Bringing the

305

book to its conclusion is an end for me. Writing this book has been another part of the process, just as much as the actual experiences I had in Louisiana and Mississippi. It was never my original plan to begin with, just a way for me to remember and remind myself of the extraordinary things that were happening around me. Then it became a way to share those experiences with a few friends and family back home; a way for me to process all that had happened to me; a way to spend the large amount of free-time God had given me; and finally, it became a book to share with everyone.

There have been at least a dozen times when I wanted to stop writing, when I felt like no one would be interested in reading my story, or that no matter how interesting the story was, I wasn't a good enough writer to tell it. But at each time, someone came along, like Aaron's friend who I met just the one time while helping him move, and told me how much they would love to read about my story. Then grad school came. I had wanted to have the first draft done before classes started, had devoted the entire summer to nothing other than getting the book done because I knew that once classes began, I wasn't going to have time to write. And I was right. For the next nine months the pages sat in a folder and I barely had time to even give them another thought. It was only after classes ended and the next summer arrived that I was able to turn back to these pages, virtually locking the door and promising that I would finish, allowing myself only time to go to work and take one daily walk around the lake.

As I come to the end, I have found an interesting connection back to where all of this began. If you remember, one of the few things that I knew when the decision to leave home and go to the coast came to mind, was that no matter what I did, my life was going to change. It was one of the few moments that I didn't have to look back on to recognize. I knew at the time it was happening that it was going to be a major turning point in my life. Either I was going to

306

answer the call to help then, or I never would. A similar feeling has returned.

I've set many goals for having this book finished in the last two years. For The first one had been by Christmas, just two months after I returned home. Then I saw it would take more time to do the job right and I gave myself until the end of May. *You just never know when you start on something like this how much time goes into it.* May quickly became August. Then school started and between a full-time course load and a near full-time job, I knew that there was going to be no time for writing. Although I had all of my notes written, I was still far from putting the last weeks into coherent form.

Just like I had felt when the weeks drug on in Louisiana and I had gotten no closer to making contact with Mississippi, I wanted to be upset and bothered during all of the next semester. I had even decided to take one less class, giving me more time to get this book finished, but in four months I only found one Saturday afternoon when I had three hours to shut my door, and move myself back to my time at Dedeaux. I was on God's schedule once again and looking back, I can see how much has changed and how much is different because I didn't have this finished a year ago. I can feel that overwhelming urge, that uncomfortable confidence that it has become now or never once again. Either I will be finished with a full draft of this book by the end of this summer (2007), or it will never happen...and my heart is breaking. *How do I bring all of this to an end? How do I satisfy my infinite desire to show, to prove to everyone just how much these two months meant to my life?*

I thought about taking another trip back through my daily entries, adding a final message to each day about what I learned and how that day had changed my life, a sort of daily devotional salute to *Doogie Howser*. But after reading over just two days of entries, that didn't work. My mind went blank when I sat down to write, or my thoughts dissolved before I could fully figure out what they were. When did I realize, "We need to put God first, then everything else will follow?" On precisely what day did I come to a new understanding of what Jesus meant when he spoke of us becoming a *New Creation*? What was the critical event that made me give up on politics?

Nothing happened in such a crisp and definitive way. While there were moments of epiphany, there was a casual flow to all of my experiences so that in most cases, I simply couldn't nail down a specific day. If I tried to force it into a sequence of *daily revelations*, they would have been artificial and defeated the whole point of writing this book. There wasn't a single moment when I realized that I had become more assertive and less reliant on the *powers that be*. There was never a *blow me of my horse* moment. I didn't have a discussion with Art that inspired me to become a teacher. There wasn't one morning when I awoke at Dedeaux and thought, "I should write a book about these experiences." Or a specific moment when I felt a sudden burst in faith exploding inside me.

From the afternoon when I got the call from Roy Sr., confirming that I would have a place to stay, I was challenged to lean outward and stretch my faith a little further. I had never before hesitated at packing up my things and moving to a different state, comfortable that I would find a job when I got there. But making the decision to ask for donations was something I had never done before. Consciously putting my faith in God to provide what I needed and not remind people to send me money may not have been a new direction, but it was another step, pulling me a little further. Leaving for Biloxi before I had actually made contact with a person and knew where I would be sleeping was yet another step. And the day that the Ice Truck pulled into the Warehouse parking lot was just one more moment that stretched my faith just a little bit more. I don't think I ever once took what you could call a *leap of faith*, maybe I'm wrong in that, but in looking back on things, what I discovered about people and the world around us, and the changes that took place in me, they were all a part of a gradual process, one step leading to another. Each one was a matter of stepping out a little further than I had previously been willing to go.

After my attempt at including a *daily devotional* failed, my next step was to try another journal entry about the first couple of months I spent back home in Colorado Springs; how that time was just as much a part of my experience as the time down in Mississippi and Louisiana. I had over fifty pages of notes, some of it was better than anything else I had written, yet nothing would fit together. It seemed like no matter where I started, everything ended up disjointed and twisting in its own circle. I couldn't put myself in the right mind of reliving those first few weeks I was back home. When I closed my eyes, I would see myself through the images of a dimly lit tunnel, sitting on the couch with a video game remote in hand. *Audible to pass play...another touchdown and if I can hold them just one more time on defense, then I might just make it to 100 points this time.* That was the only goal left for me, to score 100 points in a single game of college football. The rest of the excitement and challenge of an undefeated season and national championship was gone, only the quiet numbness of doing something that didn't matter remained.

I realized that I couldn't get all of the pieces to fit together because I was adding the sense of despair, tainting and darkening a time that was difficult, but extremely peaceful. It was one of the greatest times in my life. I could still feel God's living presence in my life, could see Him visibly making sure that I had everything that I needed. In one afternoon, as I fumbled through my computer bag looking for anything other than a penny to put in the parking meter, the window of an SUV and a woman leaned over the seat to offer me a quarter. Less than ten minutes later, one of my former coworkers at the bank simply refused to run a cash advance for me. I was going to be two days and less than $5.00 short from covering two checks. Doreen disappeared behind the break room door, returning with her checkbook in hand to lend me the money herself, while Alecia and Thuy continued to chide me about how different I looked. I thought, *Yeah, I feel bigger*, but sluffed it off, joking about how I had really spent the last two months on a cruise. Life was good.

I could feel God's warmth seeping through my feet as I stood in the palm of His hand, and the tenderness of His flesh as I hugged my face against His fingers. I wanted to learn more about God's Son, the question of "Who is Jesus Christ?" continued rolling through my head. I had always been drawn to the Hebrew Scriptures, but found new discoveries as I read through the Gospels again. When I closed my eyes, I would see the inside of a shallowly lit, empty apartment with only a rocker sitting next to a window in the corner. The wooden floors were swept clean and walls freshly painted. It was a new image for me. Only two months before, and for years before then, I would always see the same variation of two men battling with swords, often with light sabers. My face appearing with a green glow as I battled a shadowy figure whose face I could never make out. The battles were intense, our faces flashing in green and blue sparks of light. There was never a winner or looser, neither of us taller than the other, just one constant fight to maintain my balance and keep my footing against a constant pressure. But that image was gone. The clanging and watery crashing of blades hitting one another had disappeared into silence. In its place stood the quiet, freshly cleaned room and that empty chair that was rocking ever so invitingly.

Jesus tells us the story of a spirit who had been driven out of a person. Banished to the wasteland, after traveling all throughout the earth this spirit returned to the person he had left. Finding room there, it had been swept clean, he gathered seven more spirits and returned with all seven to inhabit the person again, so that this man was worse than before. It's not that before Katrina I had been possessed by an evil spirit, but my heart was cleansed. I was no longer fighting to discover my future, torn between my desire to either follow God or serve this country. I was given the opportunity to start anew and fill my life with God's choices.

I know that it sounds cliché, I really felt like everything that had been before Katrina was from another life, even though it had barely been two months since I had left for Roy's. God had cleaned the dirt and grunge out from my life, I was prepared to start something new and the only question I was feeling was: *"What am I going to fill my heart with?"* I was done with politics. I didn't even want to think about them again, but it wasn't because of my disappointment with our government's response or anything else I had seen along the coast. If you recall, it was the Red Cross, not FEMA that was bringing the tears and flaring tempers at the Cajun Dome. Neither was it because I had seen the futility and corruption in Washington, I had seen that when I interned on Capitol Hill two years before moving to Colorado. Simply put, the title of this book says it all: *Remembering God.*

I was reminded of God, shown once again that He was and is the absolute answer to seek first. Find God and we'll find ourselves. It's a guarantee that I discovered doesn't work the other way around and it was what I had been wanting to do with the Adams-Kennedy Society; to help us repair our political system as a way of leading us toward the Freedom that God both desires and guarantees us. The small stack of papers, those Articles of Incorporation that had been sitting on the corner my desk for a few weeks before I left did finally move. They were stored away in folders, right along with my drawings for a Pan-African Rail and Utility Network, and my ideas for the only lasting peace between Israel, the Palestinians and the Arab world. The saddest part of dropping the Adams-Kennedy

Society is that I never talked to Lisa again. Part of me was ashamed that it had been my idea from the start. I was the one who called her and began our first conversation with the question, "How would you like to help me change the world?" And then I became the one who gave up and didn't follow through. I knew that the least I owed her was a phone call, but then, she hadn't tried to contact me during the two months I had been gone. How interested could she still be? If she was interested, then she would call and that's when I would be up front and completely open about my decision and why I had let that momentary dream go.

I used that rationale as my excuse to decide that Lisa's heart may not have been fully behind the idea, that she wasn't as committed as I had thought. I haven't spoken with Lisa since then and I still feel a sadness well up whenever I think about her. But it has nothing to do with the decision to let go of Adams-Kennedy. It's the loss of her friendship that I miss, which was the biggest challenge I faced after returning home...I never seemed able to reconnect with my friends.

I had heard a lot of stories from other volunteers about how, after spending a week or two down along the Mississippi coast, hard it was for them to get back into normal, everyday life again. It had been hard for them to let go of the people who have to keep living without electricity, running water or even a permanent shelter; to focus on their jobs back home; to surrender the desire to continue helping; and to process the deep emotions that were welling up inside as they returned to their daily routines.

Several of the volunteers who had spent a week in Mississippi, their bodies exhausted and bones aching from the heavy work, talked about feeling guilty, having left so quickly with barely a mark made in the recovery. Many simply felt a vague disconnection from their coworkers and the daily life that was going on like nothing had ever happened. But I wasn't bothered by any of those thoughts.

When I was at the Warehouse, I had had no problem telling people when there was nothing that I could do for them. Even in the times when I failed to do everything that was humanly possible to do, I had done everything that I was able to do and quickly accepted that God would take care of the rest. Being back in Colorado was no different. I knew that I had done my part. God had asked me to help and I did what I could. Two months had been my term of service, I didn't feel any guilt or give a second thought of going back to Dedeaux, but Sherri had been right about one thing: My heart was tired when I got back to Colorado.

I was suffering from compassion fatigue, only I hadn't needed her to tell me. I knew that my temper had grown short, my tolerance for stupidity and disrespect from people had disappeared. I didn't have much energy to pursue a wedding for Rodney and his fiancé, to gather donations of tents for the thousands of people still living under tree branches and propped-up bed spreads, or to fight to keep some memory of the Warehouse open. I knew that my emotional tank was empty, that I had nothing left to give; that I had gone through so many traumatic experiences in the past two months and seen so many changes in my own life that I couldn't take any more. Even in the times when God touches our lives in extreme spiritual growth, we can only take so much before our bodies and spirits begin to crumble.

I had gone through as much as I could handle. That is why I was so thankful that no one had given me any more money, why during the last week I had been afraid that my mom would call to tell me a check for $100 had come in the mail and I would have to stay down there for a couple more weeks. It's why I was so glad that I had forced myself to accept God's plan, that He knew what was going on better than I did and had known when it would be time for me to leave Mississippi before I had even thought about leaving Colorado. The debilitating, unknown *Compassion Fatigue Syndrome* wasn't a problem for me when I got back to Colorado. Rather, what I did have trouble with was that on the one hand, I had already changed so such much that I felt like I simply didn't fit into my old life. It took me a few weeks to put words to it, but as I explained it to my friends, I was having a difficult time fitting the Post-Katrina Kendall in my Pre-Katrina life. And then, on the other hand, I was also still struggling to figure out just what the past two months had meant to my life. My biggest problem was that I had changed too much and my old life didn't fit anymore.

I have already written about how I was flooded by the desire to get to know who Jesus was, but I couldn't describe any of the friends that I hung out with at the Perk as Christian. Certainly they were all good people, and I considered most of them as living out many *Christian* values, but none of them confessed a belief in Christ as their savior. I had good friends, continued to hang out and play pool just like before, but there was a tremendous hole that they left open. I wanted to use the language of God, I wanted to learn and discover what Jesus had done with His life, to explore the miracles He performed and what they meant for our lives today. In other words, I wanted someone I could talk to whose wisdom and knowledge I could trust, but my old life didn't have that to offer.

There was also a part of me that wanted to cringe every time someone asked me about New Orleans. Part of it, of course, was that I was still tired of New Orleans getting all of the attention, it seemed as though people still forgot that it wasn't the only place hit by Katrina. But the biggest part was that I also felt like I did not know what to say, how to answer such simple questions, like what had happened and what I had been doing for two months. It felt as though whenever the question came up, something different and jumbled would jump out of my mouth. I never could get a handle on the perfect, or even reasonably good, answer to the most important thing that people should know and what I should easily be able to share. I knew that part of what was going on was that I had been down there for two months and everyday either something life changing happened to me or I learned one of those *life lessons*. Two months of life changing experiences easily meant that there was simply too much of a story for me to tell a dozen times over. At least, that's what I though was going on. So I put together a small presentation for my friends to share the pictures and a few more of the stories that wouldn't fit over a cup of coffee. But even then, telling the story of little Ni as her picture came up, the stutter in my head didn't stop. I simply didn't feel comfortable talking about it.

It's not that I was ashamed or wanted to keep quiet out of a golden sense of humility. I was excited about what had happened to me and I had no problem coming up with fascinating stories to share, but everything was twisted and it felt like whenever I talked about it, nothing came out as clear as either I wanted them to, or thought that they should be. It wasn't that I had forgotten or having trouble remembering what had happened, the events and the people I had met rang clearly in my head, I just didn't know what had *really* happened. Rather than going out to look for a job, I found myself sitting on the couch at home playing video games that I didn't even care about for hours on end.

I was troubled over the fact that I had almost no money left, was living mostly on my credit cards, the temp agency I had signed up to work with wasn't coming up with any jobs for me, and, for at least the first few days, I went into a panic. I didn't have time to sit around and go through the normal job channels of waiting three or four weeks before getting an interview and another month before my first paycheck. When I drove by the McDonald's on my way to the dollar theatre I thought, "I've done it before, I could do it again, but not yet."

I was staring at a total financial collapse directly in the face: *Is this what I get for giving up my time and energy, for selflessly giving up my job to go and help those people?* Despite everything I had been through and seen, I began to doubt God, that He would provide for me and make sure that I had everything I needed. It was crystal clear, no job means no money, and no money meant big time trouble. I had been home for about a week and hadn't heard a peep from Nancy at the temp agency about any work when the beige SUV pulled up to the stop light and I was given a quarter for the meter without having to ask for it. A few minutes later was when Doreen loaned me enough money at the bank so I wouldn't have to pay the enormous cash advance fees, again without my asking or even thinking it could happen. God was still making sure that I had everything I needed, and I could see him doing it.

That was the afternoon when I flipped things around. I realized that if I believe God gives us what we need, then it should follow that what we have is exactly what we need. I looked around…what I had was time. The reason why I didn't have enough work through the temp agency, that I wasn't compelled to wake up and hit the job hunting pavement at 6:00 am was that I needed time to figure everything out. To my roommate Adriaan, it surely looked like I was lazily and pathetically wasting my time on the couch. But I could feel invisible shapes spinning in my head. I can't tell you exactly what I was thinking, there were never any clear images that came to mind, except for the one image of that empty apartment, but I could sense that something was going on up in that empty grey.

I needed time to sort through the raw emotions and process all of those life changing experiences and lessons that I learned, much more than one afternoon of walking the streets of Waveland, Mississippi. I needed time to regain a perspective on my own life and what it all meant. I wasn't worried about not working because I was in no condition to begin working yet, and God knew that. I no longer cared that Nancy wasn't calling me with regular work, and when an assignment for one day would come up, I would mentally make a check mark next to one of my upcoming credit card payments; the next day of work would take care of my cell phone and cable bills; and I went on down the line until there was enough money to pay the rest of my bills for the year and get me home for Christmas.

It was an extraordinary freedom that I had found. I was waking up in the morning, content to spend an hour or two cooking breakfast; I no longer needed the TV turned on in the background for noise; my wish list of movies to buy had disappeared to nothing; and sleeping on an air mattress didn't bother me at all any more. I was enjoying a peaceful confidence, enjoying everything that I had because, for the first time in years, I knew where I was going. It wasn't that I felt bigger all around, while walking down the street I could feel the firmness of solid ground beneath my feet and even though I didn't know exactly how I was going to get there, I had the confidence of God that my life meant something. I had a destiny that didn't have to echo with presidential debates or an earth-shattering mission to change the world, just to learn who Jesus Christ was and to serve God.

I have come to understand that one of the reasons why this has been such a difficult part of the book to write is that everything Katrina brought into my life is wound tightly into a ball of twine. Unlike the days that I spent in Louisiana and Mississippi, sorting back through the lessons I learned and the ways that my life has actually been changed can't be organized by simply turning the page on a calendar. I could pick anything I want: the final decision on becoming a priest, spending three months teaching special ed or how I didn't believe my own journal when I went back over my time at the Cajun Dome (I had to call my mom to confirm when I left Missouri because so much had happened that my brain was

317

convinced I spent twice as long at the Cajun Dome as I did.) Anywhere I began took me off in a dozen different directions. But after writing over a hundred pages of notes for this part of the book alone, I found that I would always end up in the same place, which helped me to see the single most important thing that this entire experience has taught me: *By following God, and without meaning too, I found myself.*

Five days from now, as I'm going through some final edits and putting the final touches on the book, it will be exactly two years since Hurricane Katrina hit the Gulf Coast and it continues to be a struggle for me to hang on to the extraordinary changes that I experienced. I've finished my first year of graduate school, reluctantly gave up my hopes of completely leaving politics behind, and just this past week, I reaffirmed my commitment to starting the publishing company I mentioned in the introduction.

I'm discovering that when we come across an experience that shakes up the world we're used to, when God reaches down to touch our lives in such a personal way that we feel like we've become a different person, we have. We're seeing who we truly are and the potential of who we can become. We loose those habits of fear, our worries that draw us to failure and whatever pressures of daily life that continue to hold us back. The challenge, once we've had that glimpse of who we truly are, is in holding on to that person and turning those changes into someone permanent. I've had my days when I feel like a first grader, staring up at the adults hovering around me. I've fallen back into the thoughts of having to organize and create the next big revolutionary idea to change the world, and at times, I have even doubted whether or not God does actually want me to go into ministry of any sort. But I choose to fight through those feelings. I think about who I was before Katrina, what my life was like during those first few months back home in the Springs, and the choices become clear.

Even if I never sell a copy, one of the greatest things about this book has simply been the process of writing it. In taking the time to go back through, reading notes and editing the daily entries, I've reminded myself of some of the extraordinary things that I had already forgotten, like the importance of simply being yourself and being willing to share that person with other people. If we express who we are, challenging ourselves to be transformed into the image of Christ who has been laid out before us, that's when miracles happen and our lives become truly fulfilled…which may just be the entire mystery behind why we were created: To become something more and someone greater than who we are at this moment.

Thank you for your time in reading about my experiences and the impact that Katrina made on my life. I hope that somewhere it has touched your heart and shown you a little more about what faith is, that even in the face of something as bad as having your car break down in the middle of a Kansas on a Saturday night, or as horrible as a hurricane, God always knows what He is doing, and He takes care of those who remain faithful to Him.

From Friends

There has never been a moment when I have even begun the thought that mine was the only story to tell, or even the best one worth telling. It's simply the only one that I know well enough to tell. Yet I do have the good fortune of being able to use my story to share a small part of two others.

The first is from Deacon Art. If you recall, I mentioned in one entry that he had been writing about his experiences for a local newspaper. He has been gracious enough to allow me to include the entire journal for you to enjoy here.

The second is not a journal, or even an entry, but an email from Marlene from Minnesota. She was among the first of the volunteers to arrive in Mississippi and the first person I spoke with once I arrived. She, along with several others, made a trip back to Dedeaux over New Year's Eve. Her letter captures the sense of family and the powerful imprint that Dedeaux left on many of the volunteers who walked through her doors.

Above: Polly (Montana) , Linde (Minnesota), Seattle Bill (Seattle) and Billy Ray (Mississippi).

Below: John, his wife Dawn, father Bernie and I.

Above: Marisella and José from Miami with Tee.

Below: The Miami doctors, Marisella, Brooke and Frank, interview people outside the Warehouse.

Above: The Wawas from New Jersey

Below: One of the houses after they were finished. The Wawas made over a half-dozen trips to Biloxi.

Above: Alex and other students from the University of Dayton clear out Mimi's house.

Below: Mary Ann babysits while mom shops at the Warehouse.

Deacon Art

Katrina Support Report

Deacon Arthur Miller
Bay St. Louis, Mississippi

I Flew into Mobile Alabama at 12:10 Central time, rented a car and drove to the retreat center in Pass Christian, Ms. I will be staying at the retreat center at Sacred Heart of Mary Church. It is the Retreat center for the Archdiocese of Biloxi. The name of the place is the Dedeaux retreat center. I was greeted by Steve Sterling, a young man from Catholic Charities of Seattle. They are assisting the national office, trying to coordinate volunteers both locally and nationally. I will be working at Bay St Louis at St Rose De Lima with Fr. Sebastian and Deacon Tom Mack. Tonight there is a mass, after which, there will be time for reflection; it seems that some of the volunteers are in need of it. Most of those who have come are staying for several weeks. The need is great. I started to see up-rooted trees and tumbled down signs 70 miles from here and I am not even close to where the real horror is. As I got off route 10, the main highway I turned towards the place I'd be staying. Driving off the highway I could see how violently the winds had blown. There were few if any homes that had not been at least partially destroyed. Most every roof was covered in heavy bright blue tarp, which protected the inside from any additional damage. I kept reminding myself that it had been seven weeks since the storm. Century old trees lie around like mere sticks tossed by some great malevolent giant who'd thrown a tantrum. At the retreat center couples who had come from all over the country welcomed me. One couple Art and Polly had driven down two weeks earlier from Montana, he was the cook, and she was his assistant. Though they were not married their friendship had been formed by the years. Art spoke often of his wife Grace; the greatest sacrifice for him was being separated from her. They worked busily, preparing food for the volunteers who have come and gone. They remained like wizened parents caring for returning children, listening to each story. Another couple, who were married, Ron and Marianne, clucked around helping and preparing things, they too had been here for several weeks. They worked well together a slight smile or glance reflected their love. I have often noticed the bond that is formed in the middle of great and difficult tasks is quite often a permanent one. The shared experience is compelling and defined in time.

This evening Thursday Oct 20th, I drove into the outskirts of the most devastated region, even in the failing day's light one could see the destruction. As I guided the rented car deeper into the area, the true ferociousness of the storm began to reveal itself. Cars, suv's, and pick-up trucks were strewn about, some on their backs, some on their sides, lined the highway. Massive trailer trucks faired no better; they too felt the storms mighty wrath. Like dieing dinosaurs, they lay curled in miss-shapen forms. Having pulled their last loads they waited for the tow trucks that would take them away. The sides of the road accepted the discarded vehicles along with other debris thrown there by the winds of the hurricane

I approached a makeshift camp where the doctors I was to pick up waited. Lights glowed from tents erected to protect the people from rain and wind. Hundreds of the survivors of the devastating hurricane were gathered. They sat eating and talking at tables set about in rows under the tent. An air of jubilance sprung up from the surrounding misery. I heard guitar music and a lilting Spanish song, fill the air. The people turned and watched and listened. With the little Spanish I knew I deciphered the words of the song.

"Oh Lord, your children are here waiting
and wandering in your love,
hoping and praying that soon you will come.
Oh Lord, oh Lord, oh Lord."

I don't know if that is the exact translation, I kind of hope it is.... ..

When the song was done the guitar player smiled at the lady seated next to him. They turned and spotted Steve, with whom I had traveled, they were two of the doctors I had driven to get. There were six of them; they had volunteered their time to help. Four were students at University of Miami and were young, that is good, it is good for them to see, to experience this. For this is a life changing event, all the good of human beings, all the bad of human beings is magnified here. They are part of the good. The tent that was erected and this place in the midst of the destruction were initially set up by three friends who just came to help. I heard they arrived one week after the hurricane struck. It was said that they have fed 5000 people a day. The need is great; the volunteers' work is good.

327

After quick introductions, the young doctors piled into our cars and we headed back to the retreat center where they are staying. The conversation was lively as they disgorged their day's experiences. I was amazed at their earnest vitality and am encouraged by their youthful zeal. Upon our return the table was set and all ate ferociously as if food could erase some of the destruction that was seen. After a bit of talk and reflection all went to bed and slept well.

I called Sandy, several times today, I needed to hear her voice, I needed her to hear mine. Tomorrow will come in a few hours and I will get about the work.

1st Full Day, October 21st

Morning came early as I was awakened by the sound of loud snoring. A fellow worker gurgled and snorted most of the night.....come morning he was still at it. I yawned and decided to get up, there wasn't any possibility of getting anymore sleep. I quickly washed up and returned to my bunk, which is in a large room with 14 other beds half of which were filled. People had arrived from all over the country. Washington, North Dakota, Colorado, North Carolina, Florida,...everywhere. The need is great and many are responding. After a hasty breakfast and a sparkling conversation with Ron from Arizona and Art from Montana I was off to my assignment. I would be working with Deacon Tom and since he had arrived a few days earlier we decided that he should drive to Bay St. Louis, Miss. We took the same route I had driven the evening before. My fears were substantiated. The darkness of the night had truly veiled the damage. No words have been created that could truly describe what I witnessed, and this is seven weeks after the storm.

Boats in trees, boats in trees, there were boats in trees. It was as if some malevolent giant mocked Christmas by hanging boats in trees. Garland of clothing and tinsel of shredded roofs adorned broken trees. And there were broken trees everywhere laying one atop the other. Buildings were crumbled and torn, devastation as far as the eye could see and the mind was willing to travel, and this is seven weeks after the storm. Slowly we drove the few miles into the city of Bay St. Louis, Mississippi. I am glad we traveled slowly because it gave me time to adjust to the destruction. After dodging debris that was still in the streets we made it to our destination, St Rose de Lima Catholic Church.

We were greeted by Marilyn, a parishioner at the Church. She was the person that was to give us our assignment for today. I was relieved when I realized her richness of spirit, the depth of faith and joy exuded from her smile to her gentleness. She was a strong black woman. I was also introduced to other women of the church, Beverly, Cheri, Clementine (a Delta sister), and others. All of whom were apparently healing from their experience. The building that I met them in had been an elementary school. It had been closed for a while. But because it was large they had converted it into a warehouse. Clothing and food had been stacked everywhere. I learned that this community had begun organizing and gathering as much as they could to serve those in their parish. No concern was given to any needy person's faith, but only to their need. I was impressed but also embarrassed. I too, had come with self-imposed prejudices; I who had come from Connecticut, the richest state to Mississippi the poorest state and to a community that appeared to be just as poor. Oh, but how rich they are, much richer than I. The question came to me: How would I fare, how would my family and my community fare given such devastation? I couldn't answer those questions honestly. I'd like to think I and my family and community would have the same strength of character the same rich spirit to get through such a disaster. I'd like to think we could, but I don't know, and God forgive me, I hope I never have to find out.

Soon after meeting the lady's of the church Tom and I were given our assignment. We were given the job of tearing down a shed for one of the people in the community. His name was Mr. Adrian and lived only a few blocks from the church. Since it was close Tom and I along with Marilyn walked to the house. What we discovered was a large structure that had been toppled over by the hurricane. It was not a shed as I had imagined but a small house. I later learned it was built by Mr. Adrian's father. Now Mr. Adrian was 80 years old and it was there long before he was born. So the shed must have been at least 85 years old.

Mr. Adrian was living in a trailer that was on the side of his house, it had been given to him by FEMA as temporary shelter until his home could be repaired. The shed we were to demolish was behind the trailer. It sat on a concrete foundation. The building, originally stood approximately 12 to 14 feet high, but after the storm one of the walls had been blown out and the roof had collapsed. What was left was a huge pile of rubble that stood 10 feet high. We were to remove the rubble and place it at the front of the lot for the city workers to collect.

Before leaving the church/warehouse we gathered tools for the job, crowbars, shovels, hammers, and a wheelbarrow. The morning was warm and a stream of sweat had already begun to run down my back as we bent to the task. I hoped I was up for it. At 60 years old, over-weight and out of shape, truly the Lord was going to have to work hard today.

In the middle of my doubts, we started. It didn't take long for us to discover it was dangerous work. Splintery wood and glass was everywhere. The old wood carried termites, wasps, lizards and rusty nails. We continued to rip and tear at the old building scraping and pulling at the dieing yet not quit dead structure, it resisted us mightily. While dragging a large old blank of wood to the pile, which lay 30 feet from the building, I noticed blood streaming from Tom's leg. He had ripped it open on an old nail. He continued to work for a while, trying to overcome the pain, but it wouldn't stop bleeding so he went to the medical tent and was sent to the hospital for stitches.

I stayed at the work sight and along with Terry Ross another volunteer who lived in the area; we continued the slow task of bringing down the shed. We worked diligently in the growing heat of the morning sun. We didn't talk much, saving our breath for the work. Fortunately another volunteer from the area, Bill McIntyre arrived and we worked together, three old men, tearing at the unrelenting shed. Often we stopped for water, the sun was hot and the need to replenish fluids became necessary. But, the shed slowly, steadily fell under the unyielding pressure of chain saw and crowbar. We, the three of us, struck hard at the building and the pile of rubble grew smaller, while the growing pile in front grew higher. The people, who were to remove the destroyed and dismantled building, too would have a mighty task. But that would be their concern, this one was ours.

Around 12:00 noon, we took a break from the noonday sun and made our way to one of the many feeding stations that churches had set up to feed the hungry. And we were hungry. We ate, with little talk; I hadn't realized how hungry I was.

After only a half hour lunch break we returned to the task, hungry to finish the work. Unrelentingly we struck at the building. Hour after hour we tore at it, ripped at it. Focused our strength at that old building, then at around 3 o'clock we saw the concrete floor on which the structure had rested. That gave us even greater emphasis too complete the dismantling of the old building. It was then that Tom returned, the walking wounded, and he joined us as we swept away the century old building. The dreams of the builder lay along with the building at the side of the road. I did not know the stories that old building held, but I have a story on how it was removed. We spoke with the old gentleman who owned the place, he thanked us and said good bye. He was truly grateful as were we to have been able to help. The volunteers that joined us left for their homes and Tom and I returned to the church. I checked on the medical team to see how they were doing and if they needed anything. They assured me all was well and the room where they had set up their clinic had been busy and they were satisfied with their work.. I am happy for that, they should be pleased, they have done good work.

I walked over to the office where I was greeted by the Priest, Fr Sebastian, he asked if we would assist at masses the next couple days. Tom and I were quick to agree. Tom would be preaching on Saturday and I on Sunday. I spoke with Marilyn and she told me where they needed help the next day. The list of those in need is long, very long. I kept reminding myself, it had been seven weeks since the storm.

Tom and I climbed back into his car and returned to the retreat center. My mind stayed on the warm shower that I relished and certainly needed. As usual the gang was there. I felt like a returning conqueror from a mighty battle. Art and Polly, Ron and Marianne greeted us like concerned parents. I felt loved and appreciated. Kendal, a young man from Colorado was there as well. He's considering the priesthood and I hope he does because he would be very good at it. He has been here for weeks, mainly running a distribution center.

After a little conversation I took a gloriously long shower then I ate a grateful dinner. Renee Hudson a volunteer from Philadelphia gave me a Tastycake for desert. May God bless her generous soul. I then lay down for a nap. God, did I need a nap.

I was awakened after a good sleep by new volunteers arriving for the weekend, college students. Good, we need strong backs, and God needs the young to replenish His old flock. I fumbled for my cell-phone to see the time. I had slept for 2 hours. It was 8:45 Friday evening. I got up from my bunk and wandered into the kitchen and met the new arrivals. They were from the pan-handle of Florida and were led there by Fr. John Licari, an Italian priest originally from Long Island. He was a delightful man. The students were sparkling. I spoke with them and was pleased at their spirit and eagerness. Sarah, Bernadette, Mary, Ian, John, and Matt, a tidy group had arrived to do God's work. We all spoke and laughed together for a while bound by a mutual respect for the conviction and faith that brought us together. Jenny Hess was another worker I had seen but had not met. A hard working young lady who had considered the religious life but had discerned God had called her to marriage and family. Whichever she chose I felt she would be very successful. I pray that God lead her to find His will for her.

After a while I grew tired again, taking time however for prayer and thoughts of home. There are times in your life when you become acutely aware of God's presence. Maybe that is what drew me here.

I know God lives and his spirit is immortal because I have seen His Spirit arisen in the people here.

I went to bed tired because the work was hard, but it is the hard part that made it good work......... Good night.

2nd Full Day, October 22nd

Awakened by Art of Montana's morning song, I lay in my bunk. The early morning sun peeked into the large room where we slept. It was going to be a good day, translated that means a hard working day, and that's good. I waited a full 15 minutes as those who slept in the room scurried about to get ready for the work. After washing up I met with Tom Mack and Fr. John and said morning prayers, it was restful and filling. I am touched by Fr. John's youthful exuberance, the morning prayers were filled with his joyful halleluiahs. At breakfast Steve Sterling, the Catholic Charities coordinator, announced the Dawn Debrau was returning home. She has been here 22 days. Working hard and giving of herself. May God bless her generous soul and grant her safe passage home. After breakfast Brendan Lynch 22 and I drove back to Bay St. Louis to begin the days work.

Again we were greeted by a smiling Marilyn, already at work. She gave us our assignment and we left.

The owner of the house where we were to work was Donna, a woman I had met the day before. We were to remove wall-board from a shed in back of the home. Just an aside, I have noticed down here when they say shed they mean small house. This shed was air-conditioned, for crying out loud, and was 15ft by 15 ft. This was going to be a long day.

She however, had not removed the contents of the shed so we were unable to remove the wall-board today. There were other tasks to be done however. She needed debris removed from her backyard and taken to the front curb so the work crews could cart it away. Her yard was large with trees blown down everywhere. Fortunately Donna had a small pick-up truck which we used to transport all the broken branches and limbs to the front curb. Brendan was of great help. Young and strong and quiet, typical for his age, like my own son he responded monosyllabically. "So Brendan, why did you decide to come to help in the relief effort?" Brendan: "Saw they needed it." .... "Well, that was certainly nice of you." Brendan: "Yea." ....."Were you in school before you came down?" Brendan: "Graduated already"....... "I see. Where did you go to school?" Brendan: "Notre Dame."

The conversation dragged on until I decided to turn my efforts to the work at hand. The day was cool and that made it easier. We lifted branches large and small into the bed of the truck. I then drove it to the front curb where we piled them. After several trips the pile began to grow and that was when Donna came out to help. She was a delightful woman. I know there is hope here because I saw it in the eyes and determination of this incredible woman. She worked along with us raking and gathering branches, some small, some large and the pile on the curb grew. Eventually most of the smaller limbs and branches were moved and the only thing remaining was large pieces of wood. Evidently someone had cut the downed trees into two to four foot long logs. These we would have to get into the bed of the truck and then unload and pile them at the curb. The smallest of these logs must have weighed 125 lbs. Thank goodness Brendan was young and Donna was strong, I however felt old and weak, but the Holy Spirit gave me energy and I was able to assist them. After several hours of hauling and dragging the lot was cleared. We raked up great piles of leaves and small twigs and put them into bags and carted them to the curb as well. Donna was grateful as have been all the people here. They are an inspiration of will and determination. I am a more humble and thankful person because of the richness of the people I have met here. I now understand what Christ meant when he said "Blessed are the meek for they shall inherit the earth. Donna is a meek yet very strong and wonderful woman. She and others like her deserve to inherit the earth. I only hope there is enough left of it.

Brendan and I returned to St. Rose de Lima, and informed Marilyn that we would return on Sunday to finish the work at Donna's house. When driving back to the retreat center we decided to eat and found a Burger King. We ate hungrily, like those who have been without food for weeks. The hot meal tasted wonderful. Surprisingly Brendan spoke about his reasons for coming and about school. I think it was Donna, her infectious spirit got to both of us. I learned he had graduated in May, 2005 and has been looking for work but was drawn to the area to fulfill a personal calling to be about the work of God. I listened as he spoke softly of his church and his faith. I thought about my own family back in Connecticut hoping all was well with them.

Just before going to bed Renee, of Tastycake generosity, asked if I'd like to see her daughter's violin recital. How could I resist, even now I needed to see something of normalcy and not, not recovery from….. Most of us gathered around a small TV set up in the large gathering room and applauded grandly to the 5 year-old little girl's rendition of Twinkle-Twinkle Little Star. Renee had just received it in the mail from Philly, she has been separated from her family for the last 3 weeks. She leaves in a few days for home. Her little girl and husband must miss her tremendously.

I spoke to AJ Chan one of the young medical students who arrived from Miami and discovered he was a resident at U of Miami hospital. He was from Washington State and had completed medical school at Morehouse College in Atlanta University. His specialty was pediatrics and his wish was to work in clinics in urban centers. He had already traveled to Africa and South America in his personal efforts to heal the neediest of God's children. This young man represents the best of America. God Bless him and his work.

337

Talked to my daughter back at home, she is burdened. We promised to talk when I get back home, after all I am still Daddy. It was another good day, good night all.

3rd Full Day, October 23rd

The alarm in my cell phone beeped at 5:30 am Sunday morning, I was already awake and had been for 20 minutes. I was to preach at the 7:00am Mass this morning and I was pleased and blessed to do so. After fussing around for 10 minutes or so I walked into the kitchen to find something to eat. I was greeted by a yawning Art from Montana, up already, preparing for breakfast. After a brief chat and a bowl of raisin bran I stepped out into the cool Mississippi morning. It was still pitch dark outside. For some reason I was unnerved by the depth of the blackness. I ignored the feeling of dread that slowly crawled up my spine and walked to the car. After carefully placing my freshly written homily and borrowed alb and stole onto the back seat, I drove into the darkness. The Dedeaux retreat center is down a two-lane paved road 10 miles from Route 10, it is on what I would call an out–of–the–way, country road. I peered through the front window and into the darkness trying to find the left turn I was to make about 5 miles from the center. But somehow I missed it. I drove further into the dark morning, praying for the rising sun, so that I could find my way. I was also anxious because I certainly did not want to be late for mass, I was going to assist and give the homily for crying out loud.

I drove on hoping to find some kind of land mark, but I was unable to see anything, except shadows of misshapen forms that ghoulishly reflected the moons yellow shine. I looked into the rearview mirror, my eyes had played tricks on me, or maybe it was my growing fear, but there really wasn't an old car barreling towards me in the Mississippi darkness. It was at this moment the thoughts of Billy Holliday's song Strange Fruit, came to my mind. Thoughts of black men, women and children lynched by the white terrorist group the KKK muscled its way into my consciousness. I was a childhood friend of Emmett Till; he had been murdered not more than 100 miles from where I was. An undeniable terror crept into my bones, I was truly afraid. That was when I came to a dead end. I very, very quickly turned around not wanting to stop, knowing I wouldn't stop for anything or anyone. May God forgive me, but if anyone had stepped into the pathway of that car, on that night, I would have certainly run them over.

I frantically searched for the turnoff that I had missed. I was searching for it, praying for it, and finally slowing down from 70 miles per hour on that dark desolate morning I found it. Thank Almighty God, I found it.

I guided the rented car onto the welcoming road then quickly found the highway that led to Bay St. Louis, Miss. I exhaled fully, not realizing I had been holding my breath. After a short twenty-minute drive I parked the car in front of St. Rose de Lima Catholic Church. As I did so, the morning sun began to rise, and a sliver of light broke the darkness.

I walked to the church and into the welcoming light that streamed through the open doors. People greeted me kindly. I smiled at each of them and said hello. Strangely I had not looked into the church and walked nearly to the middle of it when I noticed something remarkable. On the back wall, behind the altar, a mural had been beautifully painted. The mural was about 15 feet by 20 feet. The back wall was shaped such that the sides reached around the altar in a semi-circle. What was painted was a huge oak tree and painted on the tree was a rising Jesus, his arms outstretched, his head enwrapped in a holy light. It was breath-taking. It was peaceful and serene, and people were on their knees praying, not to the mural, nor to the beautifully painted picture of Jesus, but they were praying in the peace and serenity the picture helped create. This church, St Rose de Lima, was built in 1926 by African American Catholics because they were not welcomed into the white Catholic churches. This is an unfortunate truth, a hideous scar that uglies our

340

church, but it is true. This is of import, because after driving fearfully through the Mississippi darkness I arrived at a historically African American Catholic church and on the mural was a rising Jesus Christ painted beautifully as a black man. Half of the people on their knees peacefully praying were white. I stood quietly, the many messages of God pouring through me, it was overwhelming. I knelt and prayed and cried. I thanked God for getting me here.

Father Sebastian arrived and guided me to the sacristy where I quickly vested. Then hurried to the entrance of the church and waited for the procession to begin. The mass started and ended in a blur. My homily was received with thankful nods by the 70 or so attendees, not bad for a 7:00 am service.

Father Sebastian ushered me over to his rectory where I was able to eat. The person that made my breakfast was Donna, the wonderful woman whose house Brendan and I had worked on the day before. She had hurried over this morning to hear my homily and encourage me. What a delightfully sweet lady she is.

The next mass started at 9:00 am, it was a gospel mass and the people rejoiced. The choir was great, the homilist was great, and God was praised, God was praised fully.

After mass, the church's Katrina recovery team had a meeting. Fr. Sebastian asked me to stay for the meeting. I agreed, reluctantly, because I had planned on driving the medical team to Biloxi. They had attended mass at St Rose de Lima which pleased me because I would have the chance to say good bye to them. I knew they were going to work that morning and then would head back to Miami. We had become good friends and I was relishing the drive. I was also relishing the opportunity to be in their company. All of them are extraordinary people and I ask God to protect them. But the meeting was more important so we said our goodbyes and they headed off to their futures and I returned to my present.

The meeting was remarkable because St Rose had developed a plan by which they could help their community. They had organized themselves and their community so that it was possible for them to direct volunteers and services to the neediest in the community. It did not matter the religion, each person in their community that needed help or services could find it here. Organizations had come to St. Rose using its structure to direct services to the appropriate people. I was amazed how they worked so well together. There was little if any wasted energy, everything was coordinated through teams that had been designated to direct information and services. If a person needed clothing they would find it. If they needed to find counseling on FEMA forms or local government access it was in place. This church should be studied and replicated. This church, situated in a community that is not wealthy, is enormously rich.

After the meeting I headed back to the Dedeaux retreat center, I had forgotten my work clothes this morning and needed them to finish the work at Donna's house. When I returned to Donna's house Brendan had already gotten their and the two of them had finished most of the work.

I pitched in quickly feeling guilty. The wallboard in her shed had to be removed because it had gotten wet in the flood brought by the hurricane. For some inane reason her shed was not covered by her insurance, nor any government program. That angered me. This woman, who was the spirit of determination, was going to have to figure out how she was going to have her shed repaired. Damn it, an unnoticed infraction on a not rich single woman, who stood up against the ferocity of this tragic storm, must absorb one more disappointment. Damn it. Damn it to hell. Forgive me Lord.

After carting everything to the curb, Brendan and I left. I hugged Donna goodbye. I pray there is someway her shed can be replaced without her paying for it. She has little money.

I returned to the Dedeaux retreat center and lay down. Even though it was early in the day, about 3:30 pm, I was exhausted and fell asleep. It was good.

Late in the evening Steve wanted to talk about organizing skilled services. This is what is desperately needed. Even Fr. Sebastian mentioned it. I am unskilled, a laborer. What is needed are skilled people, electricians, and carpenters, and plumbers. Somehow there has to be an organized way for skilled volunteers to get here in shifts so the much needed help can be given.

I will send a request to those of you who wish to help. Please send this report around the country. E-mail it everywhere. People like Donna, places like Bay St. Louis, Mississippi, Churches like St. Rose de Lima need you. Contact the numbers I will send and come here. You will be amazed at the resurrection that is happening.

Good night for now.

4th full Day, October 24th

I didn't sleep as well last night as I had before. It certainly wasn't because I wasn't exhausted, because I surely was. I believe it is because I miss my family so very much. I speak to them often….its not that…I believe it is because of what I've witnessed here…the destruction……the terrible destruction. Talking to Sandy, my beloved wife brings me a saneness I need. Today was the worse day.

I drove to St. Rose de Lima Church in Bay St. Louis and was assigned to a home in Waveland, Mississippi. It is a small town situated right on the shore of St. Louis Bay. The destruction was massive. 12-15 foot storm serge had come in and destroyed nearly everything in its path. Houses were literally moved off their foundations. Today is the eight week anniversary of the hurricane and the residents were only recently allowed into the area. What massive, massive destruction. It is necessary to understand that the buildings constructed here have no basements because of the high water table. As a consequence most sit on a shallow foundation, essentially a concrete slap that the buildings are bolted too. Paul Bunion would not have had bolts big enough to stop the buildings from being thrown about by the serge from this storm. The only way I have to describe it is to imagine a colossal child having a tantrum, throwing monopoly pieces up in the air and the pieces falling haphazardly where they may. It is sheer and massive destruction.

This area has homes that are close together, real estate value is better here on the shore of the bay. Consequently the houses are more expensive. I noticed we had to cross railroad tracks to get here. The tracks separate the two towns, a tiny physical barrier that divides them. Strangely the railroad tracks, which have a very high road bed, protected Bay St. Louis from the storm serge. The train tracks, the physical barrier between the two towns, one monetarily

344

richer than the other, protected the poorer from the richer. The church in Bay St. Louis had sent us here, because some of their parishioners lived here too.

When Tom Mack and I arrived at the house with the owner in the car, (we had picked him up at St. Rose de Lima) we hid our dismay. It was better for us not to show how horrified we were. The healing process for the people here has been underway for a while now. They do not need any whimpering do-gooders to prop up. They need all of their strength to deal with the destruction that is here. The truth is we, the volunteers as well meaning and generous as we all are, are just visitors. We, all of us, are going back home eventually where everything is sane and normal. The people here must deal with this, this literal upheaval, this massive, horrible upheaval, where all has been lost. In some cases even hope.

The owner of this house Ted Jankins, is eighty-five years old and a formal pilot in world war II. His home had been beautiful until the storm drowned it. He had taken refuge from the storm in Dallas where he had spent most of his working life. He was stoic and genteel. I liked him; he spoke softly of having met some Tuskegee Airmen. I smiled inwardly, I hadn't asked about that. I suppose it made him feel comfortable, it didn't matter, I was here to help.

When we entered the house it was clear Tom and I were in for a long day's work. Ted and his family, that being his daughter and her husband, had just started trying to salvage what they could. It was a near impossible job to find anything remotely close to being salvageable. I looked up along the wall and could see a water line about 12 feet up on the wall of the two story foyer. There had been 12 feet of sea water in the house. It hadn't lasted long; they said the water had receded in 24 hours. But in that one 24 hour span it had destroyed a lifetime of dreams and a family's memories. That is what was destroyed, a generations fond memories of their ancestors.

Tom and I tried to be gentle, but when you're a novice at home dismantling, gentle ain't a part of it. We were able to rip out a rug that was still muddy and wet from the hurricane; it smelled terribly. But when we began striking at the walls, with our huge crowbars there was a wincing evident in the old man that was physical and probably mental. He went on the front porch and wept, I did too. It is very sad. There we were an old man of the South, and a not yet old man from the North, one black, one white. The common thing between us was the tragedy he had endured, and I could only try to comfort him. I don't know if he had ever harbored racial prejudices in his life, I imagine so, but on this day he needed me, a black man to hold on to. I pray that he will be healed from his broken heart.

After a while, they asked us to stop, for there were things that they felt might be salvageable, that we might break. Tom and I decided that we should return tomorrow, after they had had a chance to go through the house. We would then return to continue our work.

Tom and I met Brendan, the young Notre Dame graduate from Holy Trinity Church in Washington D.C. at the food tent set up by a church that feeds those who are hungry. We sat with displaced residents and other volunteers who had been brought together by the storm. It is interesting to look around and see the people who have come. Every sort of people are here, from every place. It is inspiring; I wish more could come to see this. Tragedy has brought us together; too bad prosperity drives us apart.

After a quick bite, the three of us went to the home in Bay St. Louis to finish the house Brendan was working on. We were to gut the house, removing the wallboard and the ceilings as well as any insulation.

We began ripping and tearing away at the walls and ceilings, it was difficult. The crowbars we use weigh ten pounds, lifting it up and swinging at the walls in the Mississippi heat is draining. But little by little the house gave up its innards and the pile of broken pieces we placed on the curb grew. After 4 hours of back-breaking work we finished. We swept the house clean; we were done for the day, thank God.

We returned to the retreat house where a hot shower and a cold drink awaited us.

The shower was wonderful, ab-so-lute-ly wonderful. I am sore, in muscles that have long been dormant. The heaviest thing I have picked up in the last few years had been a pen. But I don't mind the soreness the soreness is good.

The crew of volunteers played poker tonight, using M&M's as chips. It was hilarious and needed and grand and wonderful. We laughed heartily together. I am so proud of them. We few, we special few, are brothers and sisters........

I am tired I have neither the time nor the energy to reread this.....To bed, for I am exhausted. Good night...Good night Sandy, I love you. Kiss the kids for me.

5th Full day, October 25th

Today, three things happened, no four things. 1st I am exhausted to my bones, period, 2nd Rosa Parks died, 3rd I almost got killed in a tree-cutting incident, and 4th, several of the volunteers are leaving.

1st the work continues, there is no difference today than it was yesterday. Yet another   home to be salvaged one way or the other. This requires much physical and mental strength, which I do not have in great abundance. However something happened that, shall we say, lightened the moment.

Which brings me to the 3rd point, I almost was killed. We had gone to Bay St. Louis this morning, they being, Deacon Tom Mack, Brendan Lynch, the usual crew of rippers and tearers, extradenaire. There we were joined by three others, Jenny Hess from N. Dakota, Mel Wrubel form Tampa Bay, and Kendall from Colorado. We gathered to cleanup a yard that still had downed trees, some leaning against the house and others in the yard with huge branches hanging from them. Since I have used a chainsaw frequently at home I was designated as the cutter of logs while the others toted and lifted the cut and broken wood to the front of the house where it would be collected and taken away. With six of us the work progressed nicely. Within two hours, and two chain saws, (one quit in exhaustion so we got another) we had cleared most of the debris. There was a huge branch hanging in a tree, however. The branch must have weighed 2000 pounds at least, but it was stuck high in the tree maybe 20 feet up. We were in luck because the owner of the house showed up in his truck and decided to tie a strong cord around it and jerk it out using the truck. That was when any reasonable person would have immediately left. We however not being particularly reasonable wanted to see the job completed, so we stood around and watched. I stood by myself in a place I felt was safe and out of harms way. WRONG! No sooner had I stationed myself in the safe spot when the owner took off in his truck and the huge branch came fly out of the tree and straight at me! Gawd, please understand I am old, sore, out of shape, slow, exhausted, etc. etc. But Jesse Owens, Michael Johnson, whoever in the world you think may be fast, would not, could not, it was an impossibility to have run any faster than I did getting the heck out of the way of that flying 2000 pound branch. I ran so fast that I got to the tree- pulling truck just as it stopped and ran into it and put a huge dent into the side of it, and Brendan videoed the whole stupid thing.

After my heart stopped racing we watched it all on his small digital camera. It was honestly funny as can be. We laughed grandly, and that was good. It was good to be alive, thank you Jesus!

Today a reporter friend of mine called on my cell phone, he told me of Rosa Park's death and wondered about my feelings. The reporter knew of the book I had written on Emmett Till's death, The Journey to Chatham, and wondered whether Emmett's Mom was overlooked in the struggle for civil rights. I assured him that her courageous response to the murder of her son was, in my opinion, of great significance to the movement. I believe her action precipitated Rosa Park's act. Additionally he was aware of this journal and evidently it is being spread around the country. I certainly hope so. If this journal can inspire others to act, and help the communities that have been so devastated by hurricane Katrina, than my efforts will be multiplied. And that would be good.

After the phone call, I went to lunch at the free food tent. As I waited in line two young women, Amanda and Emily recognized me from church. They were at St. Rose de Lima's church during my homily and were touched and thanked me for inspiring them. I was a little embarrassed but was thankful they were helped by what I hope God had directed me to say.

Lunch came and went and the new bigger crew traveled to our new assignment. It was in Waveland, Mississippi. The house was in horrible shape. Again we began ripping and tearing gutting the house. The owner had not moved everything out, which allowed us to see her cherished belongings that had been destroyed, a coo-coo-clock, small figurines and pictures. Very old pictures of little children and sand castles, marriages and picnics, disintegrating in the muck that was Katrina, memories of lives, now lost. Horrible, absolutely horrible.

Brendan leaves in the morning, as will Renee, they are such nice people, I'll miss them, Renee for her humor and smile and Tastycakes, Brendan for his blessed youthfulness and commitment to the Church. They will be missed here amongst the crew.

In time, our emotions held at bay, we finished our deadly work. We removed all traces of memories from the house and piled them in front....... for the trash-man.

This process is very difficult, both mentally and physically. I knew of the physical weariness, because even my bones hurt. The emotional part is a little more difficult, but I will heal, the moment I am in the embrace of my wife and family, I will be healed.

I will sleep tonight. I hope I don't dream. Again I'm sorry for bad spelling and punctuation. I'm going to bed.

6th and Last Full Day, October 27th

Woke up early, happy I would be going home tomorrow. This has been an extraordinary experience. However before I got ahead of myself, I had to remember there was work to be done today. I don't want to get sloppy and hurt myself or someone else.

This morning Kendall, the young man considering priesthood needed to talk. Evidently, the Director of Catholic Charities for this area decided to close a distribution center in East Biloxi. They decided to do this because she felt the people in the community were able to, and needed to begin to take control of their lives. She felt it was important for them to begin to figure out a way to start their lives again without depending on the free food and clothing offered them at the center. Kendall was in complete disagreement with this decision and confronted the director about it. As a result she felt he was burnt out. Meaning he was unable to allow those dependent on the donated items, to claim their own independence. That he was, in effect enabling them rather than allowing them to be self-reliant. I don't know, I am torn because Ken is a really kind and caring young man. He has however, been here three weeks and prior to this he was in New Orleans for two-three weeks. Maybe he is burnt out, I don't know. Unfortunately it wasn't handled well and Ken's feelings were hurt. Nonetheless it was time for him to go home to Colorado, to heal.

After our talk he appeared to be more at ease and welcomed the return home. He promised to be at the retreat center tonight for the good-byes and farewells that are offered to the volunteers. I felt certain I would see him, so I drove to my assigned workplace in East Biloxi, Mississippi.

I met the crew at the now closing distribution center; the place we were going was very close. We gathered tools, threw them onto wheelbarrows and walked over to the home we were to gut.

This area of Biloxi had been hit by a 12 foot storm serge. This house had been partially submerged in the filthy seawater for 12 hours. I could see the water mark near the ceiling. Someone had already moved the ruined belongings from the interior of the house. I have found for several reasons I prefer that. First because there is room to work and we don't waste time moving things out of the house, but secondly the private belongings make it very difficult. It is strange but I don't want to see the precious memories that were destroyed by the storm. It makes the work easier. At around 9:00 am I began my last day.

At noon a group of men arrived from Pensacola Florida. They were new at this. They started off as we did, gingerly trying to dismantle the insides of the house. A feeling of desecration comes over you when you start wielding a heavy crowbar at someone else's home. But in time they caught on and the gutting began in earnest. With eight men concentrating and working together at this grisly task the house gave up and we finished the dismantling. I wielded the last strike of the crowbar before 3:00 pm on Wednesday October 27, 2005 and I was spent.

I, may God forgive me, quickly returned to my car, I didn't help gather the tools, I just couldn't. I simply went to my car and drove to the retreat center, and took a shower, a very long hot shower. It was good and I was relieved. I was relieved that I didn't get hurt nor did I hurt anyone..........well... I did hit a plank of wood that hit one of the new guys in the head, but it didn't draw blood so......well.....he was new, so I told him

"Welcome!"

At dinner tonight they hosted Steve and I. It is a wonderful way of thanking those who have given time for this tremendous effort. What I have also found interesting is that after one day of cleaning up, or working in one of the distribution centers, or cooking in the retreat center, you are a veteran. It only takes one single day to be effected by what is happening here..

I went to bed and slept well, I awoke at 3:55am early enough to drive to Mobile, Alabama which was 100 miles away. My flight was at 7:30am. I was able to wash up quietly and get to my car without awakening anyone. The goodbyes last night were difficult enough; I really didn't want to repeat them.

The volunteers I met in Mississippi are incredible people ....I thank them, for the unbelievable strength and self-sacrificing way they have ministered to the people of God. May God bless them. I will miss them.

The end of this report was written on the plane home. I can't wait to see Sandy and my family. Many thoughts go through my mind. Most of all, there is a resurrection happening amongst the people in the gulf region. I was blessed to experience only a small part of it. I thank god for the blessings and opportunities He's given me to give witness. I know my Savior lives. He lives in the battered and broken lives of people who are being resurrected.

EPILOG

I know that we have helped people because they would not have been able to pay for the work we do, few had flood insurance. It will be of even greater importance to have their homes cleaned. Fortunately after we leave more volunteers come in to power wash and clean the interior structures of the homes we have gutted. From what I was told the cleaning crews will thoroughly clean every inch of the houses. The exposed wood must be perfectly clean or mode and other disease carrying fungi will grow. The hope is, after the cleaning, other agencies will come in and help rebuild the homes. I surely hope so.

I am unable to explain the transformation that has happened to me. I can say that I am more grounded, more in love with my family, my neighbor, and my God. I have a greater faith than I could have imagined. Even in the face of such devastation, or maybe because of it, I have found a deep calmness.

If I might, please allow me this little piece of advice before I say Good Night; kiss your families tonight, tell them you love them, even the one(s) that are not so loveable. Kiss them, and then learn to love again, it's worth it, and the stuff you've been carefully holding onto, those things, they're not.

Good Night.

Deacon Art Miller
Office for Black Catholic Ministries
Hartford Archdiocese

REMEMBERING GOD:
THE STORY OF A VOLUNTEER AND HURRICANE KATRINA

Remembering God is a story of transformation, following the life of an ordinary volunteer through his experiences working with a Red Cross Shelter in Lafayette, Louisiana; living through hurricane Rita; and finding myself in charge of an aid distribution center for Catholic Charities in Biloxi, Mississippi.

When Kendall left his home in Colorado Springs because he knew that God was calling him to help others, to serve in their time of need, he discovered that his life was transformed in ways that he had never imagined. It was an experience that turned his life right-side up, taking a recent college graduate from a promising career in politics to a ministry of social justice.

More than simply sharing his personal experiences, this book is about bringing to light an aspect of Katrina's (and Rita's) aftermath that's been left in the dark. It's about the impact that Katrina made on the life of a volunteer and sharing the *life lessons* that he learned almost everyday; To inspire people to look beyond the tragedy and destruction, and think about the incredible impact the hurricane had on the lives of the thousands of volunteers who came from all across the country to help."

TO ORDER OR FOR INQUIRIES CONTACT:

KENDALL A KETTERLIN
141 COUNTY RD 263
ARMSTRONG, MO 65230
KKETTERLIN@ME.COM